Mary Noailles Murfree

Where the Battle War Fought

A Novel

Mary Noailles Murfree

Where the Battle War Fought
A Novel

ISBN/EAN: 9783337028848

Printed in Europe, USA, Canada, Australia, Japan

Cover: Foto ©Thomas Meinert / pixelio.de

More available books at **www.hansebooks.com**

WHERE THE
BATTLE WAS FOUGHT

A Novel

BY

CHARLES EGBERT CRADDOCK
AUTHOR OF "IN THE TENNESSEE MOUNTAINS"

BOSTON
JAMES R. OSGOOD AND COMPANY
1884

Copyright, 1884,
BY JAMES R. OSGOOD AND COMPANY.

All Rights Reserved.

STEREOTYPED BY
C. J. PETERS & SON, BOSTON.

WHERE THE BATTLE WAS FOUGHT.

CHAPTER I.

IT is said that a certain old battlefield in Tennessee is haunted in these peaceful times. Often there comes out of the dark silence the sudden wild blare of the bugle, chilling the blood of distant fireside groups. Then the earth throbs with the roll of drums and the measured tread of martial hosts. A mysterious clangor, as of the clash of arms, fills the air. A flash — it is the glinting of bayonets above the grim earthworks which still loom up against the vague horizon.

And yet there are those who can hear, in the military music and the tumultuous voices of victory and defeat, only the rush of the wind across the vast historic plain; who can see, in the gleaming phantoms that hold the works, only the mist and the moon; who can feel, in the tremor of the earth beneath a charging column, only the near approach of the railway train thundering through the cavernous limestone country.

By wintry daylight the battlefield is still more ghastly. Gray with the pallid crab-grass, which so eagerly usurps the place of last summer's crops, it stretches out on every side to meet the bending sky. The armies that successively encamped upon it did not leave a tree for miles, but here and there thickets have sprung up since the war, and bare and black they intensify the gloom of the landscape. The turf in these segregated spots is never turned. Beneath the branches are rows of empty, yawning graves where the bodies of soldiers were temporarily buried. Here, most often, their spirits walk, and no hire can induce the hardiest ploughman to break the ground. Thus the owner of the land is fain to concede these acres to his ghostly tenants, who pay no rent.

A great brick house, dismantled and desolate, rises starkly above the dismantled desolation of the plain. Despite the tragic aspect of this building, it offers a certain grotesque suggestion — it might seem in the mad ostentation of its proportions a vast caricature of succumbed prosperities. There is no embowering shrubbery about it, no inclosing fence. It is an integrant part of the surrounding ruin. Its cupola was riddled by a cannonade, and the remnants shake ominously with every gust of wind; there are black fissures in the stone steps and pavements, where shells exploded; many of the windows are shattered and boarded up. In others, however, the glass is intact, and through those nearest at hand John Estwicke, standing for the first time on the long, broad portico one afternoon in 1871, caught the genial flicker of fire-light and the glow of crimson curtains. The whole place was grimly incongruous with the idea of a home, and as he was ushered into a wide, bare hall, with glimpses of uninhabited, unfurnished rooms on either hand, there was intimated something of those more potent terrors with which it was instinct — the pursuing influences of certain grisly deeds of trust, for the battlefield, the grewsome thickets, the house itself, all were mortgaged. The next moment he was in an atmosphere of goodly domestic cheerfulness, heightened by coloring so vivid and warm that it seemed to pulsate. A flaring, be-flowered, velvet carpet covered the floor of a large, square room; the crimson curtains were long and expansive; the clumsy, old-fashioned, brass fender and andirons glittered with the reflection of the blazing logs; now and then a red gleam was evoked from the time-darkened mahogany chairs, upholstered with thread-bare black hair-cloth which showed here and there the canvas beneath, for all the furniture was well worn, being scanty relics of ante-bellum days, saved by some miracle in the general destruction of the great battle. He caught a bizarre glimpse of himself in a huge fractured mirror with a showy, gilded frame, which hung above the mantel-piece, and of his host rising suddenly and turning to meet him.

"My dear sir," exclaimed General Vayne, with a certain rotund emphasis, "I am happy to see you!"

As he crossed the room and offered his hand to his guest — his left hand, for his right sleeve was empty — there was something in his manner which, despite the impressiveness of his fine proportions, his soldierly gait, his kindling enthusiastic eyes, and the grave earnestness of his florid face, savored strongly of the ludicrous. He bore himself with a noble dignity which might well have befitted Julius Cæsar, but which consorted absurdly enough with the uncouthness of the bare ruin where he lived; with his hunted condition, never out of sound of the hue and cry of his debts; with the well-worn seams of his coat — a suggestive contrast to his perfect and immaculate linen, that in making the most of its virtues only offered another annotation upon the history of his struggle between gentility and poverty. There was evident cordiality in his welcome, but it was accorded pre-eminently in his official character as host. After this the murmured civility with which the introduction of Estwicke was acknowledged by the General's slender young daughter, and the beaming amiability of an old lady, his sister, who sat on the opposite side of the fireplace, seemed a trifle irresponsible.

"My brother has told me," said Mrs. Kirby, her short gray-streaked curls waving with an animation that threatened to dislodge the little old-fashioned side-combs which held them from her plump, benignant, wrinkled face, "that you are a relative, a third cousin, of our good friend the Reverend Edward Estwicke — regret to hear of his neuralgia — so sad!"

"An admirable man," said General Vayne. He fixed his dark earnest eyes upon the fire, and with his adroit left hand, he reflectively stroked his long, gray mustache.

"I have never known, sir," he continued, weightily, "an intellect more powerful, acute, and analytic than that of that learned and eloquent divine."

The relative of the "learned divine" looked at his host with a momentary touch of surprise, for he knew his cousin only as a dull and droning old preacher in an obscure little town in West Virginia. He had not the advantage of General Vayne's moral magnifying-glass. Through this unique lens life loomed up as rather a large affair. In the rickety court-house in the village of Chattalla, five miles out there to the south, General Vayne beheld a temple of justice. He translated an office-holder as the sworn servant of the people. The State was this great commonwealth, and its seal a proud escutcheon. A fall in cotton struck him as a blow to the commerce of the world. From an adverse political fortune he augured the swift ruin of the country. Abstract ideas were to him as potent elements in human affairs as acts of the Legislature, and in the midst of the general collapse, his large ideals still retained their pristine proportions.

"I am afraid you have had a cold drive," said Mrs. Kirby, beaming on the visitor. "Our climate has changed since the war. It is much more severe."

"The loss of the trees, perhaps," suggested the stranger.

"Perhaps," said the old lady, with her gurgling laughter, "there may be something in the superstition that the Yankees forgot their weather and left it behind them. And now the malaria has gone — I wonder where! Probably we have to thank the Federal army and their cold weather for that also."

General Vayne lifted his eyes. "I thank the Federal army for — nothing," declared the unreconstructed, bitterly.

There was an unaccountable astonishment, — more — constraint in the visitor's face. He remained stiffly silent, and one sufficiently observant might have caught in his manner an intimation that he held himself on the defensive.

Miss Vayne was not sufficiently observant. She laughed out suddenly with girlish effusion, and as she changed her position, the light was full upon her delicately fair complexion, her rich brown hair, and her shabby black silk dress. She turned her joyous eyes upon the pallid heartbreak of that blighted plain. "To make light of your obligations, papa," she cried, "doesn't make away with them."

The gesture sharpened the frivolous satire, but the stranger's attention had not detached itself from General Vayne, at whom he was looking with a fiery red spark in his challenging brown eyes. This was more in accord with an alert aggressiveness habitually expressed in his face than with his suave reserved manner and his smooth and punctilious observance of the behests of polite society. His polish was like that of steel — its pleasing lustre does not deceive as to the stern possibilities of the weapon or the temper of the blade. He had a firmly moulded chin, a short upper lip, and excellent teeth. There was a dash of red in his close-clipped brown hair, and his whiskers and mustache were of a lighter tinge. His hands were smooth and white, but his face was darkened and roughened by sun and wind. He looked about thirty years of age; he was tall and heavily built, and, like all the men of this region, a military training was very marked in his bearing, despite his civilian dress.

"Ah well," said General Vayne, waving the war, the Federal army, and the nation generally into a diminishing distance with his expressive left hand, "I have — a — dismissed them — from consideration. Let them go! Let them go! Nowadays I am no wrangler. I leave all questions of public policy as a bone of contention for the Political Dogs to gnaw."

His method of enunciation might suggest to the literary mind the profuse use of capital letters.

"I am, and have always been, strictly tolerant," continued General Vayne, — "conservative in my views. Conservatism, sir," declared the tolerant man, with an extreme look in his eye, "is the moral centripetal force that curbs the flighty world."

Mrs. Kirby's interest in politics had diminished since the war, during which it had a phenomenal growth like Jonah's gourd. Now an absorption in personal matters flourished in its stead.

"I hope you find your stay in the neighborhood pleasant, Captain Estwicke — so glad," she said. "Of course you 've been to Chattalla. Charming, charming town! I am a visitor here myself. I have n't before seen my brother since the eve of Shiloh — yes, since Shiloh. I shall remain some months with him — so delightful to come back! And is it business or pleasure that brings you to Tennessee?"

This old lady possessed an unbridled imagination. She fancied it possible that people came to Tennessee for pleasure.

Once more there was that peculiar look of surprise and constraint upon Estwicke's face. He hesitated in doubt and embarrassment. It did not escape her attention this time, but she misinterpreted it as a look of inquiry, so she smilingly reiterated with great distinctness, "Did you come to Tennessee for *business* or *pleasure?*"

"I came to join my regiment," he replied, tersely — evasively it may be considered.

This information exploded like a bomb, leaving a sulphurous silence behind it.

"Ah-h-h!" exclaimed General Vayne, in a tone intended to express assent, but which was like a prolonged note of surprised comprehension. He appreciated all at once how it was that he had mistaken this man for an ex-rebel captain. His letter of introduction from the Reverend Edward Estwicke had described him broadly as "Captain Estwicke of Virginia," and when General Vayne had called upon him at the house of a mutual friend near Chattalla, where the officer was spending the last few days of his leave, no allusion as it chanced was made to the stubborn fact of his regiment, stationed at the city of Marston twenty miles away. He had subtly impressed General Vayne as a man of an inordinate personal pride and an extreme sensitiveness. To such a man the perception that he has accepted an invitation extended under a mistake can hardly be pleasant. General Vayne, versed in fine issues of internal dissension, realized how the annoyance must be aggravated by the stranger's consciousness that he was secretly regarded as a renegade, for he could but know how slightly his host would esteem the replication that he was a representative of the loyal South which had borne martyrdom between two fires.

General Vayne, however, held hospitality as the first element of religion, and it was abhorrent to him that a guest should by any mischievous mischance be rendered uncomfortable in his house. But he was not helplessly dismayed; he thought himself possessed of tact equal to any emergency, and he demonstrated this claim by bolting incontinently from the subject. The old lady beamed upon the equivocal captain with smiling eagerness to make amends. The girl's face was grave, but in her luminous eyes lurked a freakish delight in the whole misapprehension. Captain Estwicke was not in the habit of being considered amusing, but if he inwardly resented it he made no sign.

General Vayne had returned to the loss of the timber. "The aspect of the country would be almost prairie-like but for that elevation and those frowning redoubts," he said, waving his hand toward the western windows through which the huge earthworks were visible. "There are very peculiar scenic effects here now and then — very peculiar, sir, indeed. A horseman there near Fort Despair, will loom up gigantic" — lowering his voice impressively — "mysterious, wonderful. He seems a bit of materialized poetry. He looks far more like a gallant knight pricking across the plain in quest of noble adventure, than"— effective *diminuendo* — "a ploughman going out to bed up land for cotton."

"Is that the work we used to call Fort Despair?" exclaimed Estwicke, as if with sudden recognition. Something strained and unnatural in his voice struck the girl's attention. She noted too the look in his eyes — at once eager and shrinking — as he leaned his elbow upon the worn arm of the chair and bent forward to the window. Little as she knew of him she knew it was an uncharacteristic look. She did not understand it. She only apprehended the emotion that swayed him as one groping in the dark is conscious of the proximity of an unaccustomed, it may be a fearful presence.

"Fort Despair," repeated General Vayne, absorbed in reminiscence — he had lost his right arm there. "Appropriately named, too, it seems, even at this late day."

"Ah, I know!" cried the stranger passionately. "I feel its meaning! Every weed that stirs in the wind is voiced with a terrible suggestion."

Then he seemed to check himself. He leaned back in his chair and said no more. He was panting slightly; his face was flushed; a sharp pain was expressed in his eyes.

"The man," thought Marcia, watching him in a tumult of feeling, half sympathy, half inquisitive amaze, "has a morbid horror of that battlefield. And a reason for it!"

General Vayne was fighting the day over again. He saw his brigade in line of battle; he was canvassing once more the problematic strength of the opposing force; he was regretting again, as he had often regretted, that he had not disregarded his orders and pushed on through the timber; if his arm had been spared him one half hour longer! How could he notice the stranger now; he had no thought even of his guest!

And Mrs. Kirby was thoroughly tired of the war, and welcomed the opening of the door and the entrance of other visitors, a few middle-aged people of a decorously dull aspect, and, like their entertainers, so provincial that they were not even aware of it. This deplorable state of ignorance has, however, its compensations. With full faith they indorsed the old-fashioned customs that had always prevailed among them, and were free from that subtle self-distrust which hampers many very worthy people, who pay this price for the knowledge that they do not know everything.

In the general change of position Estwicke found himself beside the young lady, and nearer the window than before. Through it he could see the sinking sun, a great red globe, resting a moment on the parapet of Fort Despair. Far away a vertical line of light was drawn sharply upon the sad purple of the distant hills. The tapering shaft pierced the pale saffron belt above the horizon, and at its summit was a bright flake of crimson. It was the flag-staff, and the flying flag above the National Cemetery across the river. Certainly this was a grewsome place.

And now the sun was gone. The shadows thronged the battlefield. The haunted thickets were all a-shiver, and the viewless wind marched over the plain. The cheerful room seemed a flout, a derisive mockery, to the woful scene without.

"How we forget!" he thought. "How we forget!"

For the interior was very cheerful; the flames roared up the chimney; the shattered mirror reflected the homelike group, seated in a wide semicircle before the fire; the flush of the western sky was still bright on the girl's fair face, and there were golden glintings in her brown hair, as if belated sunbeams were entangled in its midst. A smile hovered about the curves of her delicate lips; her brilliant hazel eyes looked out from the tender shadows of long black lashes; even the genteel poverty expressed in her attire had its gracious, poetic aspects; her standing linen collar, turning slightly outward at the edges, might seem the calyx of some lovely flower as her white neck rose from it, and the plainness of her shabby black silk dress, of which the only ornament was a knot of black lace at the throat, accented all the pliant graces of her figure.

He could not understand the tranquil joyousness of her expression. She was to him the most striking anomaly of the anomalous place — so manifestly happy, so dominantly contradicting its persistently reiterated doom of death and decay; so evidently untouched by any influence of the high tragedy of these surroundings. Clearly she must lack feeling, sensibility. He looked speculatively at her, as he sat leaning his elbow on the stiff, angular arm of the chair, and with his right hand laid meditatively upon his dark red whiskers. Presently he recognized the appropriateness of beginning a conversation, and said, at a venture, —

"You have no near neighbors here?"

"No," she replied, "we have all the world to ourselves. Do you see that black line?" she added, turning her eyes toward the horizon, where the sombre hills, miles away, met the darkening sky, "that is the boundary of the world. You may think there's something on the other side, because you don't know the country; but there isn't."

For a moment he was silent. Then he laughed a little.

"I had no idea that I was to meet a distinguished astronomer, with a new planet," he said. "It has an orbit of its own, of course, and is governed by its own laws."

"That's the way with everybody," she declared. "People are always talking about 'the world,' and they only mean the few other people and the few places that they know."

"I perceive," said Estwicke, gravely, "that you are a close reasoner. The capacity for inductive ratiocination,

Miss Vayne, is the noblest faculty of the human mind. Let me congratulate you on its possession. Will you reason some more!"

He had been a trifle in doubt as to how she might receive this pleasantry at her expense, but she laughed gleefully.

"Oh, I will reason with pleasure if you will suggest a topic."

"You seem pretty expert," said Estwicke. "Do you spend much time at it?"

"At what?"

"At reasoning."

"Oh no," she cried; "I have n't the leisure for such an elegant recreation."

Her eyes were fixed upon him in delighted anticipation of what he would say next. It occurred to him that it was not often she had an experience like this; that her world did not abound with people who "amused" her.

"I should think you might indulge occasionally," he said. "When, for instance, your father is away, and your brothers"—he glanced across the room at a row of small boys, stiff in their best clothes and their company manners—"are at school, and you have your little planet all to yourself, you might find time to reason considerably."

"Oh, but they don't go to school; I teach them at home, and there's no reasoning with *them*—nor with housekeeping either."

He knew that General Vayne had been for some years a widower, and he understood now that she presided over the household. This must involve heavy cares. She was very elastic. The Juggernaut car evidently made no impression.

Already he could divine that the boys were taught at home to avoid the expense of the academy and in deference to their father's prejudice against the free school, and that the whole system of domestic education was designated in General Vayne's magniloquent nomenclature "Retrenchment."

"Teach me to reason," said Estwicke. "I assure you I am amenable."

"You have a dignified idea of my curriculum. I shouldn't try to teach you to reason," she cried delightedly. "If you were my pupil you would find yourself laboring to distinguish between the first principles of geography — North and South."

His face hardened, but he laughed and made a feint of throwing up both hands. "I surrender!" he exclaimed.

She looked at him with a sudden grave intentness. However, she said nothing, for the others were rising to repair to the dining-room. There the conversation was general, until, after a time, a rubicund, apoplectic, eager, unwieldly old gentleman of the name of Ridgeway began to preponderate, while the heavy faces of his auditors bore witness to the weight of his discourse. He talked of different processes of agriculture; of new labor-saving machines; most discerningly of the quality of land; and it was only when he began to take a morbid pleasure in humiliating himself and his hearers by comparing Tennessee soil to the alluvial richness of the buckshot cotton lands of Mississippi that General Vayne came swiftly, potently to the rescue. Then it became apparent to anyone not sodden in idiocy that God created first Tennessee, and with what was left over made the rest of the world. Nothing could live in such rhetoric. From Reelfoot Lake to the highest peak of Big Smoky Mountain General Vayne demonstrated his proposition. Its vast mineral wealth might enrich all the nations of the earth. Its water-power could run the machinery of — of the universe. On its mountain domes may be found the flora of the Canadas; its western swamps are rich with subtropical vegetation; between these extremes is every variety of soil and every grade of climate. He descanted on its geological interest, folded his napkin into strata and illustrated triumphantly. So at last the transition was very pretty to spirited sketches of angling in the waters of that mystic western lake presented by the earthquake to the State; of fox-chases through the park-like mid-land country; of hunting deer in the romantic coves and ravines of the Cumberland Mountains; of the wilder solitudes among the majestic domes and ridges of the great Unaka chain that bars off the world from our eastern borders. And as he talked it might have seemed that with his admiration of physical prowess and the loss of his right arm; with his magniloquent ideas and phrasings and the scantiness of all his belongings; with his young family growing up around him and only privation in the present and this mortgaged ruin to leave them as an estate, he was a marvellously apt illustration of the ignoble fact, failure, — a fact of which he was most profoundly, most pathetically unconscious.

The whole affair was a forced march to Estwicke; his interest lagged; the perception of the mistake under which he had been invited rankled within him throughout the evening, and even when he had taken his departure and was driving away under the frostily glinting stars.

And so the entertainment — a rare occasion for Marcia— was over. To-morrow would come again the dull routine of teaching and housekeeping — this last a matter of problems, of careful ingenuity, of reconciling large necessities and small means. But she was not thinking of that. She was ready for tears, for self-reproach, for that utter despair of youth, which, with the infinite lengths of the future before it, deems everything irrevocable. He was sensitive, she said to herself, and she had hurt him. She had let him go without a word, because she feared to speak. He seemed on the lookout for slights — but that perhaps was because he had found slights on the lookout for him. And he had had in his life some ungentle — it might even be some terrible experience; she had divined that early in the evening. And she, too, must wound him! She was so sorry — she was so sorry!

Her father's voice broke upon her absorption. "I can respect — I can even admire," he said, addressing the family circle, "a real bona fide Yankee. Born so " — he added, liberally. " But these home-made Yankees — these Southern Yankees — for my life, for my life I can't understand them."

It seemed to General Vayne a monstrous freak of nature that a man should be born south of Mason's and Dixon's line without a full set of indigenous principles warranted to stick.

His daughter turned her head suddenly. For they were not gone. Old Mr. Ridgeway was re-entering the room, stumbling over a foot-stool and spluttering and gasping in his apoplectic agitation. " I have — yes, I have " — he exclaimed. " I have broken the wheel of my buggy."

By degrees, in the tumult of his explanation, the facts were developed that Mrs. Ridgeway was not hurt in the fall, and that Captain Estwicke, who happened to overtake them at the " big gate," had kindly offered them his buggy. In order that he might not be kept waiting until they could send the vehicle back, Mr. Ridgeway desired to ask if his host could lend Captain Estwicke a saddle-horse.

General Vayne could and would, and apologized for not offering a vehicle instead. Before the war he had been "horsey" on a princely scale. Now he possessed a saddle-horse or two, and a pair of jog-trot sorrels that served alternately in the plough and in a certain dilapidation which he called his barouche. This had already rumbled off to Chattalla full of the elderly guests.

During the few moments required for the horse to be saddled the whole party waited on the front steps. The night air was keen and penetrating. A great star, in splendid isolation near the zenith, shivered in those wide spaces made dark by its own brilliancy. And the moon was bright, too — the ragged, withered crab-grass, still tufting the fissures of the bomb-riven pavements, glittered with rime as if every blade was frosted with silver. Vague belts of vapor lay upon the battlefield, and fluctuated with mystic glimmers. Estwicke watched it absently as he stood a little aside, heedless of the talk of the elders, whose black shadows and animated gestures were grotesquely defined on the blocks of limestone that floored the portico.

Marcia was silent, too. Once she cast a timorous glance upon him. Then her eyes fell. Still she did not doubt that he would receive what she wished to say as simply and kindly as it was intended.

"Captain Estwicke," she faltered, "I want to tell you — I — I — am very sorry, but — but — you won't do for a pupil at all. You can't learn to reason. You have too much imagination."

She glanced up and smiled. The next moment her heart misgave her. He was looking at her in cool surprise.

And what if she had taken too much for granted! He might not have cared at all — he might even have forgotten. She blushed painfully. She could not think to choose her words — she could not be silent while his eyes tacitly asked an explanation. She hastily stipulated —

"I alluded to teaching you to distinguish between North and South. I only meant the points of the compass — *Geography*, you know," she added, lucidly.

"I am very grateful that you should trouble yourself to tell me," he said, gravely. "I misunderstood you. I hope you will forgive me."

She was silent in astonishment. What chaos was here! She had tendered her regrets, and now *he* was begging her pardon. In the simple life of her little planet she had never before had occasion to question the appropriateness of any of her good and gentle impulses. It came upon her with a crushing sense of humiliation that she had done an awkward, a silly thing — she even thought it, at this moment, forward. She wondered that she should discern all this so late. She said to herself that he was a man of the world, whose spurious gallantry would not permit him to accept an apology from a lady. The slight wordy dexterity with which he had reversed their mutual position, and placed himself in the humble case of begging her pardon, instead of granting forgiveness, seemed to her painfully insincere. It was her first experience of the world's little feints, and it chilled her. She flinched too from the thought of how absurd the whole episode must be to him.

And in fact he laughed as he rode away in the moonlight.

"Now, that was mighty good of her," he protested. "She thought I was cut to pieces — routed!" And he laughed again.

He had pressed the horse into a gallop, and was speeding through the infinite loneliness of the moonlit expanse. When the animal abruptly swerved aside, he glanced down to recognize the shallow rifle-pits of the old picket line. He knew none of the traditions of the place, but as he reached Fort Despair, and rode along, close upon the crest of the counterscarp — dank and sodden with the late rains now, once dank and sodden with a darker current — there came upon him a mysterious sense of a mighty multitude astir in the vast, vague plain. A strange, rhythmic throb shook the earth — or was it in the air? The haunted thickets shuddered audibly as he passed. Once, when the steely gleam of a sabre was thrust suddenly forth, he turned and looked back with fierce eyes — that changed and were startled. But it might have been only the shimmering of a moonbeam on the white bark of an aspen shoot. As he rode on down the scarred, treeless bank of the river, the earth pulsated with a stronger tremor, a great white light sprang upon the horizon, and the whistle of the down train from Marston split the air.

Into the mist and into the moonlight a series of massive, isolated columns of masonry rose starkly out of the black water. They were the piers of the old turnpike bridge, burned one night long ago to cover a frantic retreat and impede a frantically fierce pursuit. He checked his horse near the brink and gazed at them. There was something so picturesque and martial in the equestrian figure, thus thrown into bold relief against the moonlit sky, that Mr. Ridgeway, in mid-stream upon the broad, flat ferry-boat, called his wife's attention to it.

"Captain Estwicke is not going back to his friend's house," added the old gentleman. "He tells me he will spend the night at the hotel in Chattalla, in order to catch the early train for Marston. The barracks are five miles from Marston."

The ferryman heard this. He lived on the highway, he saw everybody that came and went, and he had the interest of the professed gossip in small details. He noted the name, and when he had landed the old couple on the opposite bank he pulled lustily upon the rope, and the cumbersome craft, pulsing with the current, crossed more rapidly than usual under the impetus of Tom Toole's curiosity about the stranger. As he ran in to land there was a sudden, sharp change on his stolid, unspeculative countenance. He stood staring, with wild, dumfounded recognition, at Estwicke, who still sat motionless upon the horse, his eyes fixed upon the obeliscal columns, a dreary memorial, in the midst of the swift current. After a moment of doubt and hesitation, Toole tremulously held the lantern up at arm's length, throwing the light full upon the officer's face. It was no longer pallid, spectral, as it had been in the moonlight. The artificial gleam suddenly evoked all its peculiar coloring — the dark red of his hair and beard, the fiery spark in his challenging brown eyes, the warm tint of his tanned complexion.

"My good Lord A'mighty!" the ferryman broke forth, "thar ain't many men ez knows what I knows, an' hev seen what I hev seen, ez would like ter git a glimge of ye now — a-settin' in that saddle an' a-lookin' fust at the old forts, like ye war a-studyin' 'bout 'n the range o' the guns, an' then a-medjurin' that thar bridge with yer eye."

Estwicke turned quickly. Toole flinched beneath his glance, and held up one hand as if to ward it off, laughing confusedly at himself the while for the involuntary gesture.

"Ye might have knocked me down with a feather jes' now. Bless God, I thought 'twas *him* agin!" he protested, laying his hand on the rope as Estwicke pushed his horse down upon the ferry-boat. The pause was broken only by the gurgling of the water, and the rattling of the "block an' tickle" as every effort sent the broad, flat craft throbbing on its way. Then he replied to the inquiry in Estwicke's face.

"By God!" he exclaimed, wildly, "I 've seen ye hyar afore, a-ridin' an' a-raidin' on the banks o' this ruver, mounted an' armed, an' a-medjurin' the bridge with yer eye. But then — ye fired it with yer own hands — *with yer own hands.* I know it. These rocks know it. None of us hev forgot. An' I seen ye hyar agin," he added, lowering his voice, "a-lyin' dead — dead! — on the ground yander a-nigh Fort Despair, shot through the lungs, an' through the head, an' half crushed by the carcass o' yer horse!"

He paused abruptly.

There was on Estwicke's face a sudden look of recoil which imposed silence. The ferryman had loosened his grasp upon the rope, and the wayward plunging of the boat was like the disordered throbbing of some great heart. He could not interpret that look. He was wrestling with a vague, superstitious thrill. The equestrian figure seemed to rise into abnormal proportions. Its eyes — its inscrutable eyes — were fixed with some imperious protest upon him. And he remembered the face! He was shut off from the world with it — all the moonlit water was around them and all the misty air. Again he laid hold on the rope, pulling hard for the shore — for deliverance, keeping his shoulder toward the figure, but ever and anon turning, under a morbid fascination, a fluctuating glance upon it, impelled by the very strength of the contradictory desire to see it no more.

But when he was about to land, the approach to a more familiar element restored, in a measure, his self-possession.

"Ye air the livin' image o' that man, cap'n," he said, tremulously. "Of course I know 'taint *him* agin. *His* name warn't yourn. I useter know *his* name, though I hev furgot it now. I hope ye don't take no grudge at bein' called like a Johnny Reb. They hev hed the respec' o' soldiers afore now."

There was no answer. The horse's hoofs sounded loud upon the planks; the rider pressed swiftly in among the mists and the shadows; and he was gone.

Then the ferryman looked down at the boat. It had risen in the water. "He weighs!" he exclaimed suddenly. After a moment he turned about with a laugh. "Of course the man weighs. Thar's two of 'em! An' this man's name is Estwicke — an' what war t'other one's name? Ef"— he cast a swift glance at the empty embrasures of the distant fort — "ef thar ever war enny other one."

He pondered upon this problem as he pulled the boat across the river, and again while he walked up the bank toward a little log-house where the window was still a-light.

He paused half-way in his absorption, only roused when a breath of wind brought to him a strange sound from out the thicket close to Fort Despair, a sound of the whickering of horses and the heavy tramp of hoofs, and a clangor as of the clash of sabres, and a note — was it? — a note from a bugle. He remembered that a company of cavalry was literally annihilated there under a murderous cross-fire — he hastened on — and on the evening of the first day's fight, when captured and led to the rear, he saw, lying among the dead on the ground that the enemy held, this man — this staff-officer. He had reached the door of his house; he struck it with his heavy hand. He had recalled the name at last, and the recollection entered with him into his home like a curse.

CHAPTER II.

ESTWICKE slept little that night. For long hours he lay gazing at the pallid wintry moonlight as it crept, barred with the shadow of the tiny window-panes, across the floor of his room at the village hotel. The winds had died away. The world without was mute. Within, the intense quietude was broken only by the light sound of his watch under his pillow checking off the seconds. It seemed loud and strident, and its monotonous iteration jarred upon his nerves. He drew it forth presently and stopped the works. And then he could hear only his passionate pulses beat. These he might not silence so lightly.

He rose after a time, stirred the failing fire, dressed and lighted a cigar. He drew a chair to the window and sat aimlessly looking out upon the street. More than once he sighed heavily, — heavily. The shadows and the moonlight shifted about the "Square." The sonorous clangor of the clock, in the court-house tower, ever and anon warned the world how the time wore on. He watched a mist rise, and hover, and drift away. He looked to the east for the flush of dawn. But clouds were gathering silently, and in the morning they hung low and dense.

This assisted the somewhat dreary aspect of the place, for the pretty homes of Chattalla and the graces of its social life were well out of sight behind the two-story business blocks that surrounded the muddy, ill-paved Square, in the centre of which was the court-house yard and the Temple of Justice itself. A gaunt sycamore tree overhung this red brick structure; the grass was covered with dank withered leaves; to the iron fence saddle-horses were hitched in time-honored defiance of the august legislation of the county court. As Estwicke strolled out in front of the hotel after breakfast he was impressed by a certain military aspect about the citizens. The teamsters standing near their wagons, loaded with wood or country produce, shouldered their long-handled whips in a soldierly fashion, implying a similar habitude with a far deadlier weapon. An equestrian group, that might well have served a painter for a study of cavalry, had gathered about the town scales, where the weighing of cattle was in progress. A dry-goods clerk, middle-aged and iron-gray, came out of a store and crossed the Square to the bank. Estwicke's eyes followed the erect figure with its practised, measured gait.

"That man has marched a thousand miles to the throb of the drum," he said.

When the rain began to fall heavily in myriads of dun-colored lines it drove the population within doors except the teamsters, still lounging near their horses' heads, and Saturday's crowd of black humanity that surged about a row of Jew stores denominated by common consent "Jerusalem."

The contemplation of this picture from the hotel window was his only resource during the morning, and he regarded the approach of the belated train as in the nature of a rescue.

He established himself with a newspaper and a cigar in the smoking-car, and did not look up until his name was called.

"Glad to see you back," said a young man who was entering from the "ladies' car." He smiled agreeably and offered his hand, then leaned unsteadily against the arm of the seat while he struck a match and applied it to his cigarette. He was a tall, supple, dandyish young fellow, with a sparkling clever face, a girl's complexion, a long, silky, brown mustache, and hair and eyes of the same shade. The officer moved to give room, and he slipped into the place assigned him with a panther-like ease and grace that habitually characterized his motions, and made heavier and more muscular men seem a trifle awkward and clumsy in comparison.

"I'm not going to tell you we've missed you. And why? Because you have come among us too lately to believe me," he declared, lightly.

"Don't think you overtax my credulity, Mr. Meredith," said Estwicke, somewhat satirically. "I can fancy how the society of Yankee officers must be prized among you."

Meredith laughed coolly. He had been too young to bear his share on this historic plain that stretched so far around them on every side; he had grown happily into manhood under the new *régime*. He held something of the old theories, but in the revolving years his mind had been caught on the cogs of new ideas, and revolved with them. He looked with unruffled serenity at his companion.

"You are so eager in helping us to keep the peace that you never forget your mission. It had escaped me for the instant. Do you find it hard work? Very arduous, eh?"

Estwicke laughed, too. "Well, on the whole you are not so bad as the Indians," he said, temperately. "But you are duller,—far! There is some healthy snap and go on the frontier."

"That pleasing uncertainty about being scalped is the one redeeming feature of your profession — otherwise it is too painfully definite," said Meredith, philosophically. "If you keep your scalp — when it is gray you'll still be *Captain* Estwicke, unless we can get up a foreign war or a civil commotion for your advancement. Whereas *I*," with a hopeful rising inflection, "may in the course of time, and by the force of talent alone, be a Chief Justice — and then again, by the force of talent alone, I may n't. Room for speculation, eh?"

"Strikes me, on the contrary, that your prospects are painfully definite, too," said Estwicke. "Your father and his partner will take you in as a third after a while. So you'll be perpetually bringing up the rear, overcrowed by the two big lawyers. Your father will think he ought to do something for you — that's the way he'll do it."

"Not he — not he," protested Meredith. "I wish he would. My father has a theory that if a young lawyer is not helped he will help himself — to any stray litigation that may be afloat, as it were, in the air. He has left me to illustrate this theory."

"How does it work?" asked Estwicke, with interest.

"I pray God I may n't starve," said Meredith, tersely.

"Room for speculation, eh?" suggested Estwicke.

Chattalla had faded in the distance, and now the earthworks loomed up through the low-lying vapors and the blurring rain, vague and distorted but always grim and grewsome. As the train thundered with a hollow roar on the railroad bridge, there could be caught a fleeting glimpse of the isolated piers, and of the ferry-boat, pausing in mid-stream that Tom Toole might gaze after the cloud of smoke, which lay on the top of the cars, and drifted back to the redoubts and hung about the empty embrasures suggestively.

Estwicke, oblivious of the landscape, was absorbed in the conversation. He was essentially a man of this world. He craved the companionship of other men. He could not live apart from it. He had none of those intimate inner resources that make solitude sweet. Except for some principles of gunnery, bearing upon a still unperfected improvement of his own, he cared nothing for the study of science. Apart from the history of splendid achievement, some stirring martial lyrics, the biographies of great commanders, he had no fondness for reading. His books were the men about him; their experience, their lives, formed his interest, and as in the ever shifting combinations of human events they lapsed upon his own life he too bore a part in this sentient literature. He had a quick understanding of men, and a passionate sympathy with them. He did not even affect an appreciation of art; he looked blankly at its results. But an unrecognized something in the burnished sunlight, the silver-shotted moonlit mists, the haze on the purple hills, the sound of the melancholy autumn wind subtly thrilled to his heart and prevailed within him mightily. He found a wondrous sensuous exaltation in the mystery and the joy of being. He felt that his blood was swift in his veins; he stretched his limbs; he admired his muscles; he took cognizance of an involuntary alertness of his mental faculties; he knew that he was strong, and well, and graciously endowed. But he had no questions to ask of Heaven or Earth. He was too definite for mere abstractions, and adhered mechanically to the faith of the fathers.

Despite his imperfectly tempered aggressiveness he possessed certain qualities of good-comradeship, — his zest in life, his soldierly frankness, and his ardor commended themselves to Meredith, who was presently surprised in the midst of the desultory talk, which was neither wise nor witty, to see that the twenty miles had slipped past, that billowy sweeps of hills were on every side, that the city was elusively appearing and disappearing, mirage-like, in the purple distance.

They parted at the depot, and until evening Estwicke was greatly harassed with loneliness, for his regiment had but recently been stationed in the vicinity, and he knew few of the citizens. Nothing was going on at either of the theatres, and he could only mitigate the tedium after tea by lounging about the hotel with a promiscuous crowd of smokers, who habitually congregated here, for Marston boasted no club-houses. A fountain in the centre of the tessellated floor was tossing up pretty corolla-shaped jets of spray, that sparkled in the gaslight. The clerks bullied the incoming travellers. A mocking-bird in a cage sang shrilly; the cheerful click of billiard balls was heard from behind a colonnade, and through its vistas might be descried delicately poised cues and nimbly attitudinizing figures.

The scene soon palled upon Estwicke. He began to think of driving out to the barracks to-night instead of in the morning, but Meredith came in from the street, and the resolve faded.

"I'm glad to see that you are still in town," said the lawyer, as they met.

Following, as was often the case, in Meredith's footsteps, was his cousin, Tom West, a jaunty young sprig, some twenty or twenty-two years old, who effusively claimed Estwicke's acquaintance. As they shook hands the officer became aware of a close scrutiny directed upon him from over the tall, young fledgling's shoulder. It emanated from a pair of cold, fishy eyes, set in an impassive, florid face, which belonged to a stout, middle-aged, soberly dressed, responsible-looking party. Estwicke could not have said explicitly why he was so unfavorably impressed, nor why when West, with callow self-sufficiency, introduced the stranger as his friend, Mr. Casey, it seemed so very odd that he should have a friend like this. Estwicke, mechanically extending his hand, looked at Casey with wonted fierce intentness, and noted the indefinable but strong intimations lurking about him of solid commercial pursuits. Somehow his breadth of waistcoat, his sparingness of speech, his quiet, grave manner, assisted this effect. The man who knew men could not reconcile it with the look in his eye and stony countenance.

He showed a disposition to devote himself to West, and said little to Estwicke, who presently turned back in relief to Meredith.

"How do you get away with these long evenings?" he demanded.

"Professional study, generally; regular midnight oil business."

"Nice boy!" ejaculated Estwicke.

"Sometimes," said Meredith, signifying by a gesture that he desired the favor of a light from Estwicke's cigar, "sometimes clients get as scarce as hen's teeth, and the justice's court — most of my practice is in that humble modern *pie poudre* — the justice's court knows me no more. Then I make up my mind to renounce the profession before it is in everybody's mouth that the profession has renounced me. So I play billiards in the evening, or go to the theatre, or call on the young ladies."

"Oh, the young ladies!" cried Estwicke, stroking his whiskers. "That's mighty bad!"

He looked at Meredith, and laughed as he received his cigar back.

A band of itinerant musicians suddenly struck up a

popular waltz, and the rotunda was filled with surging waves of sound. "This is insufferable," said Meredith. "Suppose we go up to my room, where we can have a quiet smoke and talk."

As they passed the fountain West approached them. "Going upstairs?" he asked of his cousin.

Meredith nodded. "Will you come with us?"

"And I'll bring Casey," West declared agreeably, very slightly lowering his voice; "that is if you have no objection. I'm under great obligations to him, and as he knows nobody in town but us I feel bound to see him through and make his stay as pleasant as possible."

Meredith frowned, and hesitated. But Casey was standing at no great distance, and had evidently overheard the conversation. Estwicke experienced a twinge of uneasiness. Despite his ill-defined antipathy toward Casey, and although the suggestion that he should join them had destroyed every prospect of pleasure, it seemed to Estwicke almost a cruelty to refuse publicly so slight and apparently so reasonable a request. He watched Meredith with expectant eyes.

"Certainly, if you like," the young lawyer assented, not too graciously, and turned away.

"That's a boon," he muttered to Estwicke, who made no reply, for at that moment they stepped into the elevator, and stood silent and with their cigars held low and reversed, like the muskets of privates at a military funeral, in deference to a group of ladies within.

"I roost high," said Meredith, when they had gotten out on an upper story. "It comes cheaper up here, and there's better ventilation. 'Beggars all, but, marry, good air.'"

After they were seated before the blazing fire in Meredith's room, West seemed altogether unaware of the reluctant toleration with which his entertainer regarded the amendment to the quiet smoke and talk. With his gay, youthful self-sufficiency, he absorbed the conversation as far as he might. He was facetious, and flippantly fraternized with Casey.

"Captain," he said to Estwicke, with an explanatory wave of his hand toward his solemn red-faced friend, "there is the great original David! And I am Jonathan! Wasn't it David who saved Jonathan's life?" He pulled at his mustache and laughed and smoked his big cigar with manly gusto.

"Oh, it was nothing, nothing whatever," declared Casey. His manner suggested that from good nature he was content to lightly waive recognition of a feat.

The sharp young lawyer apprehended the intimation.

"Nothing?" he repeated satirically. "Nothing to save Tom West's life? Why, it was a public benefaction!"

Estwicke, with his quick interest in exploits, his love of danger, his enthusiastic admiration of bravery, turned to Casey with a sudden sense of respect.

"May I ask how that came about?"

Casey hesitated, and Estwicke presently recognized in this a tact which was hardly consonant with such a slow-seeming man, for West, after waiting expectantly for a moment, plunged into an account of a recent railroad accident, that might have been very disastrous, but had resulted in nothing worse than cooping him up in the debris, whence by some exercise of thews and sinews — of which Mr. Casey was amply capable — he was extricated. His rescue had evidently involved no risk, but it had served as an introduction of Casey, who was adroitly abetting West in magnifying its importance. Estwicke listened with contemptuous amusement, and Meredith's efforts to conceal his impatience had grown so lame that his relief was very evident when a knock at the door interrupted the conversation, and a card was brought in. He glanced at it in surprise.

"Show the gentleman up," he said, and the brisk, and grinning bell-boy disappeared.

The interval that ensued was expectant. Perhaps this was the reason the new-comer appeared upon the scene with the impressiveness of the principal character of a drama. Perhaps it might be that life had always cast Maurice Brennett for the leading business, and he bore himself in a manner befitting the title *rôle.* His eyes had a peculiar brilliancy, and were capable of an intent expression so concentrated that when suddenly elicited it had a sinister effect, and put its subject instinctively on guard. He was tall, thin, angular, and dressed with an elaborate fastidiousness that was somehow oddly incongruous with his pale, powerful, intellectual face — he seemed rather the type of man who scorns the minutiæ of externals. Between his mobile eyebrows many a scheme had registered itself in subtle hieroglyphics. There was a look of severely maintained repression about the hard lines of his lips as if the controlling influences of his nature had had a struggle for ascendency over other wild and turbulent forces. Even now the slight annoyance of finding a group here instead of the man he wanted had brought a quiver to the thin, sensitive nostrils of his sharp, hooked, and delicately chiselled nose. His pallor was the pallor of late hours — not such as these young fellows kept, but the anxious vigils of thought, the canvassing of opportunity, and the inception of plans. He had his hat in his hand, and the gaslight revealed such glimmers here and there in his dark hair, clipped close about a shapely head, and in his full, dark mustache, as might intimate that he was fast growing gray, which is premature at forty.

His presence exerted a singular influence upon the other men; their personal peculiarities were suddenly abnormally pronounced.

Casey seemed trebly slow, stolid, rubicund. West looked very callow, and felt very callow too; Meredith's dainty complexion, his silky mustache, his sparkle, were almost effeminate. Estwicke silently measured the stranger with challenging eyes.

"I have hardly time for this," Brennett said, as he took the cigar which Meredith tendered him. "My business with you is rather imperative."

Meredith was a trifle confused, having naturally enough supposed that the visit at this place and hour had only a social significance. Upon the word business, the others made a motion as if to take leave.

"I fear I am interrupting you," Brennett continued, looking round at the group. "I feel rather like the ghost of fiction who routs a pleasure party. It is a hackneyed theme, but no one has adequately considered the embarrassing position of the ghost."

There was a laugh at this and a momentary hesitation.

"You will greatly alleviate it if you won't allow me to put you to flight. I only want a few minutes' consultation with Mr. Meredith. I ventured to look you up out of office hours and on Saturday night," he continued turning to the young lawyer, "because I have information that a debtor of mine is about to run off his cotton on a Sunday freight, and this may be my last opportunity to get out an attachment."

"I insist that you don't go," said Meredith, addressing himself specially to Estwicke. "This won't keep me long — meantime suppose you have a game of cards. I am not going to my office — we can talk the matter over here."

He flung a pack of cards on the table; then he and Brennett turned away to a desk which was on the opposite side of the room. The trio at the table chatted for a few moments in a desultory strain, but presently West, glancing at lawyer and client now fairly immersed in business, shrugged his shoulders, gathered up the cards, and with a juvenile leer at the others, proposed to deal for "draw."

"I haven't played for so long, I scarcely remember the game," protested Casey.

West laughed jeeringly; he joyed so in his amiable wickedness.

"Oh, Casey's afraid of getting turned out of church. We'll take you in out of the wet — won't we, Captain? We belong to the 'big church'— we do."

Estwicke made no reply; he hardly relished even a "big church" membership with Casey.

"I suppose we play with a limit?" he asked impatiently, showing some eagerness to begin.

West's *was* an amiable wickedness. In fact it was only a weak-kneed semblance — that would, yet might not, be. He quaked at the bare suggestion of the alternative.

"Captain, you shock me," he declared. "Of course we play with a limit — fifty cents — say."

They talked very little when once fairly at it. For a time Meredith, who sat with his back toward them, only knew vaguely that somebody was "passing" or "straddling the blind," or "seeing and going better." Once or twice West laughed out loud and long in triumph. And again his voice rose in excited remonstrance, to which his companions seemed to pay no attention. Then the room was quiet for a time, and the lawyer lost cognizance of everything except the complications of Brennett's liens and his debtor's duplicity.

"How many bales do you suppose he has there?" Meredith asked, after a meditative pause.

There was no answer.

He glanced up impatiently. Brennett's face was instinct with an alert interest. His eyes, lighted by some inward sardonic laughter, were fixed upon the group by the fire.

Meredith turned quickly, and at this moment Estwicke, — his coat thrown off upon the floor, his hat thrust on the back of his head, the hot blood crimsoning his sunburned cheek, the perspiration standing thick in his close-clipped red hair, his eyes blazing with that most unholy fire, the gambler's passion, — cocked his cigar between his set teeth and raised the blind one hundred dollars.

West had passed out of the game, had drawn away from the table, and was gazing with dismayed surprise at the swollen proportions of the pool and at the impassive, stony countenance of Casey. Not a feather was ruffled as he looked cooly into Estwicke's burning eyes; he was as decorously florid, his waistcoat as commercially rotund as ever, but his demeanor was the demeanor of the professional expert.

He stolidly made good — and then he drew one card, Estwicke standing Pat. After this, for a few moments, each seemed cautious, making very small bets. But presently, when Estwicke raised him fifty dollars, Casey "saw it" and went a hundred better.

Then the slow, cumbrous fellow, according to his habit, laid his cards, face downward, on the table in front of him, with a single chip upon them to hold them in place, and clasping his hands lightly upon his substantial stomach, calmly awaited Estwicke's "say."

And all at once Estwicke looked hard at the man, with a change on his expressive face. There was an eager surprise in his eyes; the flush of sheer excitement deepened to an angry glow; he seemed lost for an instant in a sort of doubting confusion. Suddenly he made good, and "called."

Meredith was thunder-struck as he realized the full significance of the scene. He rose hastily. "Gentlemen," he said, sternly, "this is going entirely too far."

They took no heed. With one hand Casey laid his cards, a straight flush — ace, king, queen, jack, and ten of diamonds — upon the table beside Estwicke's jack full, while with the other hand he gathered the pool toward him, giving no sign of elation.

"I protest," began Meredith. He stopped suddenly short.

Brennett sprang to his feet with a sharp exclamation.

It happened in an instant. There was a swift movement of Estwicke's intent figure; he thrust his hand behind him, and seemed to draw from his pistol-pocket a glancing, steely flash of light; there was a sharp, metallic click — of a peculiarly nerve-thrilling quality; he lunged across the table, and held the weapon at full cock at the man's head.

Warned by Estwicke's motion, Casey had made an effort to draw his pistol. His hand grasped it in his pocket.

"Move your right arm and you're a dead man," said Estwicke between his set teeth. They were strong and white, and unconsciously he showed them. The veins that crossed his forehead were black and swollen. His breath came hot and fast and with a sibilant sound. He seemed to think as Brennett sprang up that there would be an effort to disarm him.

"If you interfere," he said, in a low voice, — "if you touch me — I will kill you — I will kill you!"

It was a moment of terrible suspense, but as Brennett moved hastily back, he laughed aloud — a short, ungenial laugh, nervous perhaps — or was the fancy so absurd that he should interfere!

Meredith's motion toward Estwicke was arrested by his next words. "Drop that card out of your sleeve — the card I dealt you."

Casey gazed abjectly at him, turning even paler than before, and made a weak, spasmodic effort to speak, to deny.

"No use talking," said Estwicke, cutting him short. "Drop the card." His finger by accident or design quivered slightly on the trigger.

The sharper shook his sleeve, and the three of diamonds fell upon the table.

"The exchange was quick as lightning — but I *saw* it!" Estwicke declared.

Without lowering his eyes or moving the weapon, he placed with his left hand the three of diamonds on the table beside the straight flush to illustrate the self-evident fact that, no matter which of the cards Casey had substituted for it, the hand after the draw was merely a flush.

"And a full out-ranks a flush!" he proclaimed, with a fierce, dictatorial air.

Casey sat before him, silent, cowed, helpless, the revolver that he still grasped in his pocket as useless as if his right hand was palsied.

"My 'Full' raked the pool!" thundered Estwicke. "I won it all! I'll have it all! Fork! With your left hand — mind."

As Casey hastily pushed the money across the table, a modest nickel that had served in the half dollar limit game with which they began, fell to the floor and rolled away among the shadows.

He had surrendered utterly — it was all over. A breath of relief was beginning to inflate his lungs, which in the surprise and fright had seemed to forget and bungle their familiar functions. The other men moved slightly as they stood, — an involuntary expression of the relaxation of the tension — the creak of Tom West's boots was to him like the voice of a friend. Then they realized, with the shock of an infinite surprise, that Estwicke sat as motionless as if he were carved in stone, his pistol still held at the cheat's head. The room was so silent that they might hear the rumble of the elevator on its missions up and down, the throb of the engine in the cellar, the faint rattle of the dishes in the dining-room far, far below the high story where the young man's room was perched. They understood at last, and it came upon them with the amazing effect of a flash of lightning from a clear sky.

Estwicke was waiting for the nickel!

The card-sharper was panting, failing, almost losing consciousness. He did not dare to stoop and search for the coin — he could not summon his voice for speech. The tears sprang into his eyes when he saw that the situation was at length comprehended by the others.

West hastily knelt on the floor, passed his tremulous fingers over the dark carpet, clutched the coin and placed it on the table.

To the two men who knew Estwicke best the episode was a frightful illustration of a certain imperious exactingness which they had discovered even in their short acquaintance was a notable characteristic of his nature. For one instant longer he looked hard at the sharper. Then he brought his heavy hand down upon the table in the midst of the pile of greenbacks, with a vehemence that sent a shiver through every glass in the room.

"Damn you!" he cried out, fiercely. "Keep it!"

He thrust his pistol into his pocket. Without another word he strode heavily out of the room, leaving Casey staring blankly at the money so strangely relinquished, and the others standing petrified under the yellow gas-jets gazing after the receding figure that marched through the shadowy vagueness of the dimly lighted hall without.

When he was fairly gone Meredith turned to Casey. The sharper had before hardly seemed able to breathe. He was on his feet now and ready to walk. His god was good to him. The touch of it had made him whole.

"I have never before had occasion," said Meredith, sternly, "to show a man the door." He waved his hand toward it.

The hardened creature insolently lifted his cold, fishy eye and grinned. His plethoric pocket-book was overflowing in his hands; he tucked the other bills into the pockets of his respectable, commercial-looking waistcoat.

"Sorry to have any disagreement, I'm sure. Your friend is a little too choleric — apt to be the fault of military men. I have to thank you for a most delightful evening. I'll come again soon. Bye-bye, West!"

He bowed and grinned and grimaced at the door. Meredith was scarlet with indignation. Tom West thrust his hands into his pockets and turned sheepishly away. Brennett flung himself against the mantel-piece and laughed with an intense enjoyment so chilling, so derisive, so repellant in its quality that Casey paused in the hall and glanced back through the open door in surprise and a vague distrust. Meredith saw among the shadows his white, heavy-jawed face, from which the smile had faded in an expression of inexplicable wonder, of fear. Then he turned once more and disappeared.

Meredith hastily handed Brennett his memoranda and, with a promise to return in a few moments, started toward the door.

"Where are you going?" West demanded inquisitively.

"To look up Captain Estwicke," Meredith replied, curtly.

The "elevator boy" knew the number of Estwicke's room on the transient floor by reason of having had the key left with him during the evening. Estwicke had hardly entered and closed the door when Meredith knocked. He looked around with a flushed face as the young lawyer came in.

"I hope you will remember how that blackguard was forced upon me," Meredith began, hotly. "I don't usually consort with cheats. I am not responsible for your meeting such company in my room."

Estwicke gave a bitter laugh.

"What does it matter to me where I met him?"

"It matters to me," said Meredith, tersely.

Estwicke was tramping back and forth the length of the room.

"I thought I had given that thing up!" he cried in a tumult of despair. "I haven't touched a card for years. I can't play in moderation. I can't, you see. I go wild — wild! It's an hereditary passion."

Meredith was a lawyer, and an acute one. He changed his base with a celerity that did infinite credit to his acumen. Estwicke was taking himself to task — not his entertainer. He briskly joined the onslaught.

"Oh hereditary!" he sneered. "I have often noticed that a man credits his father with his own pet vices. What was the reason you let the rascal have the money?"

"I had no reason — no positive idea; it was only an impulse," said Estwicke. "Somehow when I got it — I — could n't touch it. That *I* should brawl with a fellow like that for money! But why not?" he added after a sullen pause. "He is as good as I am — that is, I am as bad as he is."

"Bless me!" exclaimed Meredith, satirically, "I would n't say *that*."

"I know better. He does n't."

"But some of it was yours on the strictest moral construction."

Estwicke stood in the middle of the floor staring at his visitor.

"I mean the money you originally bet," Meredith explained.

This was a distinction that Estwicke could not grasp. "It was *all* mine!" he bawled. "My — full — raked — the — pool!" He came hastily and sat down in the green-rep arm-chair, expounding how the game stood, checking off his cards and Casey's on the fingers of his right and left hands respectively. His excited words in their confused haste stumbled and tripped up over each other in his throat; his eyes were eager and earnest; he trembled with the intensity of his interest. Even the wordy lawyer could not interrupt.

"Well," he said, when Estwicke had concluded, "I knew all that before — and it's a nice business. You told me once that you have nothing but your pay. I should think," he continued, exasperatingly, "this night's work would make a considerable hole in it. I hope you feel that you have invested your time and money to the best advantage."

"Oh, I got disgusted with the money. I could n't endure to keep step, morally, you know, with that contemptible, poor devil. I tell you he looked at the money with tears in his eyes."

Meredith stared.

"This is rather a belated sympathy with the 'poor devil,'" he said, sarcastically. "Captain Estwicke," he continued, "I don't pretend to understand you, but I feel it almost a duty to tell you how heartily I disapprove of your conduct to-night. Pistoling a man at a card-table for cheating is a practically unprovoked, cruel and abhorrent crime."

"Did n't do it," said Estwicke, grimly, on the defensive.

"You would have done it — if he had not instantly yielded."

"Ha-a-rdly," drawled Estwicke. The tone was significant. Meredith looked at him expectantly. Estwicke glanced uneasily up at the ceiling, then down at his boots. As he turned doubtfully toward Meredith their eyes met, and he broke into an uproarious peal of laughter.

"Why, man!" he cried, hilariously, "the pistol was n't loaded!"

He drew the weapon from his pocket and held it at arm's length, revolving its empty chambers, and setting the walls to echoing its sharp click.

Meredith laughed, too, partly in sympathy with the other's boisterous enjoyment of what he considered so exquisitely flavored a joke and partly in relief. "I'm glad you let me know this," he declared. "Forget what I said when I did n't know it." Presently he added with a view of contingencies of which Estwicke seemed utterly incapable — "But suppose that that fellow had persisted in heaving up the thing *he* had in his pocket?"

"Oh, but I was sure he would n't. Moral suasion, you know. There 's a wonderful deal of moral suasion in giving a man a peep down an iron tube. It puts the best of us out of countenance." After a pause he said, gravely, — "Nothing would have induced me to hurt the man — besides, I *could n't*. All I wanted was my own money."

"And you did n't want that little long."

"I feel like the devil," said Estwicke, impatiently. "I 'm so much like the devil to-night that I don't know us apart."

"Well," persisted Meredith, "you 've given us a fine sensation. I never saw a man so entertained as that fellow, Brennett."

"I don't care to set up as a show," said Estwicke, sulkily.

"A cat may look at a king."

"I doubt if it is altogether safe for the cat."

"In the light of late events, I certainly should not take the liberty if I were a cat," said Meredith, with a laugh.

"He is not a cat," rejoined Estwicke, with that sudden insight into character which was so marked a quality of his mind. "He has a hawk's face and a hawk's eyes — the most startlingly brilliant eyes I ever saw. I never met a human hawk before — though I 've known human wolves, and monkeys, and dogs, and cats. We don't want to claim kin with our poor relations. But some of us can't help ourselves. We will look like 'em, and sometimes we will behave like 'em." He stretched out his legs to the fire, and thrust his hands in his pockets. "I 'm misanthropic, ain't I?" He glanced up with a laugh. After a pause he asked — "What 's his business?"

"Getting rich."

"I could have guessed as much," declared Estwicke. "That man has his soul in his pocket. And his pocket doesn't bulge. Such a soul as that won't crowd things."

"Don't know about his soul, but he certainly has an instinct for money. He speculates heavily in cotton futures. And he owns a half interest in a mine out west that they used to say was as good as a mint."

The young lawyer had risen to take leave. With an almost affectionate impulse he paused at the door. "Estwicke," he said, "I want to tell you — you're a good fellow."

"That I am," said Estwicke, mockingly, "I'm mighty good."

He looked about him wearily, with a haggard, hunted face after the door had closed. Then suddenly he rang the bell, called for his bill, packed his traps dexterously, methodically, and in surprisingly small compass — one of his military accomplishments — and the full moon was hardly swinging past the meridian before he was bowling swiftly along the turnpike among the hills that encompassed the city. Through the carriage windows he saw it lying behind him in many an undulation, its domes and its mansard roofs idealized in the glamour and the distance to a castellated splendor. It had faded away in the dusky shadows long before he caught sight of the white-framed barrack buildings. His heart warmed at the thought of his friends so close at hand, of the familiar surroundings, and the old routine. He saw the sentry's bayonet glisten in the moonlight, and catch on its point a star of fire. And the evening and the scene he had left slipped into the dark corners of his recollection.

CHAPTER III.

HIS image, however, remained importunately present with the man whom he had characterized as a "hawk." In the days that ensued, it intruded between Maurice Brennett and many an abstruse commercial calculation, with which it was devoid of analogy in any particular. He became conscious, with a sharp surprise, of the dereliction of his trained and tutored attention. Even then he admitted to himself that this was strange, although he argued plausibly that it was but the lingering impression of a startlingly unexpected episode and a notable face.

Long afterward, in the light of subsequent events, he remembered this. And then he called it a presentiment — this man of facts and figures!

One night while it still harassed him, he chanced to come in late from the deserted streets. The rotunda of the hotel was deserted too, and so quiet that he could hear in the distance the carriage, which he had left, rolling away with a dull monotonous whir over the Nicholson pavement. A solitary night-clerk languished behind the counter. The water was motionless in the basin of the fountain. A single gas-jet served to accent the darkness and dreariness of the scene, bereft of its wonted animation. The shadows clung thick about the great pillars, and as he walked slowly and listlessly among them, he wore a grave, pondering, baffled aspect. His hat was pulled far over his brow, and his hands were sunk deep, with a certain surliness of gesture, in his trousers' pockets. His overcoat hung loosely on his shoulders, giving glimpses of his dress-suit beneath it, and of a half crushed flower in his button-hole. These exponents of recent participation in some genial festivity, were at this moment curiously at variance with his face, in which there was so marked an expression of keen intensity, and so strong, though subtle, a suggestion of latent rapacity, that it fully justified Captain Estwicke's descriptive phrase, "a hawk's face." His peculiarly brilliant eyes — so bright even in the checkered glooms — were downcast. They held an intimation of a deep dejection of spirit.

So he, too, had his hopes deferred — his far off Canaan! He, too, had some vital part that could be called a heart, where at least wounds might rankle, and disappointments chill. But once admit that idea of a latent rapacity, and he seemed an unpleasant transformation of a man into a creature of prey.

He paused when he reached the counter, and as he glanced over the register, his eyes suddenly dilated with eager intentness. His hand was poised, quivering over a certain scrawling autograph.

"When did Mr. Travis arrive?" he asked sharply of the clerk.

"Ten minutes ago," replied the impassive functionary.

Brennett hastily noted the number of the room, turned from the counter, and took his way swiftly up the stairs and through the dim twilight of the long halls. Above the row of doors on either hand, only one transom was still alight. He knocked with loud impatience, and he trembled with suspense, while the key was turned within.

"*Hello!* unexpected pleasure!" exclaimed the occupant of the room, opening the door and seeking to suppress a mighty yawn. "You *are* quick on the trigger. How did you find out that I was in town?"

Brennett made no reply. He was even more excited when they were shut in together. He tossed aside his overcoat and hat as if he were stifling, threw himself into a chair, and in hastily drawing off his light kid gloves, he wantonly tore them bit from bit with gestures that were most unpleasantly like his cousin, the feathered hawk, whom he so closely resembled. Though the meeting was fraught with a deep significance, there were no indications of the fact in Travis's unruffled demeanor, except that he now and then looked uneasily at his friend, as if in deprecation of this intensity of impatience and eagerness. His eyes were blue, finely set, and contemplative; his hair was of an equivocal shade, called golden by his feminine acquaintance, and sandy by his men friends; a very recent railway journey was suggested by the cinders on his beard. He was half undressed; his throat was bare; he had taken off his coat and vest, and they hung on the back of the chair where he sat thrusting his feet into a pair of slippers. He was tall, handsomely proportioned, and was popularly supposed to run on his looks. By virtue of his prepossessing exterior, aided by a singularly quiet and gentlemanly manner, he retained his hold on well-regulated society, and fostered a prevalent scepticism as to stories of extravagant dissipation told about him. Although far from being intellectual, he had a habit of putting plain sensible ideas into unpretentious language, which gave casual observers the impression that he was a shrewd practical fellow with solid views. He presented the anomaly of a man credited with acumen by his general acquaintance, and pronounced a fool by his intimates.

"You received my telegram?" he drawled, as he rose to his feet and stood leaning against the mantel-piece.

"Rather enigmatical it was — I did not understand it."

Brennett's tone was acrid, and Travis replied as to a reproach.

"I don't see how I could have made it more explicit, considering the circumstances. I said, 'It has all gone wrong.'"

"How has it gone wrong?"

"You know she died in London more than a month ago, and I started soon afterward for New York. Her will — you remember I gave you a copy of it — well, when I reached New York, I found there was a codicil of which I had before known nothing. It changed the former disposition of her property. She left everything available for our purposes away from me. I telegraphed you as soon as I discovered it."

Brennett fixed his eyes, sullen and lowering, though never losing that quality of searching brilliancy, upon his friend, and replied not a word.

The silence shook Travis's equilibrium.

"Say something, Brennett," he cried angrily. "There's no use in jay-hawking me. You seem to hold me responsible for your disappointment, while I — why this thing is my ruin! I have sunk in that mine every cent I could rake and scrape for years. Give over the luxury of stamping on me, and stir your wits to see if anything can help us now — or "— with anxious doubt — " do you throw up your hand?"

Brennett still said nothing, and Travis with an impatient gesture shifted his position, leaning more heavily on the mantel-piece, and struck a match for his cigar.

By a dexterous use of the system known as "freezing out," the two had become exclusive owners of a certain silver mine in Colorado. But after a time it had seemed that the biters were bitten. The yield grew meagre, the expenses continued, their perseverance had only brought them largely into debt, and now their liabilities had swollen like a gigantic boa-constrictor. Ruin was close upon them, when suddenly brighter prospects opened. If they could retain the mine now they thought it would be worth millions to them, but their necessities were immediate. A large sum must be raised within the next few months or the property, with all its inchoate wealth, would be sacrificed, possibly for the merest fraction of its value, — possibly only for the amount of the debts.

Travis had looked for extrication to the estate of his widowed and childless sister, who had been in a dying condition for months, and the result seemed only to demonstrate the long-conceded futility of waiting for the shoes of the dead.

"I tell you, Brennett," he said presently, sheltering with his hand the feeble flicker of the match from some draught that stole shivering in, "this thing came upon me like a thunder-clap. She had intimated so often — she had virtually promised me those houses. They are equivalent to cash, as you know — could be converted at a moment."

"And what do you get?" asked Brennett, with a voracious look.

"The Arkansas plantations — a drug on the market."

"You are to blame," Brennett interjected sharply.

"You can always prove that — to your own satisfaction," said Travis, with a sneer, which might have pointed a more pungent sarcasm. He threw himself back in his chair with an air of bracing himself for endurance.

"We should have taken some account of Mrs. Perrier's stand-point — we ought to have managed so as to give her a different view. I suppose," Brennett pursued, impelled rather by an incisive mental habit of stripping facts bare, than by a definite purpose, "I suppose her idea was that the plantations would give you a comfortable income always, and would be likely to stay by you — as nobody will buy them now-a-days, nor lend money on them. She intended to protect you against your own imprudence in speculation, perhaps — or your gambling proclivities."

Travis eyed his cigar sourly, while he flipped off the ash with his delicate fourth finger.

"How obvious!" cried Brennett. "And I never thought of it before! Yet I knew she had strong objections to your habits."

"Laura was religious, you know." Travis suggested this as if it were a disease, which had impaired her judgment, and was therefore a plea in extenuation of her weakness. "She was really very fond of me. She cared for nobody else, and I have no doubt the provisions of this codicil surprised Antoinette beyond measure."

"*Antoinette!* What the devil are you talking about?" demanded Brennett, impatiently, rousing himself from his absorption.

"I am talking," said Travis, with an elaborate show of placidity, "about my step-sister, Antoinette St. Pierre, to whom Laura left the property which I expected to receive."

"I never before heard of her," said Brennett, sternly. "Why did you not tell me that there was some one likely to share with you Mrs. Perrier's estate?"

"My dear fellow," said Travis, with a debonair wave of the hand, "my friends urge against me that I am indolent, but I have never been given over to such an abandonment of idleness as to have nothing better to do than to talk about Antoinette St. Pierre."

Brennett, goaded though he was, made some concession to the displeasure which expressed itself in this frivolous affectation.

"Well — tell me about her now, and how it happened that Mrs. Perrier gave her that valuable property at your expense?"

"Why, she is the same relation to Laura that I am. You see, my father married a second time, and so it came about that Laura is my half-sister. After his death his widow also married again, and Antoinette is the child of that marriage. So Laura is the half-sister of each of us, although Antoinette is no relation whatever to me — merely a step-sister. Make it out?" he asked, knitting his brows, as if he had propounded some dark conundrum.

"Of course — how can I help making it out?"

"Well," said Travis, lightly, "it is a relationship that gets away with most people."

Then he pulled calmly at his cigar.

"And you never told me this before!" exclaimed Brennett, desperately. "And this girl had the same claim exactly on Mrs. Perrier that you had."

"But Mrs. Perrier had promised," interrupted Travis. "She had written and signed her will."

"It is hard — hard!" cried Brennett, springing up and walking nervously back and forth, — "that in a matter like this I should have such a coadjutor, who doltishly keeps me in ignorance"—

"I am beholden to you," drawled Travis, airily, caressing his straw-colored beard, with a gentle gesture, as he watched, with a smiling face and incongruously fierce eyes, his friend's movements.

In a juncture like this he carried more weight than might be argued from his limited mental capacity. Brennett had found him and his resources convenient in more ways than one, and it was not yet conclusively demonstrated that this usefulness was a thing of the past.

"You must overlook something, Travis," he said, as a reluctant retraction. "But I ought to have been fully informed."

Travis readily accepted the amende, for this matter of usefulness was mutual. He was one of those fools who are sub-acutely aware of the fact. Not that he deprecated it; he would have found a ponderous brain merely a dead weight in those giddy and lightsome scenes which made up to him the pleasure and the worth of existence. He preferred to exert judgment and foresight by proxy, and he experienced unfailing satisfaction in the fact that his interests were indissolubly interwoven with those of Maurice Brennett, whose acumen had been attested by success.

"How could I imagine that Antoinette was to come into our plans? What could I have told you — that she is an interesting orphan, twenty-three years of age — and incidentally the color of her hair and eyes?"

"Where is she now?"

"She has just come to Tennessee on a visit to General Vayne's family, up there in the country somewhere," with a vague backward nod of the head. "She has a lot of friends in that neighborhood, and sometimes visits among them for months."

"Where has she been all this time?" asked Brennett.

"She has lived with her father's mother, in a rented house three miles from New Orleans, until about six months ago, when the old lady died — in the nick of time, too," added Travis, unfeelingly, "for the mortgages on her Mississippi plantation, which she had been fighting off for the last ten years, had just been foreclosed. So you see she left Antoinette nothing. Old Mrs. St. Pierre's death was the reason that Laura wanted to return from Europe. She intended to take a house in town this winter and have Antoinette with her. I don't know why you never heard of Antoinette, unless it is because she is rather an unimportant little body."

Brennett came back and sat down in front of the fire. Travis watched him vacantly for a few moments. Then he yawned portentously and shifted his position. Certainly he had had time to recover somewhat from the first poignant anguish of disappointment, but few men with interests of magnitude at stake could so readily detach the mind and so trivially catch at trifles. He glanced about the room with its stereotyped hotel furnishing; then he fell to gazing at the uncertain flickering of the gas-jet.

"What the devil do you suppose is the matter with the meter?" he suggested, lazily.

Brennett sat silent and absorbed. Presently Travis yawned again, and broke forth suddenly —

"Oh, I say — its getting on to two o'clock. And, my dear fellow, I am fagged out. I've been travelling for two days. I can't get hold of my faculties for a midnight consultation like this. Let's adjourn till to-morrow."

Perhaps Brennett had scant regard for the efficacy of these faculties when got hold of. Still silent and absorbed he made no motion. It had begun to rain, and the wind was rising. Heavy gusts dashed against the window, and in the intervals one might hear the drops trickling drearily down the panes. They beat with a resonant clamor on the tin-covered roof of some portico near at hand. The sound was chilly and cheerless, and after once more observing Brennett's impassive attitude, Travis rose and re-dressed himself completely, with a resigned deliberation of gesture; then languidly resumed his chair.

"Well, since you are determined to talk it out now I have only to say that I think we have come to the financial jumping-off place. Can't you suggest anything except unavailing regrets that you did n't know about Antoinette?"

"I can suggest a sure way to command that money," returned Brennett, taking his cigar from his lips, and glancing keenly though furtively at his friend.

"How?" demanded Travis, excitedly.

"A sure way," reiterated Brennett.

"How?" asked Travis again.

"Marry her," said Brennett, coolly, replacing his cigar.

"Marry her."

Travis looked at him in silence.

"Well," said Brennett, impatiently, "what have you to say to it?"

"Got nothing to say to it," replied Travis, shortly.

And again the man who managed him as one manages a restive horse was fain to concede the point, and give him his head.

"Well, see here," said Brennett, presently, "the division which Mrs. Perrier made is, except in the matter of convertibility, largely in your favor. Suppose you try to persuade Miss St. Pierre to exchange the houses for your plantations. Represent to her——"

"You can't *represent* anything to Antoinette. I tell you she is sharp, sharp as you yourself—and very suspicious. If you knew her you would appreciate that you can't represent things to *her*."

"In some respects the exchange would really be to her advantage. The rents of those houses are an inconsiderable per cent upon the value of the property in comparison with the income of the plantations and their market value. She would give her houses to you at the maximum valuation and take your lands at the minimum. She would exchange a small income-bearing property for a large income-bearing property. Don't you see?"

"Ye-es," Travis assented, dubiously. "Perhaps. But there are the labor questions, and the unsettled state of the country, and the low price of cotton. And, Brennett, — you don't know Antoinette!"

"There is another possibility that she might be induced to make this exchange. Her title — Mrs. Perrier's title to those houses is not indefeasible."

Travis turned with a stare of blank amazement. He took instant fright. "Then God knows," he cried fervently, "*I* don't want them. *I* won't exchange."

"You were so certain that your sister would leave you that property, that I thought it worth while to have the title looked into, in view of a speedy sale."

"And what's the matter with it?" asked Travis anxiously, vaguely aware that his friend had some intention shuffling behind all this, but as yet utterly unable to "spot it."

"Why, Clarence Clendinning, the man who fraudulently sold to Mrs. Perrier, purporting to convey in fee, was only a tenant *per autre vie*, and at the period of this sale this life estate was just terminated. Thereafter he could be regarded only as a tenant at sufferance. So you see she bought literally nothing, and all this time she has been liable to be ejected at any day by the remainder-man."

"And who the devil is the remainder-man?"

"His name is John Doane Fortescue."

"John Doane Fortescue?"

Brennett assented.

"Hm-m," said Travis, meditatively. "I have never seen him, but I know who he is. Antoinette is related to him. They are cousins — distant — but I should say she is about the nearest relation he has, for he is the last of his family." He thought it over silently for a moment. "This whole affair seems to me very queer," he suggested.

"Not so queer, after all," said Brennett. "The way of it is this, — John Fortescue's grandfather, who first owned the property, was pressed for a large sum of money — more than he could raise by mortgages — and as he had always intended to will it to his grandson he did not wish to alienate it absolutely. So he granted to Clendinning an estate in it *per autre vie*, remainder to John Fortescue in fee. This estate *per autre vie* was limited to the life of James Murray, who was then a young man and only died in April, 1857. The same year and month Clendinning — I suppose he had expected his tenancy to last longer, and wanted to make more out of it — sold the property to Mrs. Perrier for a good big price."

Travis turned upon him a face of smiling triumph. "1857! That lets us out," he remarked, cheerfully. "The remainder-man's remedy is barred. I happen to know that here the statute of limitations allows only seven years next, after the right of action first accrues, for the institution of proceedings to recover real estate."

"I talked to the lawyer about that," said Brennett. "It seems that in Tennessee an intermission or sort of suspension has been prescribed, in view of the disorganization caused by the war, during which no statute of limitations can be held to have operated. This period extends from the sixth of May, 1861, to the first of

January, 1867 — something more than five years to be added to the original seven."

"Throw in your suspension," said Travis, liberally. "Can you count, Brennett? — can you count? Seven years and your suspension — eh? We're in 1871."

"But," persisted Brennett, pressing the point, "the statute doesn't run against some people. There are minors, you know, and married women, persons 'beyond the seas,' or *non compos mentis* — all of these have three years next after the disability is removed to bring suit. The remainder-man may set up a disability and recover the property at any time within the next ten, twenty, thirty years."

"Ah, but Brennett, that is a very remote possibility."

"It is probable enough," Brennett declared, with a weighty significance of manner, "to frighten Miss St. Pierre."

Travis cast upon him a sudden glance of comprehension. "By the Lord, Maurice," he exclaimed, "what a head you have!"

"You must represent," continued Brennett, careless of this tribute, "that you are willing to exchange your solid lands for her houses, with their shaky title, because it is imperative for you to have a convertible property, and you are therefore prepared to encounter some risk."

"And I can say, too," added Travis, temporizing with a certain pulpy weakness which he called his conscience, "that the remainder-man may never appear. And I'll say it," he added with a curious inconsistency, "in such a way as will make her think he is knock, knock, knocking at the door."

He gave a short, abrupt laugh, impressed with the humor of the situation. The next moment he was himself frightened by the bugbear conjured up for the intimidation of Miss St. Pierre.

"But suppose upon these representations she does exchange — and before I have time to do anything with the property up comes John Fortescue, brisk and smiling, fresh from the Lunatic Asylum, or he may turn out to be a minor, or a married woman, or just returned from circumnavigating, or" —

"All that need not be considered by us," said Brennett, impatiently. "The man is dead, no doubt, or he would never have let this thing lie. In fact, I think I have heard that he is dead. And I am quite sure, too, he was not married."

"Never, so far as I know," rejoined Travis.

"And so, no widow," — said Brennett, with satisfaction — "and no heirs nearer than Miss St. Pierre, herself." Presently he added —

"It would be a good plan for you to go to General Vayne's place, have an interview with her, and propose an exchange of property. We can't manage it through an agent, because we don't care to take any one into our confidence."

Travis's countenance fell, but he said nothing. There was much conversation between them not expressed in words — hardly in reciprocal glances. Brennett replied to the objection in his face.

"So she does n't like you," he said, slowly.

Travis's pause was impressive.

"I should think not," he declared.

Brennett knitted his brows.

"That is a complication. Can't you propitiate her — *make* her like you."

Travis for a moment was dubious, but reflective. Then he glanced up with some hopefulness. "There is one way to please her," he said. "The very fact that I thought of it would propitiate her."

Brennett turned toward him with quick interest.

"You see," Travis explained, discursively, "Laura left her personalty to me, and among her valuables is an old heirloom of the St. Xantaine family. Laura was descended from the St. Xantaines, you know."

Brennett knew it. Everyone who had ever been within speech of a descendant of the St. Xantaines knew the fact.

"And so is Antoinette," continued Travis. "So you see it would be peculiarly appropriate for me to give this old trinket to her. She ought to have it, really. It is a very curious old cross — diamonds set in silver, in the shape of the letter X — rather handsome diamonds, but nothing extraordinary. It is not very valuable, intrinsically."

Brennett looked disappointed.

"I tell you, Brennett, the thing is famous," persisted Travis, replying to the look as the other had done. "She would value it more than something worth twenty times as much. I know her way. The stones have a history — it may be true, and it may not. I have my doubts. It is said that they were originally set in some ornament given, ages ago, by royalty itself, to some interesting member of the St. Xantaine family — I can't say how many ages — can't say what royalty — can't say what interesting member of the family." He spoke with the air of a man who had been nagged by these mythical splendors of ancestry which he did not share. "I have heard the story often enough, but the Lord knows I don't want to burden my mind with it. Antoinette, though, could tell you all about it. She would be immensely pleased to have it, and pleased with me for thinking to bring it to her."

"That will do," said Brennett, decisively. "But, Travis, talk about the business first, and bring in the cross as an afterthought."

And upon this the two parted.

CHAPTER IV.

TRAVIS was a man incapable of temporizing with lower conditions than those of his ideal, and he was acutely conscious upon arriving at Chattalla that it was not the town it ought to be. There was something fiercely inconsequent in his criticism, — certainly regarded as the terminus of a swift transition from London and Paris, the dingy little village was, by comparison, nowhere. But although they did not enter into his mental estimate the great fundamental facts of humanity were here — crowded upon this narrow stage were roaring farces, and sentimental melodramas, and elements of high tragedy, the actors all sublimely unconscious of the defects of the accessories and for the most part having known nothing better.

He was constitutionally dilatory and indolent in business, but the one o'clock dinner served as a stimulant to his industry, and with the determination never to eat another meal in Chattalla and to take the train at nightfall, he promptly prepared to call on Miss St. Pierre.

He found egress from the hotel blocked by a surging crowd which filled the adjacent section of the Square — a crowd with grave, absorbed, not to say awe-stricken faces, all turned incongruously enough toward a door bearing above it the festive sign — Saloon. He made several attempts by the use of his elbows, and also a cane with which he now and then rapped gently upon a brawny brown jeans shoulder, to force his way down from the somewhat elevated porch, that seemed in great requisition, for, jammed and creaking beneath the heavy weight, it afforded special facilities for looking over the heads of the crowd below. The cane and the elbows made scant impression upon the general pre-occupation, but at length a country fellow turned with a savage growl in response to a smart admonitory tap — as that free, enlightened and democratic animal will sometimes do — and it occurred to Travis to supplement his blandly reproving "Will you let me pass?" with the inquiry, "What's the row?"

"Why," said the countryman, casting upon him an excited eye, "Toole's brother-in-law hev jes' killed a man."

Travis looked down to button his glove.

"Gratifying to Toole," he murmured, softly.

"That's him now," said his interlocutor, leaning eagerly forward. "That's Toole."

Travis, his progress effectually barred by the press, thought it worth while to cast a glance in the direction indicated. The glance lingered upon Tom Toole, standing in front of the groggery — a tall, powerfully-built, splendidly proportioned figure, and the very ideal of a trooper. His old wide-awake hat was pushed back, showing his tawny hair and his grave, flushed face. His long tawny beard streamed down over the breast of his brown jeans coat. His feet, encased in coarse muddy boots, which were drawn up over his trousers, moved unsteadily, and his blue eyes were deeply bloodshot. He exhibited that peculiar phase of drunkenness when a man's senses have been sobered by some sudden shock, but the fire still streams through his veins and writhes among his muscles.

Travis noticed his superb physique with a flippant allusion to the dead man.

"I can't sufficiently commend his caution in not tackling Toole."

And so he fell smilingly once more to buttoning his glove, raising his hand now and then with a deprecatory gesture when some man as tall as himself jostled against him and threatened the equilibrium of his silk hat, as it towered in aristocratic isolation above the multitude.

"Oh, shucks!" said the rustic, comprehending him. "This hyar Ryder Winklegree, the man what war killed, air ez big ez Tom Toole. He war able ter pertect hisself. An' Graffy never done it a-purpus — 'twar self-defence, ye onderstand. Graffy never drawed a pistol till Winklegree's bowie-knife war at his throat. That's what some say. Though Winklegree's father an' brothers hev swore ter sweep the country ter find Graffy — the prosecution air a-goin' ter be mighty hot, now, ef they kin compass it. But they hain't fund him yet."

"Bolted — eh?" said Travis, languidly, and even while speaking to the man never looking at him and having the air of ignoring him.

"Flunged down his pistol an' kited through the back door of the groggery thar. So I hev been gin ter onderstand. The sheriff's a-riding now."

A sudden violent commotion of the crowd swept Travis and his acquaintance down the steps and upon the pavement where close at hand a carriage, of a long by-gone fashion, awaited him. Far out into the street the throng was dense, and after he had stepped into the vehicle he was detained for some minutes, while the driver loudly and fervently insisted on a pass-way.

"They couldn't do nothin' with a man like Graffy nohow — even ef they makes out ter find him," said one of the deeply interested upon the curb-stone. "He is an idjit. Jes' the looks of him would be enough for a jury."

"Graffy's a sane man, though he looks like an idjit — thar's su'thin the matter with the leaders of his face so that he can't hold it still fur a minit," declared Travis's former interlocutor — a man of speculation, for he presently added — "It always did seem ter me thar war a sorter spite in that dispensation — ef a body mought git thar consent ter think so. He's a sane man, an' he's made ter look like an idjit. I know that some folks 'low fur sartain ez he is one — an' mebbe they'll fetch that up on the trial."

"Nothing," began Travis, lounging on the seat of the carriage, his eyes on his gloves as he buttoned them at his ease — both men on the curb-stone turned sharply; a touch of embarrassment was in their manner; they were restive under the unwonted impertinence of being spoken to with contemptuously averted eyes, but their respectful attention was constrained by something peculiarly impressive in Travis's tone and bearing as if he were about to propound views of importance — "Nothing," he drawled, "is so efficacious as pleading insanity."

Then he leaned slightly out of the window.

"Now, driver," he expostulated, with that affectation of familiarity and good humor which is the most offensive form of condescension, "can't we trundle along?"

The door banged; the whip cracked; the good Tennessee horses stretched their muscles.

His lightsome mood deserted him when he was alone in General Vayne's library awaiting the appearance of his step-sister. He walked the length of the room with a swift, nervous step. The realization of the magnitude of the interests involved weighed upon him heavily. The project was clumsy at best. He was no tactician, and he knew it. How could he bit and bridle his words, and harness them in with those wayward coursers, the doubtful whims of a woman.

Perhaps it was the relief from suspense which enabled him, when the door at last opened, to drop naturally and at once into his wonted manner. It might be appropriately described as a silken manner, and it combined with all those soft lustres acquired by the habit of good society a certain brotherly ease as he approached the tall, slender girl who stood upon the threshold.

"I hope, now, Antoinette, you are going to say you are glad to see me," he drawled softly, as he took her hand. "Stretch your conscience to that extent; won't you! A little exercise will benefit it, develop its elasticity you see. A good conscience must have some elasticity or it can't be an easy fit. Take the advice of a man who experimented on his conscience before you were born."

She was evidently not quick at repartee. She looked at him with smiling hesitation, as if at a loss for an appropriate rejoinder. Then, as he laughed lightly, and, turning away, placed one of the cumbrous arm-chairs for her before the fire, she replied, at last, with conscious flatness, —

"I *am* glad to see you; very glad."

She spoke with a mellifluous, monotonous voice. She moved slowly toward the chair, the soft material of her long, mourning dress sweeping inaudibly over the gay carpet. She was so languid that in comparison even Travis seemed alert. Except for the convention which accounts all yellow-haired girls beautiful, she might be held as only pleasing. Her hair, drawn in light, loose waves from her brow, and coiled in smooth plaits at the back of her head, was of a paler, duller shade than that of the true auriferous blonde. She had a fair complexion, a ready flush, and a slender, delicate white throat, half concealed by the black crape frilling clustered about it. Her features were small, and singularly characterless and inexpressive. Despite its gentle prettiness her face, in its unmeaning immobility, was like a mask.

He sat down near her, maintaining his usual careless, listless aspect, but occasionally glancing toward her with furtive watchfulness, and doubtfully. He could not now discuss their sister's will with the callous readiness he had displayed to Brennett. The consciousness of the feelings which must naturally animate her induced in him a repulsion for the part he was to enact in the little scene, in which the two people who had profited by the death of a woman, presumably dear to both, were to canvass the relative value of the property she had left them. He did not expect open reproaches, it is true. He knew she must be keenly sensible of the futility, as well as the unbecomingness, involved in intimating to a man fifteen years her senior that he failed in the respect due to his sister's memory. She would dread the counter-intimation that her grief had been so handsomely gilded at his expense that she could afford to indulge it. The situation, however, unsettled him; the more, because the desultory conversation, on trivial topics, failed to suggest how he had best approach the subject of his mission. Presently he was fain to lay hold on his awkward project without the preliminary graces of an exordium.

"Do you know, Antoinette," he said, "that this is a visit on business."

Her smile might have meant anything or nothing.

"I should like to talk to you about the disposition which Laura made in her will of her property."

He had described Miss St. Pierre to Brennett as solidly sensible, well-informed for her age and sex, and shrewd beyond either. But she was certainly singularly inapt in conversation.

"I was very much surprised," she said inappropriately

enough. Then she checked herself, hastily, with a deep flush. For the surprise she had expressed might seem to refer to differences which had long ago subsisted between her father and his step-daughter, while a member of his household, and in which Travis had interfered to aid and abet his sister. By reason of tender years Antoinette had been a non-combatant, and she had later construed Mrs. Perrier's infrequent letters, a birthday gift now and then, or a morning call at long intervals when in the same part of the country, rather as an acknowledgment of her irresponsibility in these matters than as a manifestation of affection.

To Travis Mrs. Perrier had been the most devoted of sisters. In the relation of step-children they had formed an alliance offensive and defensive against all the world. Afterward his chosen friend had become her husband, and to the day of her death the brother and sister were on cordial terms and frequently together. The fact that Antoinette was equally closely related to her she had ignored for so long that the girl was genuinely astonished when this relationship was adequately recognized by the terms of the codicil of the will.

Travis took instant advantage of her admission.

"And I was surprised, too," he assented. Then, with his incongruous sledge-hammer mode of phrasing, he softly drawled, "I was very harshly treated." He leaned back languidly in his chair, slipping the tips of the fingers of his left hand into his trousers pocket as he glanced about aimlessly at the gay carpet, at the showy, shattered mirror, the flashing fender and andirons, and the glowing wood fire.

"The property which I received is inconvertible in the present state of the country as compared with those houses. Now I am in need of ready money, and I should like to make this proposition to you. Those plantations are, as you know, completely cleared, in full operation, and the levees are in perfect condition. Now don't you think we might make an exchange?"

He did not wait for a reply, but began to argue the question in his reasonable, plausible style, which so impressed strangers. He especially endeavored to prove that the investment was safe, and dwelt particularly on the fact that her income would be trebled, as the plantations produced phenomenally in comparison with the market value of the lands.

"I know that you are thinking it is odd I wish to get rid of the plantations when they pay so well," he said with his light laugh.

She merely smiled in her non-committal, conventional fashion.

"Let me remind you that I told you the plantations are not easy of sale. You observe I *don't* say you might readily sell them, and I tell you fairly, you can't mortgage them nowadays." He made this stipulation in a weighty manner; it was the lesson of experience. "But I do say that they will give more income than any other investment whatever. Now I am in need of a considerable sum of money. I could afford to let you have them at a great sacrifice, and I will tell you why. I know of an opportunity by which I could make an immense fortune if I had available capital, and I could raise money by a sale of those houses, or mortgages. What do you think of the plan?"

"I don't know just yet what to think," she replied, slowly.

Travis seemed prepared for this.

"Now," he drawled, placidly, "if you will permit me to advise, I suggest that you shilly-shally as little as possible in getting rid of those houses."

She fixed her eyes suddenly upon him. "Why?" she asked, with a startled intonation.

"There is an outstanding title to that property, which, if established, would invalidate Laura's title, and of course yours."

She sat silent for a moment, looking intently into his tranquil face, as if she were trying to extract more from it than he had told her in words.

"Whose is it?" she asked concisely.

"His name is Fortescue; John Fortescue. You see, Laura, who was always careless in matters of business, bought this property without having the records examined, and knew nothing of his interest. If this claim should be set up — and I suppose it will be, sooner or later — it would involve the property in a suit that might last ten years, and in all probability you would lose the whole of it. Isn't it better to draw every year the certain and large income from lands that can never be spirited away by legal chicanery than to be wound up in endless litigation like that?"

She made no reply for a time, and when at last she spoke it was irrelevantly.

"Do you know Mr. Fortescue?" she asked, with a peculiar characteristic hesitation, which might pass for mere girlish timidity, but in an older woman would indicate habitual caution.

"No, I have never met him."

"Does he know about this claim?"

"I should think not. If he knew, he would raise the question at once. A friend of mine — or, rather, his lawyer — discovered it by accident in examining some old records, and I suppose we are the only people aware of its existence. I did not know it myself until a few days ago."

"Who is this Fortescue?" she asked.

"Why, you ought to know who he is; your father was his second-cousin," said Travis, a trifle impatiently, for she was apparently disposed to give her attention to small personal details rather than to the matter of business submitted for her consideration.

"I have heard of him, but I never saw him. He used to live in New Orleans." Then, after a pause, "Where is he now?" she persisted.

"I do n't know. He has the reputation of being a wild fellow, and he has lived a riotous, wandering life, chiefly in Europe, I think. I know he has not been in New Orleans for many years now."

She leaned her elbow on the arm of the chair, and gazed reflectively into the fire. The cheap clock on the mantelpiece ticked off many seconds, even minutes, as she sat thus, gravely silent. Travis, silent too, stealthily watched her. His contemplative eyes were languid no longer, when her head turned slowly toward him. She was about to speak, and his heart beat quick with the hope that she would at least promise to consider the proposition.

She hesitated, as she always did. Then, as in his eagerness he leaned slightly toward her, she said, "Now that I think of it, I seem to have heard that that man had two sisters, and a brother. How was it? And where are they?"

He recoiled indignantly. He began to recognize in all this her ill-regulated caution, and perhaps a touch of suspicion.

"Why, what has the man, himself, to do with the matter?" he broke out, impatiently. "It is his vested remainder in the property that affects you, Antoinette. You ought to have a lawyer to examine its validity, and then decide about this exchange. The point of law is the question, not the man's relatives. Not even such a genealogist, such a respecter of persons as you, can make anything by taking account of his ma's pa and his pa's ma. *They* are not kin to the St. Xantaines!"

He gave that sudden, short laugh which he seemed to keep for those rare occasions when he perceived something which he fancied was a joke. Her face was as inexpressive as ever, but a hot flush, rising to the roots of her fair hair, warned him. This was hardly civil, certainly impolitic.

"Forgive that fling into the family tree," he said, with his careless, fraternal air, "and I'll tell you all I know about the man's brother and sisters, although they died in childhood, and have nothing whatever to do with the affair. They were drowned in a steamboat accident on the Mississippi River, when the Bellefontaine burned just above my father's plantation. Never shall forget how she looked swinging around the bend, a tower of flames."

"Oh, were *they* the children drowned there! I remember that dreadful story," she said, with a little shudder.

He looked at her and laughed. "It was nearly thirty years ago," he cried.

There was a pause.

"How that family has thinned out," said Travis, discursively. "His father was an only child and his mother's brother, Adolphe Duchene — you remember that crusty old bachelor? — died ten or fifteen years ago. This Fortescue is the last of them."

Then ensued another interval of silence.

"What sort of claim is this?" asked Antoinette.

"Well, the man who sold to Laura made a fraudulent conveyance. He had only a life estate in the property. That is now terminated and Fortescue is the remainderman. You can get all the details by having a lawyer to examine the record."

"If I should exchange with you," she said, "you would have the same difficulty about this claim. What would you do?"

"I am willing to take the risk. There is a probability that the claim may never be set up. If it should be I could possibly compromise with the claimant. A man in my financial position must make sacrifices. But you — I should think you would want to avoid the losses and uncertainties of litigation."

She made no rejoinder.

"Remember," persisted Travis, "this claim may be sprung at any moment, and any lawyer will assure you that it is valid."

"If I have no right to the property," she exclaimed, hotly, and losing for the first time her self-possession, "I don't care to keep it."

"I thought you were too sharp for that sort of sentimental nonsense," returned Travis, scornfully. "Don't you see that Laura paid a full value for the property and you can only be ousted by some legal subtlety. But law is law, you know, and many people have lost property through carelessness about titles. And, Antoinette, if I were in your place I would not talk about this affair. The mere whisper of it will cloud your title so that nothing can be done with that property for the next thirty years. And Fortescue *may* never move in the matter. There is nothing underhand in keeping it quiet," he added quickly as a concession to feminine squeamishness. "It is all blazoned on the record — as free to Fortescue as to anybody else."

Once more there was a long pause.

"Take it all into consideration," said Travis, rising. "I hope you will determine on the safest course — the only safe course for you."

He walked to the door, stopped as with an after-thought, then suddenly turned back. He caught her countenance off its guard. She was looking after him with perplexed anxiety and distrust in her eyes — a cold, hard, calculating dubitation anomalously expressed itself in her delicate infantile features. He was not a man of observant habit, but the realization of the crisis sharpened his senses. So far, it was evident, his mission had been a failure. An appreciation of this fact gave his amiable, languid manner the added charm of a gentle deprecation as he approached her once more.

"Ah, Antoinette," he said, "I had almost forgotten." Then with his blunt habit of speech — "I have brought you something that I thought you would like."

Her eyebrows were elevated in doubting surprise.

"It really belongs more properly to you than to me — that old St. Xantaine cross, you know."

Her face changed; her color rose; her eyes were suddenly aglow; her lips parted in a smile of unaffected pleasure.

"Oh, how kind of you — how kind and thoughtful! There is nothing in all the world that I should so delight to possess."

The genuine ring in her voice thrilled him. As he placed the gleaming gaud in her hand there was a certain picturesque effect in their attitudes. It might have seemed a moment of some splendid homage — the man was so handsome and so intent upon pleasing; she was so graciously pretty and so evidently agitated by a sweet emotion. The scene would have suggested an episode in a romance. Surely there was no possible intimation that the presentation of the cross was devised by a crafty schemer to lubricate the stubborn machinery of a clumsy project.

Certainly all was much smoother now. The girl held up the diamond X all a-glitter, and laughed with pleasure. Travis found it easy enough to say in a casual, off-hand, brotherly fashion, —

"I'll write to you about that matter of exchange, Antoinette, and give you in detail all the points."

"I shall always be glad to hear from you," she replied, prettily, and he was struck anew by the change in her voice.

"By the Lord Harry," he said to himself as he stepped into the carriage and was bowled rapidly away, "Maurice Brennett himself could n't have managed that more adroitly."

Then his flexible attention turned from the subject, and as he cast a glance out of the window at the desolate waste that encompassed him on every side, something in the terrible solemnity of its aspect smote upon the chords of his trivial nature and set them all to jarring.

"Damn such a God-forsaken country!" he exclaimed with a sudden unreasoning anger.

He struck a match, lighted his cigar, lifted his boots to the opposite cushions, and thus as comfortably established as circumstances would allow, gazed out upon it with a contemplative contempt into which entered an element of self-gratulation that it was none of his.

And so he saw before him a bleak barren; he knew that it rained and sleeted and hailed alternately; he heard the frozen drops of water dashing against the glass, and he was chilled.

But did he see, as he passed, a spectral wavering in the haunted thickets, where even the weeds were dead and sheeted with ice? Did the wind bring to him from across the plain the shrill tones of a bugle, piercing the clamor of some woful invisible rout? Did he quake with an unnamed fear when he skirted a heavy work and the pallid mists came suddenly down and interposed an impalpable but opaque barrier between mortal eyes and some fierce assault upon the grim redoubt, which threw the earth into a strong tremor and shook the air with a terrible sound? Was he even aware of the presence of a woman, who heard and saw all these things, as she stood in the rain, and the hail, and the sleet on the steep slope of the great traverse in the midst of the terre-parade plein of Fort Despair — or was his glance so cursory that he hardly distinguished her among the bushes, and the mists, and the looming works? Sometimes she turned her head slowly, fearfully, impelled to look backward, yet hardly daring for the horror of what she might see. Sometimes she rose to her full height and, panting with her exertions, leaned upon her axe-handle and gazed far away at the billowy sweep of the wire-weeds — all whitened with the hail and lashed by the wind into a surf-like commotion, and stretching and stretching across the level, until, though only weeds, they touched the blurred sky. Then she bent once more to her work.

And it was strange work for a woman — and a slight, timorous, weakly woman like this. She dug for the wood as well as cut it, for, although others had been here before her on a like errand, the timbers of the old powder-magazine still lay deeply embedded in the heart of the great traverse. They would kindle more readily than the green, soaked, ice-girt saplings close at hand, and make better fuel for supper. This heavy, unaccustomed labor, and the terrors of the spectred place were a check on some grief which beset her. It was only at long intervals that she fell to sobbing, and dried her tears with the backs of her hands, or upon the sleeve of her dark blue cotton dress, or upon the red worsted tippet tied over her yellow hair, which hung down about her neck after the country fashion, and glittered here and there with frozen drops of water. Then with a tension of muscle and nerves that sought to be substituted for strength she lifted the axe, and again the burnished glimmer of the steel cleft the pallid mists. There was a flash of a different kind struck out when the metal clashed sharply upon a minie-ball, spent so long ago, and sunk into the clay, or a curiously fashioned, flint arrowhead, — for often these implements of warfare of far different ages and far different peoples are found lying side by side, washed by the same rain, lighted by the same sunshine, turned sometimes into the same peaceful furrow. Once there was projected into the dim, gray atmosphere a fiery darting gleam, brighter and fiercer than all the others. She drew back hastily, then she stooped and took from the earth a great solid shot, and tossed it down upon the terre-plein. "Ef that thar thing," she said, as she watched it break the ice in a standing pool, "ef that thar thing hed happened ter be a bomb, the way that fire lept up mought hev busted it. An'" — with a sudden change of countenance, — I wish it hed! I wish it hed!"

And yet again her fears broke upon her weeping. Suddenly her eyes were dilated with a new terror. She had become strongly conscious of a vague presence near at hand. She fancied that it sometimes flitted to the shapeless fissure where once was the door of the powder-magazine, but as her glance turned thither it stole back silently into the glooms within. With a morbid fascination she was continually peering over at that black gap below, as she worked high up in the rain outside. She saw only the mists shifting in and out of the useless vault-like place. But when she averted her eyes she knew that something had slipped to the door and was looking at her.

All the full-pulsed courage that had once beat so high here where the battle was fought had ebbed away long ago, and there were those stronger than she who avoided the place as if there were a ban upon it. She only wondered now that she should have come at all, as she hastily packed the wood she had cut into the barrow, and wheeled it away through the outlet and into the midst of the battlefield, along the road that the movements of mighty armies had worn,— a meek successor to the flying artillery! But here the whirl of any wheel was suggestive, and it roused the cavernous echoes. Even when it was silenced by the distance the bright colors of her garments were visible from the spot she had left — now a fitful gleam of red and blue against the hail-whitened weeds, and now adding to the Protean illusions of the place and flaunting like a battle-flag from a far away misty lunette.

And when it was gone at last a sound issued suddenly from the silence of the old powder-magazine — a sound as of despairing hands struck together. A man came out abruptly from the jagged fissure and stood gazing wistfully at the point where she had disappeared, — a man with a face such as one does not care to look upon twice, a face which Nature seems to have intended as a flout at humanity. There was some painful affection of its muscles which would not let it be still for an instant. He mowed and grimaced like an idiot, and only the expression of his eyes gave evidence of his sanity. He was further set apart by the red brand of a birth-mark above his left eyebrow. His yellow hair, of a deeper hue and a silkier texture, but like the woman's, hung down to the collar of his brown jeans coat. Here only was the hand of Nature laid kindly upon him — even in the gray light of the sad day it glimmered like burnished gold.

When he spoke, each syllable was flung out from his agitated muscles with the force of a projectile.

"Mirandy might have holped me some! Jes' one word would have holped me some! But I dilly-dallies ter the door—an' then I dilly-dallies back—too skeered ter let her know. An' now she's gone! An' ef I war to gin her a call to fotch her back, them ghostis would set up sech a charging cheer I'd most drap dead ter hear it."

He too glanced dubiously over his left shoulder, and his own mowing face set in the pallid mists was as frightful an object as any he could dread to see.

As he stood out hatless in the rain and the sleet he noted the deepening gloom of the day. The early nightfall was close at hand, and he welcomed the change.

"It'll be cleverly dark by the time Mirandy gits ter her house," he said, unconsciously speaking aloud, the rural proclivity to soliloquy strong upon him. "An' along 'bout midnight I kin slip down thar an' see Tom an' her—an'—" What to do then? Once more, with a realization of the utter futility of scheming or effort, he held his despairing hands above his head and smote them together.

Then he turned back into the old powder-magazine for safety. Sometimes when the terrors of the law were strong upon him he lay silent, motionless, scarcely daring to breathe, listening to detect some alien sound in the surging wind, and the ceaseless rain, and the turmoil of the ghostly forces that had died in the vain struggle to carry the work, and vainly struggled still. Then there were times when fear loosed its clutch upon him, and he rose up and strode about his narrow bounds, the grotesque distortions of his mowing face more horrible than ever in contrast with the misery expressed in his eyes—times when he could take no comfort from the distinctions between murder, and manslaughter, and excusable homicide. He only knew that there was blood upon his hands. And he wrung them.

The woman wheeling the barrow had need of the guiding gleam of light which she caught from far across the battlefield. It was like the glister of some great, lucent, tremulous star, but it was charged with a meaning foreign to cold sidereal glintings. It was the light of a home and the fact can dignify a kerosene lamp and a log-cabin.

She burst into her ready tears as she saw it. "Thar'll be a mighty differ in that house arter this!" she exclaimed.

The red fire-light flared out into the night as the door was opened and a burly shadow came forth to meet her.

"Gimme a holt o' the handles o' that thar barrow, Mirandy!" said Tom Toole in penitent haste. "I clean forgot thar warn't nothin' lef' at the wood-pile." He meant the place where the pile ought to be. "Did ye hev ter go a-pickin' up of doty wood off'n the groun'?"

"Thar warn't no doty wood nowhar ter pick up," sobbed Miranda. "I got this off'n the old forts."

Her husband turned and looked hard at her as she came into the light.

"Ye hev hearn 'bout it all," he said, conclusively.

"They kem hyar a-sarchin' fur him," she replied.

"They ain't fund him yit," he said, breathing hard as he thrust his hands into the pockets of his brown jeans trousers and strode heavily up and down the floor. His wife had knelt upon the rough ill-adjusted stones of the hearth, and was stirring the live coals with an old bayonet kept in the chimney corner for the peaceful offices of poker. But when he spoke she turned her head and looked after him breathlessly, the bayonet still in her hand, her loose yellow hair tossed back, a deep flush hot on her cheeks, her eyes wide and bright, the kindling of a sudden hope revivifying the early faded youth in her face. She had expected only a terrible tale of capture and despair. And she had dreaded it.

Toole was a man of a discriminating conscience.

"Ef Graffy hed done it a-purpose I'd be the fust to say — 'Take him.' An ef Graffy hed done it in a fair fight I'd say — 'That's agin the law. Take him, too.' But thar air mighty few men ez hev got the grit ter stand still with the p'int of another feller's bowie-knife ter thar throat an' be carved. Ev'ybody said 't war no wonder that Graffy drawed his pistol then. He'd hev been a dead man ef he hedn't. Leastways, that is the word they tell in town."

Caution prompted this last stipulation, for Toole was conscious of having been too drunk at the time of the occurrence for the evidence of his senses to be of any value, even to himself.

His wife hesitated, the bayonet still poised above the glowing coals. Then with suddenly developed cynicism she said — "Thar's nothin' like humans. A man air obligated ter be mighty peart ter git away from twelve other men a-settin' in jedgment on him."

"Waal," said Toole, "he air fur enough away from hyar by now, I reckon. 'Twar self-defence, but ev'ybody 'lowed that the prosecution would hev been mighty fierce."

"How'd he git the money ter go?" asked the woman with an anxiously knitted brow.

"Somebody mus' hev lent it ter him, I reckon," said Toole with preposterous hopefulness.

Equally ignoring the probabilities she assented to this view and then fell silent.

Every faculty was absorbed in brooding upon the various phases of the event, and she went mechanically about her preparations for supper — broiling the salt pork upon the live coals, and baking a johnny cake on a square flat board propped up before the fire and thus exposed to its heat. There was "salt risin'" bread in the oven with coals beneath and upon the lid. This she lifted off now and then with the bayonet-poker to judge how the baking was progressing. Once she let it fall with a heavy crash.

"An' whar he will go," she cried, with a sharp note of anguish, "it will all be strange to him. He air a man marked for a purpose by God A'mighty — but what air the purpose nobody keers ter know. Thar 'll be laffin' an' mockin', an' a-follerin' of him always. An' stones will be flung at him in the streets. 'Pears like ter me ez I kin feel 'em now. The Lord is mighty hard on some folks."

Toole paused in his heavy striding to and fro. He looked upon his wife as a sort of moral pilot, and he felt that he was now among the breakers.

"That ain't religion, Mirandy," he said, severely. "An' ye air a-talkin' of foolishness. Who hev got the moest friends — you, or me, or him? Why, thar ain't a yaller dog in the county that don't wag his tail when that man goes by the fence. An' wharever he 'll drift to thar 'll be the same pack o' chillen, an' idle, shiftless niggers, an' no 'count white trash a-hangin' round ter hear him play on the fiddle, an' beg or borry his money — he can't keep his money no more'n ef it 'twas red hot — an' git him to do 'em faviors. And' they 'll traipse arter him jes' like they done hyar. An' he'll crap — he'll rent land from somebody. An' he'll go fishin'; he'll go fishin' of a Sat'day like he always done. He ain't so 'flicted, nohow; he hev been respected by all. An' this thing war self-defence.

Lawyer Green was speakin' 'bout it jes' afore I kem out'n Chattalla, an' he said he thought so, jedgin' from town talk an' them that stood by. Law, Mirandy, he'll go fishin' all the same, an' the chillen, an' the dead-beats, white an' black, all will hang round him, an' he'll hev so many friends that they'll hardly leave him a nickel for himself."

Somehow the idea of this friendship, albeit of a dubious advantage, made life seem more tolerable to Miranda. The fire flared joyously up the wide chimney, casting a ruddy glow on the faces of the children as they trooped in to supper, and conjuring up quaint shadows on the dark walls and the rafters, from which depended strings of red peppers, and hanks of blue and yellow and white yarn, and a picturesque swinging-shelf where the humble store of groceries was kept safe from the rats and mice. And there was the sound of childish laughter in the house, that had been so sad to-day, and the baby grew excited amidst the hurly-burly, and after the others were tucked into the trundle-bed he was hard to get to sleep. But at last quiet came again. Toole lounged in front of the fire smoking his cob pipe, and his wife, her foot still on the rocker of the box-like cradle, sat in a low chair mending the child's clothes until, succumbing to the soporific influences of the heat after her long cold tramp, she fell asleep over her work. Very still it was within; you might have heard the drawing of the wick in the kerosene lamp, for the oil was low. There was a bed of pulsating coals where the hilarious flames had been. The gnawing of a mouse among the rafters now and then annotated the silence. Without, the rain fell in a low muffled roar — sometimes a volley dashed against the shutterless window. The mists pressed their pallid cheeks close to it and looked in. Far and faint a bugle sang out suddenly in the night and the wind redoubled its force.

It was with a movement as if a galvanic thrill were all at once astir in every fibre, that Tom Toole became conscious that something beside the mist was looking in at the window. Roused to a wild alarm he sat rigidly upright, his pipe in his hand and his eyes fixed, expectant of the re-appearance of the vague presence of which he had only caught a glimpse. It might have been hallucination, suggested by the subject uppermost in his mind; it might have been the distortions of the rain and the grimy glass; it might have been the strange uncanny effect of the mist, but it was like a mowing human face. And he knew it when it came again.

He cast a startled glance upon his wife; her sleeping head had sunk down on the edge of the cradle, and her yellow hair streamed over the baby's torn red dress which she still held half mended in her unconscious hand. No creature was awake in the house except himself and the mouse gnawing among the rafters. He crept cautiously to the door — so cautiously that the loose boards of the ill-floored room scarcely creaked beneath his heavy weight. That short instant was charged with the force of years. He always felt afterward that in shutting himself out into the rain, and mist, and darkness, with the man who awaited him there, he had shut himself off forever from all his former life — a life so different from what was to come that it often seemed to him that that other reckless, buoyant, undismayed self had died when he closed the door.

Henceforth he was a changed man, for he carried a heavy secret. He could not so much as be boisterously drunk of a Saturday evening, according to the immemorial custom of the dwellers about Chattalla, lest some fatal allusion escape him. He was of an unthinking habit of speech, and the perpetual guard upon his tongue, even when alone with his wife and children, was a perpetual effort. He actually feared that he would tell in his sleep that a man whom the law sought, lurked in hiding near at hand. He could scarcely support the strain of feigning, when among his boon companions; speculation was rife as to Graffy's flight and refuge. Whenever his boat was in mid-stream, and he faced the east, as he pulled on the ropes his heart waxed faint and his sinews failed, and he labored hard in the old accustomed vocation that used to be but a slight matter for his strength. He was aware, too, of a change of countenance in nearing the cruel old redoubt, and grew painfully conscious of the powder-magazine in the distance, where, as in a cell, a man who had slain another in self-defence expiated a deed that the law forgives.

Sometimes for the sake of the light and air, Graffy stole cautiously out from the jagged fissure where once was the door of the powder-magazine, and lay at length on the banquette. He could see far across the battle-field through the outlet, narrow though it was. The sun came out and shone upon the young ice-covered growth fringing the long lines of earthworks, and then those grim parapets seemed overhung by a glittering network of stellular scintillations. Even the humble wire-weed was an incredibly magical and refulgent thing, and all the level expanse was bestrewn with myriads of glancing frosty points of light. The skies, vast as the skies above a sea, shoaled from blue to orange, and thence to the purest green, in the midst of which the red sun went down to the purple hills. There was much splendor before the sad eyes so full of tears, and half unconsciously he missed it as the thaw came on.

He grew very lonely after a time. He eagerly watched for Miranda as she went back and forth from the house, and he was glad to know that she thought he had miraculously secured the money to go far away, and was safe somewhere, making a new life for himself in a new place. He learned to look for the ferry-boat, slipping to and fro across the river with some wagoner and his team, and he took an interest too in the passengers. His idle gaze followed Tom's motions as he cut the wood, or fed the pigs, or pulled the boat and set the air vibrating with his melodies.

For with no appreciation of his voice, and no adequate appreciation of his motive, Toole sang at his work, though his heart was heavy, thinking the sound might give a sense of companionship to the solitary wretch hidden away there in the empty powder-magazine. Even the stern old rocks along the river were instinct with a wild, barbaric, melodic spirit and responded in strophe and antistrophe. Sometimes there were war-songs; sometimes quaint antiquated ditties which his great-grandfather had brought here when he came and settled in the cane among the Indians; often he sang a certain old hymn, and its dominant iteration — "Peace — peace — be still!" — resounded in its strong constraining intensity far and wide over the battlefield — echoing from parapet to parapet, thrilling through the haunted thickets, and breaking the silence with a noble pathos where the shadowy pickets lurked and listened in the rifle-pits.

A long unseasonable drought succeeded the thaw, chill and calm, with a clear sky, and a pale suffusion of wintry sunlight. The traffic on the distant pike was slight, and the dust lay motionless. But more than once on the battlefield when the earth was a-throb with that strange tremor, and a vibratory blare rang faint in the distance, and a dull weird clash as of arms pervaded the drear and lonely sunshine, Graffy heard the swift wheels of artillery whirl by with a hollow whir, and he saw the dust spring up from an old redan and, without a breath of air, whirl too in a reeling column after the invisible battery. He had seen often before this simple phenomenon of dry weather. But its coincidence with the sound gave it a new meaning, and then he came to fear the dead hardly less than the living.

And so when Tom Toole, under cover of the midnight, slipped down into the old magazine with his tin pail of bits, stolen from his own larder, and his canteen that had not yet forgotten a certain trick of joviality, and a cartridge-box full of tobacco, he would find these creature comforts disregarded by Graffy in his frantic importunacy for the money to get away and be gone forever. A promise to "skeer up" all the cash possible without exciting suspicion, supplemented by warnings that an inadvertence would certainly precipitate capture while all the world was yet on the alert for the reward offered, could reconcile Graffy to the "harnts" for a time — so long in sooth as Toole lay there and smoked his pipe, and talked in whispers, even though his topic was not cheerful. For Toole grew prone to dwell upon the experience of various malefactors who had fled from justice with an inadequate supply of funds, and who were finally glad to choose between surrender and starvation among strangers, fairly falling upon the sheriff's neck for joy when he came with the Governor's requisition.

But when Tom was gone Graffy would relapse into his anguish of loneliness. He pined for his friends — who, stimulated by the reward offered for his apprehension, sought him by bush and brake. He pined for the sound of his crazy old fiddle. He yearned for the light. One afternoon when he crept out from his burrow he found that clouds had gathered at last and portended rain. He hardly feared to lie here on the tread of the banquette, for in these days there were no laborers in the fields. The last " dog-tail," as the frosted remnant of the cotton is called, still hung on the black and withered stalk, and not a plough was yet bedding up land for the new crop. In these early sunsets the cattle that broke down the fences, or were surreptitiously let through the bars by their enterprising owners that they might utilize General Vayne's fields as pasturage, came lowing by on their homeward way. Sometimes an estray was sought with a loud, beguiling call of "Suke!—Suke!"— which echoed far along the level stretch, and heralded the cow-boy's approach. Now, however, there was no sign nor sound of life. The earth seemed as lonely as the lonely skies. As he smoked, a coal fell from his pipe upon the ground, and in the very abandonment of idleness he watched the golden thread, which emanated from it, steal along the edges of a dead leaf and trace in a fiery arabesque all the graces of the maple. Then, spark by spark, it died, and the leaf was a cinder. Another had been touched by the coal — another and another. Here and there a twig caught, too, — and at last a tiny blaze was kindled. Its presence cheered him. It was a friendly, domestic thing. It seemed instinct with the spirit of home. "It's ez much company ez a human, mighty nigh!" he exclaimed.

Somehow the sight of it deadened his fears. The sound of it lulled him. As he lay on the ground beside it he dropped into a reverie — so deep that even his morbidly sensitive nerves were not startled by the thud of rapid hoofs until they had approached very near.

It was a terrible moment. He sprang to his feet. Then he seemed stricken into stone — he could not move a muscle. He had no consciousness save a repentance of his temerity. He understood nothing but the imminence of his danger as he looked over the parapet at a horseman galloping past close along the crest of the counterscarp. He remembered afterward, rather than noted then, that this man's face was meditative, and that his downcast eyes were fixed absently upon the ground, heedless of what he saw. The sweeping gallop bore him speedily into the distance toward the great house looming up in the closing twilight.

The fugitive from justice hastily flung a heavy stone upon the fire to crush its life out. Then he skulked like a shadow, like the skulking shadows whom he feared, through the jagged fissure and into the deep glooms within the powder magazine, and his world of lunettes, and redans, and redoubts, knew him no more.

The sky was gray. The earth was black. The wind was dead. The only motion in all the still, sombre expanse was the upward curling of a tiny wreath of luminous smoke from beside the heavy stone that had served to smother the fire. Its fall had displaced a single coal. This glowed, and flared, and reddened in the melancholy dusk encompassing it.

And the night came on very dark.

CHAPTER V.

THE battle-field, the cannon-shattered house that rose like a monument in its midst, had so impressed Estwicke, that when he was here once more he had a strong sense of familiarity with all the details of the unaccustomed place. It seemed to him that he had often sat in the dim light of the flickering fire and the shaded lamp, watching through the window the weird new moon in the cloud rifts, as it hung, a curved, red blade above the dark glooms of Fort Despair, then fell like an avenging sword in their midst; that he had often noted the bizarre reflections in the shattered mirror, which gave distorted glimpses of the gay carpet, the crimson curtains, the stiff mahogany furniture and the family group. And perhaps because of this savor of old associations he was quick to detect something which he did not recognize. The young lady looked at him with changed eyes. They were more brilliant than he had thought them, and colder. A deep, rich flush glowed on her delicate cheek. She seemed older, more formed. Her manner was collected, and he observed with a sense of loss that her smile lacked a certain spontaneous cordiality which he had supposed was characteristic of her. For a time he could not understand this change. It roused him to a keener interest in his visit, which had been prompted only by duty, and perhaps unduly postponed, for it was a drive of but eight miles from the barracks to General Vayne's plantation, these being intermediate points between Marston and Chattalla. The mistake under which he fancied he had been invited still rankled, and he had promised himself that, after taking due cognizance of this involuntary hospitality by a call, he would drop off and trouble the Vaynes no more with his acquaintance.

He often glanced toward her as she sat close to the table in the mellow dimness of the shaded lamp. The pliancy of her figure and the soft, black folds of her dress were prettily accented by the stiff, angular outline of the old arm-chair. Sometimes as she turned her head her brown hair caught the flicker of the fire and sent out a golden gleam. Her silence struck him as significant. It seemed tense and studiously maintained — unlike the mute quietude of the young stranger, Miss St. Pierre, which had the ease and languor that suggested habit. Miss Vayne was alert in every fibre and vivacious in every impulse. He saw in her eyes the interest with which she followed the conversation. She was denying herself in that she took no part in it. He had a vague idea that he had something to do with this — that she sedulously forbore to claim his attention.

Was it possible, he asked himself in swift alarm, that he had so received her unsophisticated little apology as to induce in her restraint, even resentment? He made an effort to recall the interview — it had not since recurred to his mind — and it seemed to him that what he had said was peculiarly neat, even more appropriate than he had thought it at the time. Surely she could not know that he was secretly amused by her contrition; that he had laughed because she had seemed to fancy him so susceptible to her unintentional sarcasm. Even then he had recognized how gentle an impulse had prompted her. He valued it adequately now that he had apparently forfeited her kindly feeling. He was all at once eager to recover lost ground.

To win a proud and alienated young lady to graciousness, in a general conversation founded upon so recent an acquaintance that only platitudes are in order; with her father and her aunt solemn sentinels on either side; with a silent, observant young stranger to mark all lapses from established usage, was, he felt, no easy matter. Still he took advantage of the earliest hiatus in that weary subject, the state of the turnpike — which had certainly been a sufficiently severe trial while he travelled it.

He addressed an observation directly to her, although he could think of nothing more felicitous to say than —

"As the spring advances the road will be better, and I assure you, Miss Vayne, it is a very picturesque drive to the barracks. I hope that some Sunday afternoon you will come with your aunt and Miss St. Pierre and witness dress parade."

Marcia looked smilingly from her aunt to Miss St. Pierre, as if submitting the question.

"Oh, delightful!" cried Mrs. Kirby, amiably effusive.

"No doubt it is very interesting," murmured Miss St. Pierre.

Mrs. Kirby's face grew abruptly grave, as if the sins of many sinful years had suddenly found her out.

"Oh — but, dear me — now I come to think of it — *Sunday* afternoon — yes," she said, in an appalled *staccato*, her waving curls stilled into becoming solemnity.

An ethical discussion with the old lady was hardly what Estwicke wanted. Once more he fixed his eyes on Marcia.

"Do you think it too frivolous an entertainment for Sunday afternoon? All the ladies in Marston come."

The girl's cheek dimpled. Her sudden laughter broke upon the air.

"Thank you for suggesting 'the ladies of Marston!' In a case of conscience nothing is so valuable as a precedent," she cried, joyously.

Estwicke was a trifle confused by having this sentiment attributed to him, and Mrs. Kirby rustled hastily to the rescue.

"Not that I mean to imply that the dress parade is in itself sinful on Sunday. I — well — I, myself — I don't judge of that — yes — I don't judge — for military men have no — no —"

"No souls to be saved?" suggested Marcia, raiding like a guerrilla through the conversation.

"Oh, my dear child!" protested Mrs. Kirby, aghast.

"I beg your pardon, Aunt Alice. Don't let me interrupt you. You were saying that military men have no —" She paused, expectant.

In breaking her silence her mood had changed. A daring spirit was shining in her eyes. She had a freakish delight in her aunt's embarrassment and involution of explanation. Mrs. Kirby was eagerly desirous not to seem to reflect on Captain Estwicke and his Sunday parade, but was bewildered by Marcia's conduct, which she supposed was inadvertent.

"I meant that military men have peculiar duties, and —"

"Very peculiar, if one of them is to break the Sabbath," cried the bushwhacker, harassing the enemy's march.

"Perhaps the life does not tend to foster a sense of religious responsibility," said Estwicke, demurely, commiserating the old lady's anxiety.

"I did n't mean *that*, exactly. I meant — I meant —" Then Mrs. Kirby plucked up a little spirit. "It is very hard that *I* should have to fight the battles of the *military men*," she said. "You should resent these reflections, Captain Estwicke."

"I am too wary a soldier to give battle to a superior force," Estwicke declared. "I am retreating in good order."

The girl had the grace to be a little ashamed. She was still laughing, but she did not look at him, and she blushed.

"And you ought to remember, Marcia, that your father is a soldier, too," said Mrs. Kirby, reprehensively.

"Oh," cried Marcia, altogether reckless, and rejoiced to throw a bomb into the cowering circle, "that kind of soldier has — has gone out of fashion."

She was frightened when she had said this, and a sudden grave pause ensued.

"How far are the barracks from Marston, Captain?" asked General Vayne, feeling bound to interfere. He was a serious and earnest man, a little slow; he had had no large experience of the world, and he did not pretend to understand women. In a girl, the general feminine incomprehensibilities were enhanced by the caprice of youth, and he made no effort to tackle the problems which Marcia daily suggested. What she had just said seemed to him singularly inappropriate, but he did not even wonder how she had happened to say it. He was relieved to see that she had subsided at last, and that Estwicke entered with unimpaired gayety upon the new theme.

For Estwicke was pleased and flattered. It is true he began to understand that she regretted her apology and had repented of her repentance. She evidently wished him to think that it was a matter of no such paramount importance to her as it had seemed then; that she had no special solicitude about hurting his feelings and jarring his prejudices. In order to convince him of this she was handling them sufficiently carelessly now. But she only succeeded in convincing him that she had thought much about him, and that she had schemed in her innocent and inexpert fashion to produce these impressions upon him. He deprecated infinitely wounding her pride and sustaining her resentment, and once more he sought to conciliate her. With that smoothness and suavity which were evidently only superimposed upon his manner, having no root in the rougher material of his character, and which affected her as an exponent of worldliness and insincerity, he again addressed her.

"What amusements do you have in Chattalla in winter — no sleighing nor skating, I suppose?"

"No; I hardly know how to describe the amusements. We have the rain and the mud."

Estwicke laughed. "Oh, that sort of gayety! You have been deprived of it for the last three weeks."

"Singular drought, sir, for this time of the year; protracted, sir, — very, indeed," said General Vayne, with a planter's chronic disaffection with the elements.

"It looks like rain this evening — very cloudy," said Estwicke. He watched the glowing fire for a moment in silence. "The wind is rising," he added.

A meditative pause ensued.

"That sound," said General Vayne, slowly, "is not the wind."

His eyes, too, were fixed absently on the fire, but as Estwicke lifted his head he became all at once conscious that the others were watching him with some strange, furtive meaning, some intent expectation. A yearning sense of desolation had struck suddenly across the warm domestic atmosphere, and although an alien it shared the hearth with them. The hickory logs flung jets of sparks and long, quivering plumes of flame high up the chimney; the fender glittered as if set with scintillating jewels; the faces of the girls bloomed like rare exotics. In this quiet sanctuary of home even the hot hearts of the men were fain to beat calmly. The shattered mirror reflected the sheltered, peaceful group; but oh, for the battle-field without! and oh, for the graves beyond the river!

The earth pulsated with a strong tremor; the windows shook with a responsive vibration; all the air thrilled and shivered with a tumultuous throb.

"It is a drum!" cried Estwicke.

He was unprepared for the effect of his words.

"Oh, don't say that!" exclaimed Mrs. Kirby.

"Oh, surely *you* don't recognize it, too," cried Miss St. Pierre, her soft voice strangely agitated.

He faced round and looked at them in amaze.

"I beg your pardon?" he said, interrogatively. They made no reply, and he turned toward Miss Vayne. She was softly biting her under-lip, and looking at her friend with eyes suffused with laughter.

"I begin to think, Antoinette," she said, "that you are superstitious; you really believe the battle-field is haunted by the dead soldiers."

Only Mrs. Kirby observed that Estwicke recoiled as if from a blow. His face was pale, rigid, and very grave, but it had, even in its gravity, a consciousness of self-betrayal. He visibly strove to regain his composure.

"I hardly think *I* am superstitious, Marcia," returned Miss St. Pierre, speaking with more animation than usual, and with a shade of annoyance in her voice, "but *you* have positively no imagination."

"What you call your imagination seems to be only a thorn in your side."

"Perhaps what she calls her imagination might be translated as a heart," said Mrs. Kirby, blandly allying herself with the visitor.

"And what is a heart but a thorn in the side!" cried Marcia, joyously.

General Vayne began to explain. "The country, sir, is so cavernous that the gradual approach of railway trains produces very peculiar effects of sound."

"I lived here," said Mrs. Kirby, significantly, "for many years. I never heard those sounds before the war. Of course I don't believe that terrible story — but — but this is one of its inexplicable points."

"There is the wind, at last," said General Vayne, with the air of a man impatient of nonsense, and striving to effect a diversion.

It came with a hollow roar through the vastness of the night and the plain. There was a sense of a mighty movement without. The tramp of feet, that long ago finished their marches, rose and fell in dull iteration in the distance. The gusts were hurled through the bomb-riven cupola, which swayed and groaned and crashed as it had done on the day when even more impetuous forces tore through its walls. Far — far and faint — a bugle was fitfully sounding the recall.

"Ah-h!" said Mrs. Kirby, shuddering a little — "hear that!"

Estwicke mechanically turned his eyes toward the window. They distended suddenly, and he sprang to his feet.

For the empty embrasures of Fort Despair were belching flame and smoke once more. The haunted thickets, visible in the lurid light thus projected into the midst of the black waste, were in grim commotion; and here was a prickly growth that might be bayonets — for who could say, in this strange glow and this strange place? — and here was a triumphant, waving hand — and one might fear to look at the ground, remembering what once lay there. The pallid horizon alternately advanced and shrank away as the fire rose and fell. The deep, surly glooms of the night pressed close about, but veins of flame were beginning to pulse through the thickets wherever a dead leaf might cling, and a glittering rim had encircled the dry crab-grass, and was flaring and broadening round all the field.

"Some miser-r-able boy," exclaimed General Vayne through his set teeth — he was a man of punctilio, and even with this provocation he did not forget the presence of ladies — "some miser-r-able boy has been hunting over the plantation, and his gun-wad has set the grass afire. Ten to one the fence will burn!"

Estwicke was still standing near the window, his hand upon the red curtain. Mrs. Kirby looked at him speculatively. Certainly he — a man and a soldier — could not be afraid of ghosts like Antoinette, who was morbidly timid and afraid of everything. She could not thus translate the emotion he had manifested. Here was something different, deeper. It baffled conjecture.

No trace of it was on his face when he turned. "The wind has shifted," he said. "That fence must be in considerable danger now. General, we had better make a sortie."

Marcia's face grew very grave. "If the fence should catch, papa, would the fire be strong enough to blow to the gin-house?"

There was a pause. "I hardly think that," her father replied, "but it is possible. I couldn't spare the gin — and — and I've a good deal of cotton there still."

"We had better go at once," said Estwicke.

General Vayne glanced hurriedly about him for his hat, and strode after his guest out into the night.

There was no moon; there was no star; tumultuous clouds surged over the battle-field. The glare showed the great, gaunt waste in its immensity. The wind rioted fantastically with the flames. Here and there a ball of fire was thrown from the empty embrasures of Fort Despair, and fell into the midst of the crab-grass, and burst into a thousand waving plumes, and expanded and glowed into a thousand more. Now and then, as a dead branch crashed to the ground in the thicket, a fiery flag waved so high that one might see the livid sky look down — then the flag was struck amid a shower of sparks. A deep, steady glow in the distance suggested that the flames had given over these airy effects, sustained only by leaves, and dead-wood, and crab-grass, for the solid business of burning the fence. They quickened their steps, and presently the younger man began to run. He was not a light weight, but he was swift on his feet, and he soon left General Vayne far behind.

And as he ran, a thing happened which seemed to him strange at the time, and afterward still more strange. He was not so far from the blazing redoubt as to believe that what he saw was imagination. Among the slender growth that fringed the parapet, some of which was already aflame, there appeared suddenly two figures that walked with a measured gait, presently accelerated to a soldierly double-quick. He had not a touch of superstition — he instantly suspected that General Vayne had secret enemies, who had fired his field of set purpose, so that his gin-house and cotton might be burned as if by accident.

Estwicke, with characteristic inconsequence — without an idea of what he should say, how he should deal with them, or how they might deal with him — held both his hands, trumpet-wise, to his mouth, and shouted to them with all the force of his lungs. The crackling brush drowned his voice. They had halted abruptly upon the parapet, arguing with each other, to judge by their excited gestures — one of them was so wild of demeanor that Estwicke fancied him drunk. At the second stentorian halloo, they faced round suddenly. Perhaps in the far flickering vistas which the flames revealed among the dun shadows they caught a glimpse of Estwicke. With a simultaneous movement they dropped out of sight, leaving him staring at the blazing panorama in blank amaze.

As he pressed on he began to overtake other men, both white and black, chiefly tenants of General Vayne, all running toward the gin-house. They were inspired only by friendly feeling, for their rents were already paid, and the cotton still there belonged to their landlord. The figures of a distant group loomed up, gigantic and distorted, through the smoke, and seemingly in the midst of the fire as they knocked down the burning fence and scattered the rails. With these grewsome effects the simple significance of the gin-house was oddly incongruous as it came in sight, mounted grotesquely on its stilts, and distinctly defined against the black whirl of skurrying clouds, and the lurid, unnatural glare. The out-door press, which stood near, was like some menacing monster, with its levers, huge, uncanny black arms, poised above the negro who with a balky mule was trying to plough a few furrows to hold within bounds the impetuously burning crab-grass. The sharp, ringing strokes of an axe sounded high above the roar of the flames and the clamor of voices, for a dead apple-tree, a fatally near neighbor, had caught fire from the fence, and was blossoming white and red anew. Before the sharp steel had pierced through its rotten trunk it had fallen, sending up myriads of sparks into the dark sky, and a moment later the cedar shingles that roofed the gin-house were blazing timorously. When Estwicke came up the smell of burning cotton was on the air.

They made an effort, however, to save what they might. After a few minutes of such desperate exertion as left a soreness in his muscles for days, Estwicke happened to glance up in the midst of tearing out the soft, fluffy, infinitely bulky masses of unginned cotton. He caught the steady gaze of a man with a pallid, frightened face, who stood idle on the outskirts of the sweating, struggling, panting crowd. Save for that frightened pallor Estwicke might not have recognized the face, but he had not forgotten the scene on the ferry-boat, and Toole's expression recalled both it and him.

"Hello, my man, lend a hand here!" Estwicke called out fiercely. Do you find nothing to do but to stand and watch us work?"

The man fell to without a word.

But once or twice afterward Estwicke came in contact with him, and noticed that, big fellow as he was, he was doing no good. His hands trembled; he was confused; he seemed to see nothing; he was in everybody's way. And he *was* a big fellow. Estwicke measured him critically, noting closely his gait, gestures, build; then silently fell to work.

The gin-house and press were burned. The rescued cotton, scorched, begrimed with cinders and dirt, lay, nearly worthless, upon the ground hard by. The air was still dense with smoke, and pervaded by the pungent odors of charred cornstalks and crab-grass, and of the burnt cotton. It had grown intensely dark; the very outline of Fort Despair was swallowed up in the black night, and except the sullen glow of the embers of the press and gin-house, there was no spark nor gleam in all the vast stretch of country. Estwicke was looking about for his coat, which he had flung upon the ground when he went to work at the cotton. He stumbled upon it presently, and, as he picked it up, he accosted Toole suddenly.

"You're one of the men I saw on the parapet yonder to-night. I know your build. Did n't you hear me call?"

So imbued was he with the idea of incendiarism that he wondered the man did not affect surprise, — did not attempt denial.

Still Toole seemed agitated, anxious, almost piteous.

"An' I knowed it war ye ez war a-callin' of me, 'kase I seen ye ez well ez hearn ye. But it got so hot thar that I war obleeged to scoot outern them works, an' dust away in a hurry."

But for the man's tremulous deprecation Estwicke would have thought all suspicion of evil-doing absurd. "Who was with you?" he persisted.

The other's face was very white; or perhaps some livid flame had started up among the ashes and cast a pallid gleam upon it.

"'T war Tim Jones ez I started away from the turnpike with, but I dunno ez I had n't caught up with that darkey Bateman — no, I overhauled him down ter the spring. 'T war Tim, or mebbe Pete Winsley."

Estwicke turned away, half ashamed. Then with his insistent exactingness, he looked over his shoulder. "How did you happen to go up on the parapet? That was a queer manœuvre."

Why should the man tremble? The reply was so obviously natural. "Waal, Cap'n, I lives not fur on t'other side o' that redoubt, an' it had n't been long burnin' when I seen it, an' naterally I run ter whar I seen the fire fust. Then it air toler'ble good walkin' up thar on them old forts, an' I jes' thought I could run along the parapets till I got hyar; but the fire got het up so hot ez I war obleeged ter come down."

If he had resented any of these questions, which must have seemed to impute to him some evil intent, Estwicke would have dismissed the subject from his mind. As it was, he spoke to General Vayne when they were tramping back together through the darkness toward the lights beginning to be faintly visible in the windows of the distant house.

"My dear sir," exclaimed General Vayne, "he is my good friend, although a very humble one. Why, he served four years in my Brigade!"

"That settles it," said Estwicke, satirically; but he said it to himself.

However, he felt justified in throwing aside his suspicion, since the man most interested refused to entertain it.

He was sorry, of course, that General Vayne's cotton and gin-house and press were burned, and wondered that the loss should be borne so calmly, knowing that it must be disproportionately large to a man in his financial condition. But Estwicke's was a temperament to which excitement is always grateful, and he strode into the bare, echoing hall, flushed and warm, but feeling all the more active and alert for it. He looked like a young blacksmith, with his soot-begrimed face and hands, and his hair and whiskers powdered with cinders, and his collar and shirt-front ornamented with arabesques in charcoal. He was distinctly deprecatory of the presence of the three ladies, as they surged out into the hall, eager for news. Mrs. Kirby did not scruple to hold up her hands at the sight of him.

General Vayne noticed this. "We will go and get rid of some of these cinders," he said. "Then we will give you an account of the affair."

But when they returned, he did not at once mention the fire. Estwicke was speaking as they entered the library. "I assure you, General," he protested, in a tone that sought to veil impatience and annoyance, "it is nothing — nothing whatever."

"I am afraid, Alice," said General Vayne, gravely, addressing his sister, "that Captain Estwicke has burnt his hand severely."

There was a sympathetic chorus of "Oh-h!"

"You must let me bind it up," exclaimed Mrs. Kirby.

Marcia turned to the door. "I will get bandages, and sweet oil, and flour — and what else is good for a burn?"

Estwicke glanced keenly from one to the other, as if doubting their seriousness; then he flung himself into a chair, held up his hand, looked at it, and laughed aloud.

"If I go back to the barracks bearing such desperate wounds as these, it will demoralize the men. They will mutiny — desert. They won't stay in a country where such horrors are possible."

But his ridicule had no effect. And in fact their sympathy was not altogether misplaced, for the burns were sufficiently severe to cause great pain, which he had borne with the stoical pride of a man who piques himself on his fortitude, who has known the poignant anguish of serious wounds, and who is supported by the consciousness that this is no killing complaint. He had intended to say nothing of it, and at the earliest opportunity to bid his entertainers good evening, but his host had accidentally discovered it. He was soon reconciled, however, to the offices of these gentle Samaritans, as he sat by the table while the three stood in anxious absorption around him. He thought the pain would be considerably assuaged if one of the young ladies should bind up the injured member; but as that might not be, he was in a measure consoled that Marcia held the saucer, and Antoinette the bandages, while Mrs. Kirby's gentle, wrinkled hands were soft and soothing to the touch.

He could not forbear a gibe at her old-fashioned remedies and the amateur performance. "I can't let this stay on till I get back to the barracks," he declared.

"But you must — and why not?" asked Mrs. Kirby, sternly, repressing him as if he were a refractory boy.

"I wouldn't — I wouldn't have the surgeon see this extraordinary bit of work for — " He looked at the bandages and the slow, tender hand hovering above them, and shook his head silently.

"Good surgery as any!" cried Mrs. Kirby, strong in her faith in herself. "I assure you, Captain Estwicke, *I* am not ashamed of it."

"Oh!" cried Marcia, abruptly — "his wrist!"

"His *wrist* is burned, too!" exclaimed Mrs. Kirby in an animated *crescendo*. "The flesh is baked! yes — fairly baked! You will carry that scar to your grave!" she prophesied with grieved solemnity.

Estwicke broke out laughing afresh.

"What a pity! What a pity!" he protested.

"Oh, how it must pain you," exclaimed Marcia. "And to have burned it *here* — trying to save our cotton!"

Estwicke was daring at best. This sympathy did not tend to decrease his courage. He lifted his head and looked straight at the girl, with a sudden meaning kindling in his eyes.

"To make amends you must promise that you will always think kindly of me after this," he said.

Mrs. Kirby paused, her head inquiringly askew. She looked quickly from one to the other of the young people. His eyes were still fixed upon Marcia's face, which had crimsoned from the roots of her hair to the lace knot at her throat. Her long eyelashes dropped. The hand that held the saucer trembled visibly. And she evidently could not speak. Mrs. Kirby answered for her.

"You must be very wicked indeed if you make us"— *Us* was the word the punctilious old lady used — "think unkindly of you — on so short an acquaintance."

But Estwicke did not care for this thrust. He saw that the young girl understood him, that Mrs. Kirby did not, and that the episode had been unnoticed by General Vayne and Miss St. Pierre, who were now standing near the hearth listening to the account which one of the boys was giving of his experiences at the fire.

Marcia was very silent and demure after this. And Estwicke was demure, too. He got away as soon as he could, and as he rode off he said to himself that it was a pleasant little circle, and he would come again next week.

"That young man has a very wilful temper," said Mrs. Kirby, thinking of his resistance to the blandishments of flour and sweet-oil. "But," added the judicious old lady, "he is as handsome as a picture."

Miss St. Pierre was more discriminating.

"He has fine eyes, and he carries himself splendidly, but I can't say I think he is handsome. His features are too irregular."

Only Marcia said nothing.

One of the boys broke the silence. "He's got a red head on him," he submitted.

"Reg'lar sorrel-top," drawled Dick. And this was *his* contribution to the evening's entertainment.

They did not linger long about the hearth, for it was growing late. The haggard anxiety of General Vayne's expression began to be reflected on his daughter's face as on a mirror. She became very grave. She seemed absorbed. But he talked with his habitual manner of lofty cheerfulness, and bade his sister good-night with a smile. As he rose and with his dexterous left hand moved a chair from Miss St. Pierre's way, she said mellifluously — "I hope your loss is not very severe, General."

"I have been apprenticed to pessimism," he evaded, with a smile. "This is the way I learn the trade."

He opened the door, stood aside, and bowed her out with his old-fashioned ceremoniousness.

Marcia had gone to the dining-room on a household errand connected with laying the cloth for to-morrow's breakfast. She came back presently. His eyes were on the door as he sat by the embers alone. He had expected her, but for a moment he said nothing. She looked at him eagerly — very anxiously.

"How much of the cotton was burned, papa?" she asked, placing her right hand on his left hand as it lay on the table.

"Nearly all, Marcia, nearly all," he groaned.

"And the rest is ruined? — and the gin, and the press?"

"Ruined — yes, ruined," he assented, with a sigh.

In the days of his wild enthusiasm he himself had put the torch with his right hand — a misguided hand that, and better gone perhaps — had put the torch to a thousand bales on his Mississippi plantation rather than risk the capture of the cotton or smuggle it through the lines, and, to use his own rotund phrase, stain his palm with the enemy's gold.

It seemed the veriest fleer of fortune that now he should have such bitter cause to sigh for the loss of perhaps twenty bales, which at the best could be but a sop to Cerberus, to meet the interest of impending debts, to stave off the foreclosure of the mortgage that menaced forever the shattered and quaking old house and the grewsome fields about it.

She still kept her hand pressed upon his hand — one of her ceremonies in their councils of war.

"Papa, what will the creditors take?"

"Anything they like, Marcia," he said, bitterly.

She glanced instinctively about her; it was not a cheerful home, with the wild waste without and the gnawing anxieties within, but they had no other.

Then she turned her eyes upon him with a pained intensity that was pathetic in its helplessness.

"How will we live, papa?" she asked, in a tense voice.

The strain on his nerves suddenly gave way. "God knows, Marcia," he exclaimed, tumultuously. "I don't!"

He rose and walked heavily out of the room. The tears started to her eyes, but she forbore to follow him, and presently she heard him tramping, tramping, back and forth, the long length of the dark, unfurnished drawing-rooms opposite, according to his wont when he could not be still for the throes of his financial distress, or when he was only reflective.

For sometimes his anxieties seemed to relax their clutch, and then the interval, empty of pleasure, of interest, gave him opportunity to review the most important events of his life, and he busied himself with those distraught questions — settled, thank God, long ago — which involved the righteousness of the Lost Cause. Doubts thickened about him. Doubts! And his right arm was gone, and his future lay waste, and his children's lot was blighted. And he had flung away the rich treasure of his blood, and the exaltation of his courage, and his potent enthusiasms, and the lives of his noble comrades, who had followed him till they could follow no longer. So he was glad when the screws of the usurers came down again, and the present bore so heavily upon him that he grew dulled in suffering for the past.

No one suspected this — not even his favorite child. She only knew that he was on one of his "forced marches," as she called these demonstrations. To-night it was more prolonged than usual. His soldierly step resounded through the empty rooms and echoed over the quiet building. The faint glimmer from the windows guided him — he would not have had it more. In the intense darkness it seemed as if he were rid of himself — annihilated.

The house had been still for hours, when he saw with surprise a long shaft of light steal past the door. He walked out into the big, bare, black hall, and looked up at the landing of the wide stairs.

Marcia was standing there, her crimson shawl caught about the shoulders of her dark blue dressing-robe, her hair floating in confusion over it. With the aureola of the candle, held above her head among the dusky shadows, she looked like some pictured saint. She smiled at him, and waved her hand toward his room, which was on the ground-floor, and reproached him in pantomime for disturbing, with his heavy tramping, the sleep of the guests in the house.

She kissed her right hand to him, and he kissed his left hand to her. She silently watched him walk softly to his own door, enter and close it after him.

Then, with a wild gesture born of a sudden, mad impatience with this troublous world, she smote the candle upon the balustrade, and in the instantaneous darkness she burst into stormy tears. She had had her touch of martyrdom to-night. As she leaned sobbing against the wall, the extinguished candle still in her hand, she heard the heavy rain begin to fall in the vast waste outside. She recognized once more in the wailing wind those sad sounds which, it was said, were the dead soldiers' cries.

"Oh, my poor fellows!" she exclaimed. "Life is so hard! Be content that your battle is fought — and rest — rest!"

As she went groping up-stairs, blinded by her tears as well as by the darkness, she thought of that hopeless warfare her father was waging now — she had a bitter prevision that it would end only with his life. It might have been happier for him, perhaps, if this new sordid struggle had never begun — if he were now with his comrades outside — outside of the world! Then she shrunk back shuddering from the unspoken thought.

She lay awake for hours, her mind busy with the deep significance of this disproportionate loss. She canvassed the relative obduracy of the creditors, for from her father's experience she knew their respective characteristics better, perhaps, than they knew themselves. In many an anxious struggle since the war the cannon-shattered home had had more hair-breadth escapes than even in those three terrible days when the world about it went mad, when the air was powder and smoke, and the light was flashes of flame, and the rain was lead. She tried to remember what she had heard her father say of the various complicated liens that lay on the property — even on the worn chairs and tables, even on the jog-trot sorrels that munched their hay in replevied jeopardy. She computed the interest with a dexterity acquired in her daily task of teaching arithmetic to the boys. Sometimes, when the total was less than she had feared, she brightened. But in a moment some forgotten item would recur to her mind, and she would fall to sobbing afresh, and bury her face in the pillow. Then she would resign herself to this additional load, and begin again her expert calculations. Once, in the midst of her tears, she did not lift her head — gradually they ceased to flow. Sleep had overtaken her, and had even crowded out the debts.

It was not a restful sleep. She rose in the gray, wet morning, harried and fagged out, with heavy eye-lids and pale cheeks. As she went down stairs she met, in the hall and on the landing, trickling streams of water, that insidiously slipped in where the great shot and shells had made way for the rain. She paused at the door of the empty drawing-rooms — a mass of damp plaster, fallen from the ceiling of the bay-window, lay on the floor, and moisture was still dripping down upon it. She looked up at the grinning laths. She gave a little laugh that was more bitter than tears.

"It's a poor roof you are," she cried, "that we make such an ado to save!"

With all this ruin to clear away, it was to be a field-day with the house-keeping, and when breakfast was fairly over, she made haste to be at it. She went back presently to the dining-room door to admonish her brothers, who sat learning their lessons at the side-table, where it was their habit to partake of mental refreshment, convenient to the household duties of their preceptress. As she looked in a frown gathered on her fair brow. There they were, ostensibly hard at their books, but panting and flushed, as if to master the rule of three were a matter of physical exertion. A tell-tale marble was rolling over the floor, and she noted the swelling and hastily stuffed pocket of the middle-sized boy. His face was grave, studious, but the green cover of the table was drawn aside, and she could see his hilarious, brass-toed boots kicking his brothers, to gleefully call their attention to the fact of how ludicrous was their task-mistress, as she stood apparently deceived by this show of devotion to duty. The stalwart kicking legs must have inflicted severe pain on the other boys, but they made no sign, except to actively return it in kind.

"Boys," she said, sternly, "attend to your lessons. I will keep you in two hours by the clock if you don't recite perfectly." Then in an altered tone, "Don't let me have to do that," she pleaded. "I'm not well, and there's so much work to-day about the house."

"Bet on me, Marsh," said the roguish, middle-sized boy, with a gravely reassuring face. "I'm just a-stavin' ahead on these here old 'rithmetic sums."

"Me, too, Marsh," the others promised in concert.

But what a tumult of the silently deceitful feet under the table! How much they expressed of the gayety of the games of marbles when she was away. How they congratulated each other on her ignorance of these pastimes. How they jeered and gibed at her in their fantastic gestures.

She gave no sign of her consciousness of this sly pantomime. In her normal state of feeling the discovery would have resulted in more trouble to the little miscreants than to her. But now she was greatly depressed, mentally and physically, and she regarded it tragically. She walked away along the hall and into the empty drawing-rooms, her face flushed, and with a swelling, indignant heart. Was she such a tyrant that she must be secretly scoffed at and derided among them? They cared nothing for her, she said — she had expected the recompense of their affection, for young as she was, she did all for them that a mother might. She made their clothes — no dainty work; she taught them and kept them in order; she schemed and contrived for their comfort; they and their rough ways rendered the housekeeping a heavy burden. She worked for them till her hands were hard — *hard* — she protested with despairing iteration. She held up these hands and looked critically at them. They were shapely and white, but the palms were a little roughened, and this was a grief to her.

As she stood in the midst of the fallen plaster, waiting for the one house-servant with brooms and pails, General Vayne chanced to pass the door.

Instead of his lofty cheerfulness there was a pained resignation, almost meekness, on his face. It smote upon her very heart-strings. That dominant impulse of her nature to help to lift up, was suddenly all astir within her.

"Papa," she cried, passionately, "when ill-fortune takes the field in force like this there's nothing for it but to form in line of battle and give it the bravest fight we can make."

There was a tense vibration in her voice; her face was replete with feeling, and all aglow; her eloquent young eyes looked at him from out the ruins of the big rooms that had been so fine in their day.

He had paused abruptly. His hand stole slowly up to stroke his mustache.

"That is very true, Marcia," he said, with weighty conclusiveness. And again, — "That is very true."

The dignity of the metaphor could efface for him the sordid aspects of the situation.

Her words were to him like the blast of a bugle. They rallied his courage. He had lifted his head. He turned away, twirling his long, gray mustache, and strode out buoyantly into the rain.

And she herself had experienced a sudden revulsion of feeling. She went back to her work with a light step, already beginning to evolve plans. She had a full realization of the terrible menace of the future — of the pitiable straits of the present. But now that she had formed anew in the face of these inexorable facts she returned to the charge with the desperate ardor of a forlorn hope.

Despite her youth and her effervescent girlish gayety she had a broad and mature appreciation of the seriousness of life; — her experience warranted this. Even the terrors of her childhood were never the hobgoblins of the nursery tales; instead, she had known what it was to quake in the cellars of bombarded towns and listen to the shriek of the shell. Her imagination had been tutored by the imposing spectacle of a gallant division in line of battle. She derived a commensurate idea of the grim tragedies of existence from the sight of the same crack troops, before the sun went down, decimated and demoralized, mangled and routed. Her only impressions of the gala-world were reminiscences of those hurried festivities in the Confederacy, when she had watched with precocious eyes the unprescient gayety of spirited young officers, who danced all night and marched out and were killed in the morning. Her only experience of travel was in the rôle of refugee, knocking about with her mother through all the South, a prey to a deadly anxiety about the distant "command," and in terror of a newspaper lest she might read her father's name among the long lists of the killed. Her participation in those mad, panic-stricken flights of non-combatants, sometimes in the dead of night, to escape an unexpected insidious approach of the enemy, had sharpened her comprehension of an emergency. Perhaps all this had added to her decision and force of character, and gave her that practical element of precocious management which had been of infinite service in enabling her and her father to readjust the fragments of their shattered home.

All the plans she was revolving now had a certain phase of feasibility. She was utterly lacking in his marvellous susceptibility to abstractions. The case was so desperate that little could be done, but she projected with a sense of triumph small savings here and there in the small supplies. She would hope for the best, and work for it, too.

When the debris of the night's rain had been cleared away she went blithely back to the boys and their ill-learned lessons. She was no longer occupied with the tragic aspects of their callow ingratitude; here, too, the wonted practical element of her management reasserted itself. Not one second was abated of the threatened two hours' penance — even after the others were released she watched above her sewing the roguish middle-sized boy — roguish no longer — alternately weep and "wrastle" over the doctrine of projectile forces as set forth by his primary philosophy. Who so skilled as he in the great feat of plumping out the middle-man from taw — who so reluctant to recognize the scientific principles thus illustrated.

As he was gathering up his books at last his hard-hearted tyrant put her dimpled elbows on the table and looked across at him with a smile. He returned it by a surly, mutinous stare.

"I am going to make," she remarked incidentally, as it were, "— Royal pudding for dinner — on account of *Somebody's* sweet tooth."

A reluctant smile broke upon his face. This beguilement he could not resist.

Thus she made amends for having had "hard thoughts of the poor boys," as she phrased it to herself, and silently forgave the nimble iniquities of those brass-toed kicks.

CHAPTER VI.

THE days that ensued were very anxious days, but with a stoicism inconsistent enough with the impulsiveness of both father and daughter, they sedulously repressed all manifestation of this anxiety, and life in the maimed old house had to its guests as cheerful an aspect as usual. The excitement occasioned by the fire gradually smouldered away with its smouldering embers, but there were other incidents of the evening that Marcia wondered should slip by so lightly.

She constantly expected her aunt to canvass, with all the fervor of feminine curiosity, Captain Estwicke's pointed requisition that she should always think kindly of him now. As time wore on, and Mrs. Kirby said nothing, Marcia was angry with herself for experiencing so vivid a sensation of relief. In extenuation, she declared that if she were asked she would not hesitate to — to — explain — and then she realized suddenly how difficult it would be to unravel for a dispassionate examination this tangle of thought and feeling — or rather this subtle and sympathetic divination of feeling — in which she and a "strange man" — for thus she called him — had contrived to involve themselves in two short interviews.

She dwelt so much upon this episode, and the "strange man's" part in it, that the idea of him became familiar, and might have earned him the right to be accounted an old acquaintance.

Oddly enough, Mrs. Kirby had forgotten it; but perhaps this was not so odd after all, for the day after the fire she dined by appointment with Mrs. Ridgeway, the gossip of the county, and there was greatly entertained. When she came back, even before she got her shawl off, she was absorbed in rehearsing to the family circle all she had heard. The news was dramatized by the expressive play of her blue eyes and her wrinkles, her airily waving curls, the explanatory gestures of her plump, jewelled hands, and the animation of the swinging, swaying veil that clung to the crown of her old black bonnet. Before these excitements had fairly palled, a new interest occupied her.

"Antoinette," she said, one afternoon, breaking a long silence, as the two sat in the flicker of the library fire, and the ever-reddening bars of sunlight that struck aslant through the dusky room, and set all the motes to dancing, "Antoinette, you are reflective, I see; you garner up your thoughts; I hope you make good use of them, my dear. Now, with me," she declared, with her gurgling laughter, "every trivial subject cries, '*Largess!*' and I am generous; yes, I fling away my choicest ideas in words. Anybody may have them for the asking. So, when solitude and silence pounce upon me unaware, I can't think; I haven't an idea to solace me; I have talked them all away; yes, I've nothing to fall back on, you see. And I'm destitute now, my dear; so say something, do. Tell me what you were thinking about."

Antoinette had raised a flushed, perplexed face. She seemed a little confused, perhaps because the thread of her meditations had been so suddenly broken, perhaps because she was conscious of her conversational deficiencies.

"I was only thinking of a letter which I received yesterday — a letter from Austin Travis, my step-brother, you know."

Mrs. Kirby stared. She felt that girls were not so naïve in her day! So he had written to her, had he? And he had come so far to see her — yes, indeed! And he had brought her their sister's diamond cross, so interesting from its associations, and so beautiful! A long vista of romantic possibilities was opening before Mrs. Kirby's contemplation. For this old lady was given over to reading novels, and had a cultivated imagination. Despite her sixty odd years, all that is delicate, and true, and tender in sentiment appealed to her as vividly now as when this dull old world was freshly a-bloom and she stood in her eighteenth summer. Thus she was exceedingly susceptible — vicariously. Under normal circumstances she would have regarded Mr. Travis only as a drawling dandy, and felt for him that robust contempt with which the substantial provincial magnate favors the superficial syllabub circles of fashionable life. The moment he loomed above her mental horizon in the interesting guise of lover, he had acquired all the dignity appertaining to the passion. Mrs. Kirby was suddenly impressed with the conviction that he was a very handsome man, well educated, of good style, according to the modern standard, of excellent social position, and well endowed with this world's goods. He had known Antoinette all her life; doubtless this was an attachment of long standing, and it would be a charming match. To be sure, people said he was wild; yes, (regretfully) a *little* wild. But then, people said so many things. They talked; yes, they talked too much. (Thus the crony of Mrs. Ridgeway.) She had an idea now to solace her, and she experienced a little wistful curiosity, good soul, about the contents of that letter. She sat silent, meditatively gazing down the rich crimson and orange vistas of the fire, where the chips had burned away between the logs, giving glimpses of the white heat beyond; here and there a purple flame, completely detached in the air, quivered with so lucent a gleam that it might seem the vivified spirit of an amethyst; the red coals close to the hearth pulsated visibly, as if the heart of the fire beat there. With these stimulants to her imagination, she wrought out and shaped a letter, such as she wished it might be — so eloquent, so tender, so delicately fervid, that Travis could not have written its like were he to hang for it.

This aerial epistle was a great waste — and there was a great waste, too, of her sweet sympathy. She looked with a motherly yearning at the girl, who had always been lonely enough. An unwonted depth was in the old lady's blue eyes — a little moisture, too, perhaps. She was so happy in her foolish fancy that others were happy. She refrained from speaking, however. She said only to herself that the Balance of Life swings at that delicately adjusted and perfect poise but once. No word nor glance should jeopardize its equilibrium. Curiosity might consume her first! And so she gazed once more at the fire and fell to retouching her letter.

It was very different from Travis's actual letter. He had inclosed with it an abstract of the record which bore him out in all that he had said concerning Fortescue's claim to Antoinette's property. To the inexperienced girl the document had great impressiveness — her title seemed far more shaky than before. Her appreciation of the value of money, of a solid competence, of a provision for her future, had been greatly sharpened in that short interval after her grandmother's death when she stood penniless face to face with the world. She was ill-adapted alike by training and by her constitutional timidity for its conflicts. She had no wild enthusiasms to serve merely in underrating them. Inquiry and effort only proved how overcrowded was the profession of teaching — that favorite recourse of reduced gentlewomen, and for which alone she was well fitted — and dependence or semi-dependence, the greatest dread of poverty and pride, was not altogether below the horizon. The unexpected remembrance of her in her half-sister's will, after so many years of neglect, had changed the aspect of the world for a time. But the knowledge that her title was not indefeasible had reopened all these anxieties and possibilities. Therefore she had concluded it would be best to risk nothing, to exchange with Travis while his financial condition rendered this desirable for him as well as for her. The plantations, it was true, were cumbrous of management, of uncertain value, and impossible of sale. But they gave a good income, and were not liable to be spirited out of her possession by some technicality. As she reflected on this she said to herself that it was high time she made her decision known to Travis — that it would be well to have a lawyer at once examine the state of the titles, both of the town property and the plantations, and confer with her step-brother as to relative values and final arrangements.

By a strange chance, however, which presently befell, her resolution was suddenly reversed, and this came about in the simple routine of life here, where the battle was fought.

On this same day these grave cogitations were still uppermost in her mind when she and Marcia, according to their custom, started for an afternoon walk along the quiet plantation road. The air was crisp and cold, and as they descended the broad stone steps to the pavement, rent here and there with its historic fissures, they heard, distinct in the distance, the ringing thud of a horse's hoofs. A moment more and a swift equestrian figure appeared galloping along the serpentine drive, and Marcia was first to recognize the "strange man." As he rapidly approached them, he was smiling and lifting his hat. Seen in the crude light of the day, which was full upon the unique tints of his dark red hair and beard, his bold, quickly-glancing, brown eyes, his tanned complexion, and his clear-cut but irregular features, his face could less than ever be called handsome, although it was notably striking. There was a suggestion of great vitality and alertness in the pose of his fine figure, but that air of dash and mettle owed something of its effectiveness to the high-couraged animal he rode, for he was gallantly mounted. Her father's daughter could not look upon such a horse save with emotion.

He threw himself from the saddle and walked up the bomb-riven pavement to meet them.

"Adopt Bishop Berkeley's theory, I beg," he cried, gayly, "I'm no matter — and therefore can't interfere with your excursion — or perhaps" — he added with a laugh, "you might allow such an impalpable essence to join you."

"I have an idea," said Marcia, as the three began to walk on slowly together, "that there is just enough reality about you to keep off the cows. Antoinette is dreadfully afraid of cows."

"I perceive a purpose in my creation!" Estwicke exclaimed.

"Oh — I'm afraid of everything," Antoinette admitted, with the shamelessness of the feminine coward.

"And you?" asked Estwicke, glancing at Marcia.

"It is all the other way," she boasted. "Everything is afraid of me."

"I can appreciate that," he declared.

She flushed, and looked away and laughed.

"I hope your burned hand is better," said Antoinette, mellifluously.

"Oh, no!" Estwicke insisted. "It is *not* better — much."

He looked from one to the other — but this, after such a lapse of time, was so empty a bid for sympathy that even they triumphantly withheld it.

Antoinette had paused to pluck a spray of cedar from a little tree by the roadside. She showed the berries to Estwicke. "They are pretty — don't you think so?"

"You won't find many now," he remarked, glancing at the great charred expanse of field and thicket, whence that fiery besom had swept the withered grass and leaves. "Is that the object of this expedition?"

"Oh, no," she explained, "we are only going up on the parapet of Fort Despair to see the sun set."

"We have a glimpse of something like scenery from that elevation," said Marcia.

Estwicke made no rejoinder, and somehow after this there was an indefinable change; perhaps only the wind, blowing from the red west, chilled them — for they were facing the wind now and rapidly approaching the heavy earthwork which loomed, silent and grim, against the gold-flecked splendors of the crimson sky. A scanty fringe of peach and plum trees had sprung up along the slopes, where the soldiers had tossed away the stones of the fruit they ate, and the red clay showed through the bare branches. On the opposite side of the road was a blackened, leafless thicket of young dogwood, hackberry, and aspen trees. The wind was surging through it. The shadows here were deep. In skirting the dense copse it seemed close upon nightfall.

And now the besieging force made its way into Fort Despair, which offered no resistance, and walked slowly around on the parapet and watched the sun go down. All the clouds assembled to do him honor, and color and rejoicing filled the sky. Then the dull, sad shadow fell upon the landscape, and the wintry twilight came on apace.

Antoinette stood watching the fading west, the wind stirring the waves of fair hair which her bonnet permitted to be visible on her brow, and fluttering the semi-opaque veil of black crape that floated backward from it.

"Such melancholy suggestions in that sky!" she exclaimed, with a gentle inflection.

"The day is dead," said Estwicke, mechanically striking with his light riding-whip at the charred bushes about him. "It's gone forever. There's no resurrection for a dead day. It is the type of the irrevocable. And what is done — is done."

Marcia glanced from one to the other, her eyes brightening beneath the gray mists of her tissue veil.

"I only see that the sun has gone down," she declared, with her blithe laughter. "To-day has left its mark on the world — a vast deal of useful work has been done everywhere. And 'To-morrow' is already sailing on the high seas, and bright and early in the morning she will be here."

Estwicke looked hard at her as he offered his hand to assist her down the steep exterior slope of the parapet. The shattered old house was visible in the distance, its upper windows still aflame with the sunset, as with some great inward conflagration. He thought of its maimed and ruined owner. What a support her sturdy optimism must be to a man like this!

With a sudden acute discernment he saw her life — she was all heart and hands. Instead of bewailing the ruin of the war, she busied herself in picking up the pieces. Her courage — the virtue of all others which appealed most strongly to him — roused a quick sympathetic throb, which was half pity that so young and gentle a thing should know this desperate struggle, and half admiration of her pluck — such as he might feel for some stripling soldier's fine deeds of valiance. It was nothing more tender. As they paused on the berme to rest, and stood there motionless for an instant, he was all unaware that he held the helpful little hand in a close clasp — as he might have pressed with friendly fervor the hand of that brave young comrade. He did not notice how deeply she blushed beneath the shimmer of her silky gray veil; that she shrank away shyly from him after they had crossed the ditch, and climbed the counterscarp and were once more on level ground; that she was confused, agitated; that she did not speak. He sighed — he was only reminded of the faith and affection which bound together that little home-circle in perfect peace, here where the battle was fought — such simple virtues — so widely possessed — and yet he sighed. So he walked on, silent and absorbed, thinking — not of her — only of what she suggested.

He had forgotten Miss St. Pierre. She hardly needed his assistance. She only missed it because it was becoming that he should offer it. To cover the slight embarrassment thus induced, she busied herself once more with the cedar, for, as she followed them over the glacis, she caught the gleam of the berries against the dark green of a funereal little tree on the verge of the haunted thicket. She paused to gather the spray while the others walked on unheeding. And so it happened that the moment of their pre-occupation came to be an era in her life.

The fire had been very fierce just here, and the charred tangle of vines and the prickly stubble of the burned bushes and weeds showed how thickly matted was the growth thus cleared away. As she moved forward into the midst of the thicket, she said to herself that no other foot had pressed this sod since the days when the battle was fought.

The next moment a cold horror clutched at her heart. There — almost at her feet — was a ghastly row of excavations of a shape and size that told their own story. These were the empty graves of the soldiers whose ghosts walked here, and would not follow their transplanted bodies. She stood motionless, looking down in terrified fascination. They were shallow; the rains had washed the earth into them; the wind had helped to fill them with leaves. And as she looked, a sudden fitful gleam caught her eyes. It flashed up from the bottom of the nearest grave. Perhaps it was the fading light on a drop of water; perhaps on a bit of tin; — but it was like the burnished glimmer of precious metal. She did not understand her courage afterward. She was suddenly impelled to step swiftly forward, she knelt down on the brink of the excavation, and picked up a small fragment of a watch chain. At one extremity it had been cut smoothly off — perhaps by the bullet that had carried death to the heart of the man who had worn it here. From the other end depended, encrusted with clay, stained, too, she fancied, with some dark current, a gold locket — the memento of a romance it might be, a love token. The dead soldier had left it in his grave, and here it had lain all these years, overlooked and unmolested. And here his story ended.

No — not ended yet! She had mechanically touched the spring and the locket was open. She had only a glimpse of a tress of dark hair beneath the shattered crystal — and then with the shock of an extreme surprise, her pulses seemed suddenly stilled. For within the lid were engraved these words: —

JOHN DOANE FORTESCUE
from
"ADELAIDE."

Her blood came back with a rush. The pathetic interest of the bauble, found here and now, was merged in its prosaic significance. John Fortescue was dead. This discovery proved the fact. Did it prove something more — that Travis was working on her fear of litigation to weaken her hold upon the property he coveted? To be sure he might not know that the man was dead, but he doubtless had reason to believe it. She remembered that he had alluded to the fact that Fortescue had been singularly alone in the world — he was probably aware, too, that the dead man had no relative nearer than herself to urge their rights as his heirs. Thus, in exchanging undesirable for desirable property, Travis would acquire also her indefeasible title.

She recollected where she was with a shudder, for as she stood with the trinket in her hand, the earth was suddenly a-throb with mysterious vibrations. Loud voices rang on the wind in its wild, unimpeded rush across the plain. The shadows in the haunted thicket were swaying back and forth with a convulsive motion — the fantastic shapes began to assume a dimly realized resemblance to human forms. She hastily thrust the bit of chain and the locket into her muff, and as she turned, it was a great relief to see her friends strolling leisurely along the road close at hand.

They were still silent, and she was silent too when she joined them. Already her caution was warning her that the discovery she had made had so serious a connection with the title of her property that it was not well to provoke an indiscriminate curiosity in the matter until she could have the advice of a lawyer, and take the proper measures to restore the little trinket — valueless except, possibly, from association — to its rightful owner, if, indeed, the dead Fortescue had a closer relative than herself still surviving. But was he dead — was this sufficient to prove it?

Her strong sense of justice, too, combated the impulse to canvass with her companions the wonderment of this episode, that was so strange in that it should aptly fall into her experience, and so natural in that it had happened here, where the battle was fought. But it involved the honor and honesty of a *quasi* member of the family, and this touched her pride. She knew that its recital could not fail to suggest to them the identical suspicions which she entertained of her step-brother's motives in the proposed exchange of property, and had she sufficient proof to warrant her, for the mere love of sensation, in exposing him to this grave discredit?

Thus it was that she said nothing.

Night was falling. The evening star shivered in the wind. The mists were crouching in the rifle-pits of the old picket-line, and had silently entered the works. Now and then she glanced back at the desolate stretch of country, its heavy redoubts so grim, so gaunt, so doubly drear, projected against an infinitely clear sky. The scene, in its vast loneliness, was burnt into her brain — she saw it years afterward as vividly as she saw it now — as all must forever see it who once look upon it. Even the house, standing stark and silent in the distance, gave no sense of life, of a future, of the domestic world, of humanity. One might sigh to see the pallid, wintry moon peering curiously through the big rifts of the bomb-shattered cupola.

CHAPTER VII.

IT chanced that Maurice Brennett's varied cotton ventures took him to New Orleans in February. He found the city ablaze with illuminations and wild with excitement, for it was the evening of Mardi Gras and the Mystick Krewe procession was on the march.

In the enchantment suddenly turned loose in the streets, the past and the present were fantastically blended. The Pickwick Club-house lent the radiance of a thousand gas jets to the triumphal pageant of the "Faërie Queene." A salute of artillery thundered from Lafayette Square, and made the hero of those mystic weapons, "Caliburn" and "Ron," acquainted with the realistic magic of modern warfare. In front of the City Hall the procession halted, and Prince Arthure dismounted to exchange the compliments of the season with his honor the Mayor of New Orleans.

It seemed as if all the nations of the earth had gathered here between the Mississippi and the Swamp. From among the banners fluttering from every balcony and open window, and house-top, looked out creole eyes, potent enough to have laid their languorous spell upon the splendid, glittering swarm, and held it there motionless for all time to come. These southern beauties had a pretty contrast in the fairer faces from the north. And below, jostling along the sidewalks, sternly repressed by the police, was a motley throng of every grade of swarthiness, from the broadly grinning African, the mulatto, the Indian, the cream-tinted Chinaman — gazing with oblique smiles at the wild vagaries of the "Melican man" — to the Sicilian, and the dark-browed Spanish vagrant, wearing his tattered garb with the dignity of a hidalgo.

And beneath the inspiring melodies, and the cheers of the enthusiastic populace, and those louder iron-throated plaudits of the guns, were all the echoes of Babel. One heard here a resonant German "ach!" and there the nimble Gallic tongue demanding of a just Heaven if this were not *too* magnificent, and the neat, precise Yankee pronunciation, and the languid, Southern drawl, and the Englishman's broad "a," of which the swelling proportions overlapped all the other letters of the alphabet. The mirthful guttural negro dialect rose too, mingled with unique clippings known as pigeon-English, and that *vox populi*, slang, which, like "don't care," has no home, was loud upon the air.

Orion looked over the western house-tops at this strange red constellation wheeling through the streets so far below. Cassiopeia sat in her splendid chair, and Berenice's shining hair streamed athwart the moonless heavens. But the stellular display of the *ignis fatuus* of the Swamp was soon over; the Opera House was reached, the ruthless door shut the rabble from "faërie land," and it hung hungrily about outside, reluctantly making way for the richly-attired freight of carriages privileged to behold the tableaux within.

Among those thus favored was one who had less greedy an appetite than the untutored mob for the gracious and splendid. Only a very short time elapsed before Maurice Brennett emerged and walked up Toulouse Street — slowly, meditatively, as if he had less an object in view than a desire of the motion and the fresh air. Little affinity had he with this night of enchantment, these beautiful presentations and responsive enthusiasms. The dominant instinct of his nature was the instinct of prey. He pursued it in his varied speculations with as little conscience as his cousin, the "feathered hawk," pursues his own peculiar line of business.

Now, as he walked on listlessly, his mind was filled with complex calculations, with rigidly severe retrospections as to whether he might not have been more adroit even than he was, with careful reconnoitering of tortuous alternatives of future policy. They all led him to the wall. This realization roused him. He raised his head and looked tentatively about him in the darkness as if he sought an inspiration. Slowly a purpose began to shape itself in his thoughts. He paused irresolute for a moment. Then he slipped on his overcoat and took his way briskly toward the levee.

A silence had fallen with the night upon the great embankment that lies like a guardian dragon along the sinuous borders of the city. Numbers of steamboats — dark and silent — lurked at the wharves, their smokeless chimneys rising high, high into the mists that hovered about the great river. One felt the presence rather than saw that leafless forest of masts where the sea-going craft was lying. The monotony of the interval, while he waited, was broken only by the measured tread of watchmen echoing along the planks, and once by the swift sibilant rushing of a locomotive upon the branch line of a railway close at hand, the glare of its cyclopic eye rending the darkness.

He was about to turn away in disappointment, when suddenly from up the river sounded three husky, remonstrant whistles. They conjured up a hundred twinkling lights among the glooms by the water side, and soon the levee was swarming with the dusky figures of roustabouts, running hither and thither with clattering steps and an uncouth chatter. Presently the white mists up the river were gemmed, first with a ruby, then with an emerald gleam; both appeared close together, and from that moment until he could see all the side-lights of the great illuminated floating palace; until he could hear the water surging in the darkness about her wheels, and the throb of her machinery; until she was swinging, with a slow, easy grace, to the sharp jangling of her pilot's bells, into her allotted berth by the levee, the man who watched her landing was in the grip of a strong emotion. It brought a quiver to the hard lines of his parted lips; it shook his hand; a faint flush sprang into his cheek; his eyes were eager — so eager and so fierce. He accosted the first man ashore — one of the deck hands, who was making the boat fast.

"Is that the Marchesa?"

"Yes, sah."

"Why is she so long behind time?"

"Well, sah, disher boat jis' run aground ob a sand-bar up dere in Choctaw Bend — stayed dere twenty hours. Den we kem a-bustin' down de ribber, makin' de fastes' time eber seed on de Mis'sippi. Did n't do no good, dough. An' dese yere passygers, wot's gwine ter be landed too late fur de Moddy-Graw is a-tearin' deir shirts 'bout it. Sich cussin'!"

As Brennett scanned the passengers crowding down the stage-plank, he stepped forward with a sudden look of recognition.

"Have you heard from *her?*" he exclaimed, with quick impulsiveness, as he mechanically grasped Travis's outstretched hand.

His manner was so pronounced that a lady who was

passing at the moment, and who caught his words, glanced at him with covert sympathy. This was surely a phase of some delicate and tender heart-drama, which is forever on the human stage, but which shirks an audience, who may only catch a glimpse of a scene, now and then, by some chance lifting of the curtain, such as this. And so she went her way, speculating futilely about this important "her."

"Got a letter just as I started," said Travis, slowly separating an envelope from a dozen missives which he had drawn from his pocket, and handing it to Brennett, who hastily slipped out the inclosure, and read it by the lamps of a carriage near which they stood. Miss St. Pierre's letter was in response to the one which her stepbrother had written immediately after his visit, urging still further the proposed exchange of property. The reply was a marvel of non-committal temporizing. To reconcile its cool and formal tone with the sanguine expectation which Travis had deduced from her delight in receiving the cross was difficult. He had believed, when they parted, that she was far more kindly disposed toward him than ever before, and that, thus propitiated, she could be readily influenced.

But now her feeling, as expressed in this letter, had changed to distant reserve. There was even, indefinably suggested, an undercurrent of distrust. She had come to no decision; not a word foreshadowed her ultimate course; she might have written chiefly with a view of gaining time.

"She will or she won't, Brennett," drawled Travis. "It's like her to want to eat her cake and have it too."

As he stood in the light of the carriage lamps, listlessly twirling his gloves in one hand, and glancing about him with that disparaging superficial interest characteristic of the professional loafer, there was nothing in the contemplative placidity of his manner to suggest disappointment or irritation. In fact, he had given with the letter all anxiety for the future into Brennett's hands. For he was an expert in the matter of shifting responsibility and "taking it easy."

But Brennett's was a face on which every emotion and thought had left its mark. He read and re-read the letter without speaking, but with a perplexity, and a baffled avidity, and a doubt, which nearly approached dismay, vividly expressed on his sharp features. At length he carefully folded and returned the delicate sheets, with a significant glance, and a smile that was curiously related to a sneer.

"Well," said Travis, "I'm afraid our getting hold of that property is a thing that will never come to pass."

"Travis," said Brennett, laying his hand lightly upon his friend's arm, which was swinging the gloves, and thus arresting the motion, "other men expect events to come to pass. *I make* things happen."

Travis's contemplative eyes, staring intently for a moment from under his hat-brim, held a sharp touch of surprise, and he laid his hand meditatively on his silky, straw-colored whiskers, which the lamplight seemed to burnish to a deeper yellow.

"Stick to that!" he exclaimed, gradually taking in his friend's meaning. Then, as Brennett's grasp relaxed upon his arm, he fell once more to twirling his gloves, and glancing casually up and down the levee.

"Well!" he presently exclaimed, with a cheerful intonation, as he turned toward the door of the carriage, "I have to go and dress."

"What for?" demanded Brennett, rousing himself with difficulty.

"For the ball. I might as well see what is left of the poor little show."

And when they were rolling along the street toward the hotel, he had no graver absorption than swearing at the bar in Choctaw Bend, and asking questions, that were hardly answered, concerning the relative splendors of the procession and tableaux to-night and those of former years.

Travis was like a cork. The surface was his element. He knew nothing below. Perhaps, however, he might not have been able to maintain his constitutional buoyancy had he divined that, behind Brennett's boast, was an absolute chaos, in which not even an indefinite plan of action was vaguely shaping itself.

With secret wonder at his own poverty of resource, Brennett only suggested, after a day or so, that Travis should write to her again.

"If this produces no appreciable result," he said to himself, "I must try heavier artillery."

As the time went by no more letters were received from Miss St. Pierre.

And for the nonce Maurice Brennett was at a loss for his ordnance.

One lingering sunshiny morning it chanced that he and Travis were in the reading-room of the St. —— Hotel. The murmur of the streets below rose drowsily, and within it was very still. The other occupants of the room had dropped out gradually one by one, and only the rustle of the journal in Travis's hand broke the quietude as he hastily turned the sheet. Brennett was not reading. There was a folded newspaper on his knee, his eyes were fixed absently on the floor, and his thoughts were busy with that baffling perplexity never in these days far from them.

"The Tichborne case!" exclaimed Travis as he glanced at the head-lines. "I'm devilish tired of the Tichborne case. What do you think of it, Brennett? Is the claimant an impostor?"

It was as if he had touched a match to a fuse. The air was full of strange forces hitherto latent.

Brennett sat silent, motionless, looking at his companion with an expression in his brilliant eyes difficult of analysis.

"Eh! What do you think of the Tichborne case?" reiterated Travis.

And still on Brennett's face was a fixed expression of introversion — as of one who ponders deeply, who is carefully evolving an intricate train of sequences. A new idea had been projected on his mental horizon — vague, diffuse, but soon to be focussed in action. Even Travis, unobservant though he was, felt that his friend's mind was coming back through wide spaces as Brennett replied, absently, "The Tichborne case? — why, I hardly know what to think about it."

And then he was silent again.

And so Travis left him.

He remained there for an hour or two, sunk in this new absorption, uninterrupted by friend or acquaintance. Then he wrote and mailed a letter, and by four o'clock that afternoon it was on its way to New York.

Travis's ruminant moods — the mental process could scarcely be dignified as reflection — were rare. One of the most memorable of his life was superinduced within the next week by a casual meeting with Brennett in the lobby of the Opera House. The performance was over, and Travis was in the midst of the surging crowd near the door when he first caught sight of his friend in the jam on the stairs. Brennett made a slight gesture with the opera glass in his hand, which Travis interpreted as a request to wait for him without. He went on, experiencing at the moment a faint and fleeting amusement that a man like Brennett, who seemed, however illogically, harder and sharper than the hardest and sharpest, whose whole heart and soul were in his eager haste to be rich, should nevertheless affect a sentimental interest in music, and to enjoy the gentle illusions of the lyric stage. There recurred to him, too, a vague perception, of which he had often before been conscious, that men of Brennett's stamp usually care little for externals, and that there was a sort of incongruity in the glitter of diamonds on his shirt-front when he moved beneath the gas-jets, and in the fact that he was always so carefully plumed.

As Travis lounged in the gloom without, beside the posters which announced in gigantic letters the resplendent attractions of "L'Etoile du Nord," billed for Monday the 6th of March, he watched carelessly the erratic orbits of the carriage lamps far up the instarred perspective of the street. Presently Brennett came out, and slipping his arm through Travis's they took their way along the thoroughfare together.

"I have something to say to you," Brennett began.

"Say it, my dear fellow," rejoined Travis, lightly.

The next instant he was struck with a sudden surprise that Brennett's arm should be trembling within his own. The circumstance was significant. He grew abruptly grave, and turned an expectant face upon his friend.

Brennett seemed to hesitate. It was only after they had traversed the broad belt of moonlight falling athwart the crossing, and reached the deep shadow of the opposite block of buildings that he spoke.

"I have heard from Fortescue," he said.

Travis stopped short in the street.

"Not John Doane Fortescue?" he asked, with a sharp intonation of dismay.

"He is the man," Brennett assented.

Travis stared hard at him for a moment. He was only a black shadow sharply outlined upon the dim, gray background of the street. Even the light in his eyes was eclipsed. But somehow it seemed a keenly vigilant shadow. Its attitude was intent.

Travis's observation was the mere embryo of a faculty. But he had an instinctive aversion to being watched, and, although hardly realizing that he stood in the moonlight and the other in the gloomy obscurity, the instinct prevailed. The words and the gesture were almost mechanical as he said, "Come, let's get out of this," and passing his arm once more through his friend's they walked on together.

"I thought that man was surely dead by this time," he said, desperately. "He has not been heard of for years."

"He is in New York now," said Brennett.

"How did *you* hear of him, Brennett? How did it come about?"

"I remembered that a friend of mine in New York speaks of him occasionally. I wrote and ascertained that Fortescue has just arrived there after a prolonged residence abroad. He expects, so my correspondent says, to come to New Orleans very soon."

"Of course, then, he will get scent of his right to that Tennessee property before long. But, Brennett, now I think of it, I don't see how that can affect our chance of securing it. His remedy is barred by the statute," said Travis, striving to fling off the anxieties that had so suddenly beset him.

"He will rely on the disability of continuous absence," said Brennett, eagerly, showing a strange insight into the intentions of a man whom he had never seen, and who was as yet presumably in ignorance of the vested remainder in these houses in Graftenburg. After he had spoken he recoiled slightly, and was savagely biting his lip.

But Travis's sense of the artistic was too blunt to recognize this lapse from veri-similitude. "Ah, the game is up!" he cried, despairingly. Then with a bitter gesture of renunciation he flung the stump of his cigar into the street, feeling as if he had put from him in the moment every cherished prospect of the future.

The air was soft and full of vernal suggestions. The moon hung low in the western sky. The elongated shadows of the two men dogged their progress down the deserted streets, and for a time the silence was unbroken save by the rhythmic beat of their footsteps, and once when the multitudinous brilliant notes of a mocking-bird's nocturnal melody burst forth suddenly.

"In thinking it over," said Brennett at last, "I doubt whether we are so much damaged by this new development after all. The project of exchanging property was beginning to seem very hopeless."

Travis made no reply. He was wondering whether Brennett's apparent astuteness, hitherto so prominent in the invariable success of his enterprises, might not have been instead only the heavy backing of circumstance — luck rather than brains. And now, if luck should fail him, and the man who relied upon him — what would remain?

Brennett presently resumed. "It seems to me that, if we are adroit, we might make the appearance of the claimant serve our interests. Perhaps we can manage her all the better for it — through him, as it were."

Travis hardly recognized the caution which, even at

midnight and in the empty streets, used a personal pronoun for a proper name, but under the magnetic influence which Brennett exerted he unconsciously followed the example.

"But he, himself! his title is superior to hers."

"Still he is not in possession, and the law is proverbially uncertain. We can manage him through her."

Travis shook his head.

"I don't altogether make you out, Brennett," he said.

"Why, see here. When the claimant appears she will stand in immediate danger of losing the whole property. Perhaps she would be willing to compromise. Now view the matter from *his* standpoint. It is doubtful whether he can dispossess her or secure any concession. It might be that for a pecuniary consideration he would let us get the advantage of the compromise if it can be effected. One half of that property would give us the money we need."

"You mean buy his claim?"

Brennett assented.

Again Travis shook his head. "It would be a cut-throat sacrifice on his part for anything we could afford to pay."

"You lose sight of the uncertainty, Travis," said Brennett, eagerly. He seemed anxious that his friend should regard the scheme as practicable. "It is very possible that Fortescue would get nothing at the end of a long suit, and have all the costs to pay. And it is possible, too, that she will not compromise at all. Don't you see that a substantial sum, planked down at once, is rather an enticing alternative — especially as the man is a gambler, so my correspondent intimates, and given over to riotous living. Men of that stamp prefer ready money to anything in the way of distant possibilities."

"It may work," said Travis. "But it will surprise me. And, Brennett, we haven't time to prosecute the suit. You know that."

"If she will not compromise that is the end of it — at least so far as the mine is concerned."

"Well, if I understand you," said Travis, in great dissatisfaction of spirit, "the proposal is this — He takes the ready money. And if she can't be induced to compromise she takes the houses. And we are left with the bag to hold."

"The money we pay him is only a stake. We take the risk. But I am confident she will compromise. Otherwise she jeopardizes her whole estate. She has nothing else, you said?"

"Nothing else."

A pause ensued.

"Look here, Brennett," said Travis, presently. "This arrangement with Fortescue is what the lawyers call, in their confounded jargon, 'champerty.' It is against the rules of the game, as I understand it."

"That amounts to nothing. We must keep the affair a secret between ourselves and him — that is all. The proposal for a compromise will have to be made in his name, and through his lawyers. And it is much better that this is the case. It strikes me that, after all, his coming is rather opportune, though it will bleed us a little. She distrusts you, and she is predisposed to oppose you. It is very well that you will be obliged to lie low and seem to have nothing to do with it."

"But this thing of champerty," said Travis, dubiously, "it is no offence, is it? There is no fine, nor penalty, nor" —

"Practically none. That has all fallen into desuetude. But, of course, we shall take care to keep it quiet."

"I ask," said Travis, "because I never had the grit to run against the law. I am a very Jonah for being found out. It's my policy to be above board — else I'm overboard in about a minute and a quarter."

He laughed a little, in a low-spirited way, at his hobbling witticism. Then he said, gravely, "Make the thing straight, Brennett, and keep it straight. I depend on you."

"I'll take care of that," said Brennett.

Then they both fell silent.

The moon was slipping slowly behind the western roofs. The melancholy tones of a bell close at hand clanged out the hour. Others far away sounded like its echo. The world was lost in the immensity of the night — even their shadows seemed to have deserted them, only recalled now and then by the sudden glare of a gas-lamp as they passed beneath.

And presently, still silent, they turned into the familiar hotel where they always sojourned during their stay in New Orleans, and which seemed to them as much like home as any other place.

Shortly after this interview the races began and Travis's anxieties and forebodings lost their hold upon him.

CHAPTER VIII.

IN the darkness of the night the snow slipped down, and the morning broke on an unfamiliar world. Chattalla was idealized like a town in a dream. Pavements, smooth and unblemished as marble, had replaced the wretched sidewalks. "Jerusalem" was a picturesque row of low, white-roofed buildings, softly defined against the sad, gray sky; here and there delicate tendrils of blue smoke were beginning to timidly ascend. The dome of the court-house was begirt with icicles; its gilded weather-vane seemed to touch the low-hanging clouds; the leafless sycamore in the yard was blanched to a yet more pallid effect by the snowy lines traced on every branch and twig. A great black crow was cawing from its top.

The first faces that appeared were of the unmistakable Israelitish type, and soon all Jewry was alive. Then groups of freedmen, silhouettes against the snowy background, slowly slouched along, grumbling because of the weather. Last of the three classes came the soldierly clerks, and lawyers, and doctors, their morning greetings complicated with comments on the unprecedented depth of the snow, and disputes as to the relative depth of the "big snow" of 1843.

There were no carts in from the country, but the streets were soon enlivened with every manner of fantastic expedient — from a goods-box to a wagon-bed — that could serve as a sleigh. Some of them were of such grotesque contrivance that the very dogs barked at them in frenzied surprise. After the one o'clock dinner these vehicles became more numerous, and Captain Estwicke met upon the turnpike nearly all Chattalla, on pleasure and pleurisy bent.

But it was lonely enough when he had turned off from the high road and reached the great, ghastly battlefield, that after all its woe was laid at last in its motionless, white shroud. The stillness was something dreadful. The vast snowy expanse stretched out indefinitely beneath a livid sky; only the sombre tints of the haunted thickets broke the monotony, until the great dilapidated house rose up before him, and he caught through the library windows the flicker of firelight and the glow of crimson curtains.

"De Gen'al's done gone ter town, sah," said a small major-domo, with an air of importance disproportionate to his inches, and an expression of affable regret on his black face, as he opened the door in answer to Captain Estwicke's ring. "Mrs. Kirby went yestiddy to spen' de night at Mrs. Ridgeway's, an' de snow, so onexpected, kep' her f'om comin' back. Miss Anternette went up ter Mrs. Percy's place las' Wednesday ter stay a few weeks wid her"—

Estwicke's heart lightened as he listened, and he received the next item with a sense of elation.

"— but Miss Marshy — she's at home. Won't yer walk in, sah."

It was the first time that Estwicke had found the library unoccupied, and he was conscious of a certain alert expectation as he waited; not, he stipulated, because he was in love with Miss Vayne, — he often told himself that he was not a susceptible man, — but she possessed a unique charm and interest, and he had more than once felt that he could, with an admirable degree of fortitude, dispense with the less congenial presence of the others.

"You have disappointed me," he cried, gayly, as she entered the room, and he rose to meet her. "You told me that spring was coming."

"And so it is."

"And so is the millennium — after a while."

"Well," said Marcia, with an air which seemed to dispose of her delinquency in the matter, "life is a mosaic of disappointments — the art of life is to adjust their jagged edges together so nicely that they form an harmonious whole."

"Do I understand this?" said Estwicke, knitting his brows in mock gravity. "Are you trying to inculcate the moral lesson of contentment?"

"Oh, no," cried Marcia, with a blithe laugh, "I am only admiring your patience."

Somehow he greatly relished these strictly personal themes, and sought to conserve them. He was silent for a moment, then said, ponderingly, as if reaching a weighty conclusion, "I thought so — I thought so from the first. You are very satiric."

He was hardly prepared for the degree of pleasure expressed in her face. She was delighted that her little ill-feathered shafts of wit should be dignified as satire, for she was possessed by that youthful admiration of cynicism which is so marked a phase of intellectual adolescence.

"Oh, you are altogether wrong," she returned, with the air of waiving a compliment. "On the contrary, I am very"— she paused, at a loss, then meeting his intent, expectant gaze as he leaned slightly forward, his elbow on the arm of the chair, and his hat held motionless in his hand, she laughed and blushed, and turned her eyes away.

There were wonderful depths in those happy eyes, shaded to softness by their long, black lashes. They held some spell that touched his imagination. They suggested to him deep, enchanted waters, overhung by the mystery of some wild, romantic legend. And was there ever a line like that which gave a gentle curve to her under lip, and defined her chin, and swept away with its long, lithe grace to be lost in the knot of black lace at her throat! He was struck anew by the charm of sudden contrast between her dark eyebrows and the shade of her light brown hair, with its flashes of gold all a-sparkle. As it waved back from her forehead, he could see, from the opposite side of the fireplace, the blue veins in her temples.

But why was he on the opposite side of the fireplace? There suddenly seemed a needlessly immense distance between them. He rose and stood by the table, taking up one of those frightful Japanese fans which lay there, and affecting to be interested in its grotesque design. He idly opened and shut it, and when he again seated himself, he selected a chair nearer her.

"You remarked just now that you are 'very,'" he said gravely; "I beg to agree with that. I have found you 'very' indeed. Especially on the subject of the weather. Why, I could have drummed up more sympathy at the barracks."

"About the weather?—why, *they* must be in their element this morning!" she cried. "I can imagine that at every blast *they* exclaim —'How nippingly this reminds me of home!'"

Estwicke laughed. "*They* ought to hear you say that. *They* stand up manfully for 'home.'"

She looked down meditatively at the fire. "They are a long way off," she said presently, in a sort of speculative commiseration. "I wonder if they never mind it. Do you?"

"I have no home," he said, harshly. "I have never had a home."

His tone startled her. It was like a passionate reiteration of some long-cherished grievance. His sudden frown was upon his face. He passed his hand hastily across his brow, as if conscious that a fierce intentness had gathered there, which he sought to obliterate. Then with a short, angry sigh, that yet was not all angry, he slightly shifted his position in the crimson glow of the fire, and turned his eyes upon the shrouded battlefield, lying stark and cold beneath the sombre sky. He looked out with moody reflectiveness, so long that she wondered when he would speak. Some inward monition swayed her, and held her mute.

"How still it is here," he said at last. "An impressive silence broods over this landscape."

"All strangers say that. Antoinette declares it makes her melancholy."

"Sometimes," pursued Estwicke slowly and thoughtfully, "it does not seem like silence. It is as if there were a great sermon or solemn oration in the air. I know it is being pronounced. I am thrilled by the electric eloquence. But somehow my nerves won't respond. I don't hear it. I am too gross, too sordid, too coarse. Now and then I think I have caught a whisper, but when I come to analyze it — nothing!"

He had forgotten her for the moment. His eyes were still fastened upon the scene without, and her surprised eyes were fastened upon his face. She did not know how it was — all that he was saying seemed wild and strange — but her heart was beating in painful sympathy, and her tears were rising fast. She made an effort to regain her self-control. He would think her silly — he would not know what to think. For an instant she fought her emotion, and then said, in her ordinary tone of voice, "It is a lonely place."

Her words roused him from his absorption. "Yes," he rejoined, detaching his attention with obvious effort. "And are you never lonely here — so far from any other house?"

"Oh, no," she replied. "Whenever I go away I almost *die* with homesickness. I think I could n't live anywhere else. It is so peaceful here — so still and peaceful."

Estwicke looked at her without speaking. So peaceful *here* — where the battle was fought!

"Life seems a long struggle everywhere else. Why, when I go to Marston I am oppressed with a sense of all the movement, and strife, and hurly-burly in the world. And yet at the same time everything is so narrow — so contracted."

"I can well understand that — after these large skies," said Estwicke. But he was thinking what a narrow, contracted life hers would seem to those of her age in a wider sphere — with her educational cares, and the succession of dull old guests of faded gentility. He regarded her speculatively. How unconscious of her beauty she seemed. Had no one ever told her? Was he the first to discover it?

She became a little restive under his gaze. Her color rose; again she glanced out at the snowy landscape. There she caught an inspiration. "You are fond of peculiar scenic effects," she said. "If *you* should look out of the window, your artistic eye would perceive that that horse, with the grayish slope of the snow below him and the sky — just the same shade — above, seems as if he were miraculously poised in the air."

"And what do *you* see?"

"Well, I — with my practical eye — looking out of the window, see only a horse that belongs to me, that is named Hotspur, and that ought to be in the stable this minute. But you would be in an artistic ecstacy if you could see him from where you are sitting."

"Come with me to the window so that I can go off in an artistic ecstacy," said Estwicke.

They walked together across the room, and he held back the heavy crimson curtain with one hand that she might stand in the recess. The peculiar reflection of the snow was upon her face, which was all the fairer for it, and yet the delicate flush on her cheek was fresher and purer. He silently watched her while she looked out smilingly, and talked of the "scenic effects."

"And there is the line," he said presently, fixing his eyes upon the horizon where the sombre woods, miles away, met the sky, "that you told me once is the boundary of your world."

"Oh, did you remember that?" she exclaimed naïvely.

He looked at her quickly. "Remember what you say? I forget everything else," he protested with a sudden mental illumination.

A moment of surprise, the color intensified in her cheeks, and her eyelashes quivered and dropped. His heart was beating tumultuously; there had broken in upon him a realization of those subtle processes which had of late changed his own world. It had crystallized within closer limits than hers. This curtain and this window were the boundaries of his world.

He never knew what he was about to say in that first ardent, full-pulsed rush of emotion — but all at once there sounded a great clatter of feet in the hall, and here were Mrs. Kirby and General Vayne, bringing a cold blast of air to the fire with them, and bringing also Mrs. Kirby's chosen intimate, Mrs. Ridgeway.

"Oh, Marcia, my dear!" cried Mrs. Ridgeway, shortly after the salutations, "the sleighing! We went all the way to Mrs. Percy's. You could never imagine it!"

Mrs. Ridgeway was a short, rubicund, stout old lady, and in all her sixty odd years she had never before been in a sleigh.

"And that reminds me," she continued in so animated a tone, that it riveted general attention upon her. "Mrs. Percy told us to-day that her son is coming home in a few weeks."

"Won't that be rather early for him to leave New Orleans?" asked Mrs. Kirby, blandly.

"Well, yes. I should think so if I were in his place. But I suppose he is soon tired of town. There seems to be some powerful magnet in this dull country neighborhood for Horace Percy. He is always coming back."

She glanced at Marcia with an archness which seemed to Estwicke odiously knowing. He turned his eyes instantly upon the young girl. She was blushing and embarrassed.

The mere mention of this man, of whose existence he had hitherto been unaware, sent a hot thrill through his blood. The man's name was Percy. And she called her horse — Hotspur.

In the few moments that he remained after this, there was an alteration in his manner. He was pre-occupied, and an accession of formality was noticeable in his voice, his phrasings, even his bow, as he took leave. And presently he was gliding over the snow in the crisp cutting air, remembering only how she had blushed and faltered when she was told that man was coming.

That man's name was Percy. And she called her horse — Hotspur!

It was dark before he arrived at Chattalla, and intensely cold. He had taken out a cigar, but found, in great annoyance, that he had no match. He made the last mile in very quick time, and when he reached town he pulled up at the book-store. A tattered black urchin was lounging about the sidewalk, and to him Estwicke tossed the lines as he alighted.

"Hi, boss!" shouted the little darkey after his employer, shrewdly desirous of settling the amount of his emolument beforehand. "Yer've got ter gimme a quarter for holdin' disher hoss in disher kind o' wedder. You heah me!"

"I'll give you a quarter and confound you!" exclaimed Estwicke, irritably, as he disappeared within.

The book-store served Chattalla in the stead of a club-house, but it was almost deserted now, the coteries that were wont to assemble here having gone home to tea. The clerk behind the counter, and a solitary figure sitting by the stove at the further end of the store, were of a lonesome aspect. Estwicke recognized in the latter Mr. Ridgeway, and after a momentary hesitation he strode back into this dim perspective. There was to be a political meeting and speaking this evening at the court-house, and Mr. Ridgeway had come to town to attend; he was now awaiting the time appointed for the political potentate to give his fellow-citizens the benefit of his newly discovered method of saving the country. He took his cigar from his mouth and greeted Estwicke with —

"Come in, Captain, come in. Almost frozen, hey? I should think you would be more accustomed to the cold."

"Don't know why," said Estwicke shortly.

"That's a fact. I always forget that you are a Southerner."

Estwicke sat down, placing his feet companionably beside Mr. Ridgeway's on the fender of the stove.

"Can't say, Captain, that I think this Arctic weather improves Chattalla."

"Chattalla seems on the down grade," returned Estwicke. "No business, I should think — except in the line of the Jews. They seem to have a pretty soft thing."

"Taking the town," assented Mr. Ridgeway.

"Raise cotton?" asked Estwicke, jerkily, pulling at his cigar.

"Jews don't," replied Mr. Ridgeway, also jerkily. "They raise greenbacks. Don't plant at all; show their sense; planting these days will break any man. Speak from experience."

"I mean the people generally," said Estwicke.

"Oh, yes; *they* raise cotton; all the old set do. It's their ruin — prices down to nothing, and still they keep planting — straight along. But, Lord," continued the old gentleman, sweepingly, "everybody is broke — flat as a flounder, sir. It really makes no difference what they do now, I suppose — impossible to aggravate that fact. There's not a man in this county who is not wofully reduced — *wofully* reduced, sir, except, of course, Horace Percy, and he is richer than he ever was."

There came a sudden change into Estwicke's face. His eyes were lighted with interest, and his color rose. Still he would not ask a question. But after a long, retrospective pause, Mr. Ridgeway — waving aside the wreaths of smoke that floated about his head — continued of his own accord.

"Horace's good luck is all owing to his uncle, old

Colonel Percy — Colonel by courtesy, you know. Between you and me and the gate-post, old Walter Percy is a fool about everything in this world except money. But he is the longest-headed old sinner about money that ever was seen. When the war began this young fellow had a fine estate by his father's will, and his uncle was his guardian. By the time the first guns were fired old Walter Percy had sold plantations, negroes, stock, *everything*. He knew their day was over. He foresaw how it was all going to end. What do you suppose that old fox did with the money? Bought United States bonds. People thought he was crazy! The lower bonds went the more old Walter Percy bought. Well, the event justified him. His finesse has made Horace a rich fellow."

Estwicke smoked in silence, and after another long pause Mr. Ridgeway continued, —

"People are so fond of exaggerating — liars, you know. They say Horace Percy is worth a million — and that's bosh. I am in a position to know. Five hundred thousand would amply cover all he's got. *Half* a million, sir — scant."

"Is *that* all?" said Estwicke, satirically.

The old gentleman misapprehended him.

"Of course I know there are vastly richer men elsewhere, and were here before the war. General Vayne, for instance, could have pocketed all the Percys, scot and lot. But here, and now, a man as rich as Horace Percy is a rare bird. If anybody deserves good fortune Horace does. You have never met him? Well, you will, probably, as you come down here once in a while. Yes, Horace Percy is a fine fellow; good as gold, and generous to a fault — a little too reckless and headstrong, perhaps. But that is the natural effervescence of youth and animal spirits, you know. Horace is a whole-souled, high-mettled, ardent "—

— "A sort of a Harry Percy of a fellow — Hotspur," suggested Estwicke.

"Tha — that's it," spluttered Mr. Ridgeway, in cordial approbation of this apt translation of his idea. "That's Horace, exactly. Hotspur!"

CHAPTER IX.

EVEN bores have their *raison d'être*. Maurice Brennett had long speculated on the purpose of Colonel Percy's creation. One sunshiny afternoon in New Orleans he seemed to have solved this problem, for, chancing to meet the old gentleman, he detained him in conversation for a few moments on the street, and then, arm in arm, they turned into the St. —— Hotel, close at hand, and repaired to the reading-room.

Colonel Percy's natural manner, if ever he had a natural manner, had been so long and so utterly submerged beneath his mannerism, that not the faintest vestige of the hypothetical original tissue was discernible. He conserved, mentally and physically, a pose of portly pomposity and benign condescension, which would have implied repletion of self-approbation but for its covertly insatiate demand for responsive homage. He was emphatic, and oracular, and eminently Socratic — not that he was verbally interrogative, but the whole man was himself a huge interrogation point, seeming to ask continually, "Do you comprehend — can you appreciate *Me?*"

He was an exemplification of the driving force of prosperity. It had carried him far along the grooves of convention, and he occupied an enviable place in public esteem. To the impartial observer, however, seeing things as they are, uninfluenced by tradition and worldly consideration, he merely proved how very creditably a man can sustain a high social and financial position on how very little mental capital, confirming the old belief that fools are Fortune's favorites, and making wise men "ambitious for a motley coat."

But in his happy, ignorant pomposity he thought he knew it all. He took it for granted that his brain-pan was as handsomely furnished as his purse, and the world in general took it for granted, too.

It was not Brennett's habit to fly in the face of established usage. He did not resent the old gentleman's condescension, for, when it suited his designs to take a low seat, it mattered very little who said, "Sit thou here." Conventionalities are the pawns of the chess-games of life, and by their adroit management he frequently gave checkmate without mooting graver radical questions — the expediency or the inexpediency of the relative position of knights and bishops.

"You have seen the evening papers, eh?" said Colonel Percy, as he sank into a chair. "Sad state of affairs in France — sad state — sad state. Riotous."

Colonel Percy had a habit of iteration. He chanted continually an acquiescent refrain to his own words. His speech was like a Greek chorus, strophe and antistrophe blending in one harmonious whole.

"I had expected to go to Paris this spring," he continued. "But now, I hardly know, I hardly know."

He looked as if the Commune were especially invented for the frustration of this praiseworthy intention.

"It has been some time since you were abroad, I believe," Brennett remarked.

"Years, years. I have not been off American soil for years; not since my brother and I made a little tour together — a little tour."

"He died in Germany, did he not?"

Was Brennett talking merely for time, that he should thus steer the conversation into the dull channel of these personal interests? An eager expectation, foreign to the subject, was in his countenance. An intense anxiety and excitement had kindled in his eyes. Once he turned his head toward the door — only once — and afterward there was a rigidity in the muscles of his face and neck, as if he would avoid, by an effort of the will, the gesture to which an unruly impulse rendered him prone.

Nothing of all this did old Walter Percy see or imagine; absorbed in the subject, he prosed on.

"Yes, yes; his health was not good, and travel was advised by his physicians. He was a great sufferer during his latter years, and died at last from spinal meningitis — he died from it."

"I remember meeting him at Interlaken."

"Interlaken? Yes, Interlaken. I recollect Interlaken, Mr. Brennett. Nice scenery there, very nice scenery indeed. The scenery at Interlaken is certainly very nice," repeated Colonel Percy, with about as much imagination as a primary geography.

"Very nice," Brennett assented.

The afternoon sunlight was streaming in at the windows; the lace curtains stirred softly to and fro in the fresh breeze, and, as they moved, the long, yellow rays were broken and deflected into fantastic shimmers. Now an arabesque of golden light in a network of gray shadow — the etherealized similitude of the curtain itself — was waving on the frescoed ceiling; and now it was slipping insidiously over the carpet. Sometimes the radiance encircled the old man's white hair like a halo; sometimes it played over his withered features with a scornful brilliancy; sometimes it flashed full on Maurice Brennett's bright eyes. Once it surprised a strange expression there. He was looking intently at the pier-glass — not at his own reflection, for he was so placed that he could see only the indistinct image of a man in the dim perspective of the hall without. And the man could see Maurice Brennett's reflection, lounging in a green velvet chair as he talked to a garrulous graybeard. Could it be that a swift glance, charged with a deep meaning, flashed between the *simulacra* in the mirror? Or was it only the vagary of the wanton sunshine, flying on the wings of the wind, and filling the room with its quiverings, and bright distortions, and bizarre effects?

Suddenly the shadow in the hall was merged into substance. There was entering a tall, well-dressed man, with a handsome face and a singularly effective manner. He had a certain air of high breeding, but his appearance gave a sharply contradictory suggestion of reckless living. He looked as if he ought to be the finest type of gentleman, and yet could not, or would not — for there was something distinctly vicious in his handsome eyes.

The two friends by the window were rising; their conference was terminated. The stranger had paused near one of the tables, and was listlessly glancing over a newspaper as he stood. Occasionally he looked with faint and fleeting interest at the other occupants of the room, until his eye chanced to fall on Colonel Percy. Then he laid the paper down and advanced.

"I believe I had the pleasure of your acquaintance a long time ago," he said.

The smile of amiable condescension which had for so many years adorned Colonel Percy's face had become the habit of his muscles. Just now it was more bland and mollifying than usual, because he was in the painful position of not recognizing the man who knew him long ago.

"Why, you have forgotten me," cried the stranger, with a fresh buoyancy of laugh and manner simply indescribable. "You used to know me well enough — John Fortescue."

"Ah, my dear sir," exclaimed the old gentleman, eagerly extending his hand, "I had only mislaid your name for a moment — yes — mislaid for a moment. But as soon as you came into the room I knew I had seen you somewhere. And yet you have changed greatly in personal appearance. Appearance, you know."

"Everybody tells me that," said Fortescue, carelessly. "Very few of my old friends recognize me at first. It is hardly a matter for wonder, and I ought not to expect anything else, as I have not been in this part of the country for nearly thirty years."

He bore himself with a most discouraging affability, before which even the condescending old gentleman wilted a little. When Colonel Percy partially recovered from the novel sensation, he sought to assume an air as of taking Mr. Fortescue under his wing, and the stranger, with a certain imperious good humor, permitted himself to accept the position of *protégé*.

"I am glad to welcome you back," said Colonel Percy pompously. "Yes — glad. I knew your father well. Intimately. In some respects you remind me of him — yes, very much, — especially in your manner and the tones of your voice. You have the family traits very strongly marked. A chip of the old block — eh? Yes — a chip."

The several groups about the room observed this scene with some interest. Maurice Brennett was still standing near the window. The old gentleman suddenly recollected him, and at once introduced him to Fortescue. The two men looked into each other's eyes in the agitation of elation, and gravely shook hands.

Thus in re-entering New Orleans society Mr. Fortescue had as a voucher Colonel Walter Percy — a man of great wealth and social consequence, and as well known there as the custom-house.

In these early days of his return, Fortescue often dined with the punctilious old Pattern at his club, went about with him to exclusive reunions of the very elect, had the run of his house.

"I pledge you my honor, sir," the old fellow said to a mutual acquaintance, "I feel rejuvenated after a choice symposium of this sort. Symposium. I talk. I tell about my college days — his father was my chum — great times we had. Great times. He is fond of hearing me talk about his father; he likes our old-world stories. I tell him that he is his father over again — build, gait, voice, manner — wonderful resemblance — wonderful! But I *don't* tell him," added Colonel Percy, with a sort of cumbrous slyness, "that he is his father — *sublimated.* He is the only *handsome* Fortescue I ever saw. He has far more than fulfilled the promise of his youth — oh, yes — I remember him when he was an ugly, harum-scarum, smooth-faced cub. Yes — ugly cub. The only handsome Fortescue I ever saw — he is, now. They were all men of fine presence — but a hard-featured race — hard-featured to a degree."

That notably exclusive circle in which John Fortescue had been welcomed by virtue of the high position formerly held by his family sustained something of a shock when *outré* stories of his extravagant dissipation began to be bruited abroad. A few people with long memories now recalled sundry mad pranks of his early youth, and said he was exactly what might have been expected, — as the twig is bent the tree is inclined. He persistently sought to conserve the hereditary consideration which had been accorded him, but he also greatly affected a certain clique of fast men, in which he rapidly became a prime favorite. His never-failing gayety, his vitality, his prodigality, above all, his talent and invention in the noble art of killing time, were qualities not to be lightly appreciated. A sudden impression here prevailed that he was a man to be imitated, and many a young fellow's merely frivolous tendencies took a turn downward to positive dissipation that might be dated from Fortescue's reappearance in New Orleans.

Now and then, over the smooth surface of this shallow-seeming life, there played ripples which might have told of strange movements in the unmeasured depths below. Several of the incidents that stirred the waters came about in this way: —

In some sort, Maurice Brennett had begun to dog John Fortescue about, and although not philanthropic, and by no means a temperance man, he made every effort to restrain this chosen intimate from inordinate drinking. One day, as Travis opened the door of his friend's room in the hotel, after a slight annunciatory tap on the panel, he heard Brennett call out in a strained, excited voice —
"You are drinking like a damned fool! And if you keep it up, I'll cut the whole thing, by God!"

The sound of the opening door interrupted Fortescue's reply, and both turned sharply.

"What does it matter to Brennett how hard Fortescue drinks," thought Travis, in great mystification. But the impression was soon effaced, and the occurrence forgotten in the vicissitudes of fighting the tiger and cognate pursuits.

A very observant man might have detected the fact that Mr. Fortescue was merely veneered, as it were, by his seigniorial manner — the wood beneath was of coarse grain. Then concerning his age there was a strange discrepancy. He said that he was fifty-two, and he looked barely forty. And the life he lived does not tend to preserve youth. It was noticeable, too, that he seemed at first singularly unfamiliar with the streets of New Orleans, considering the circumstance that he was born and bred in that city, but he explained that many places about it had in the thirty years of his absence slipped from his memory, for he had "no head for locality." He possessed other peculiarities, one of which occasioned some remark, slight, however, and transitory enough. When he was to a certain extent under the influence of wine he did not answer readily to his name. He was known to sit in motionless silence after some direct appeal, such as — "Will you come, Fortescue?" as though another person were addressed whose reply he was awaiting. When roused to a perception of the fact, he was deft at subterfuges, and the matter passed as an accident.

Once a more significant episode took place in Brennett's presence. While walking with Fortescue along Canal Street one day they encountered Colonel Percy, who with wonted benign condescension paused for a few words. He was accompanied by his nephew, of whom he was superlatively proud and fond, and, as he could never have done with making an impression, his manner of bland importance in introducing his kinsman to Fortescue seemed to say — "This, you will note, is Horace Percy, — a man, young, rich, of fine parts, and greatly favored in that he is my nephew."

The flourishing nephew was a tall, lithe fellow of twenty-four or five years of age, with regular features, a fresh complexion, black hair, dark gray eyes, and a delicate dark mustache that curled upward at the ends, and had rather a pampered appearance. His deportment was a contrast to his uncle's. He was unconstrained, propitiatory, and seemed altogether unaware of his consequence. It may have been that from the plenitude of his self-satisfaction he could afford some concessions, but the very sight of him predisposed one in his favor.

His superficial glance changed suddenly to an intent gaze as it rested upon Fortescue, and the idea slowly percolated through Colonel Percy's thick skull that instead of impressing his own merits his nephew was distinctly impressed. And certainly there was something peculiarly admirable in Fortescue's manner. Those strong intimations of pride, a fine candor, and a generous ardor, gave value to his imposing bearing, his height, and personal effectiveness. A marked individuality was attendant on his slightest gesture. His light laugh was full of an infectious gayety. He was like a high wind — he brought his own exhilarating atmosphere with his buoyant, untamable spirit.

With the bookish man's carefully cultivated sense of the picturesque, all this addressed itself intimately to Percy. It promised a perpetuity of interest in the midst of the arid barren conditions of common-place life. Naturally he had expected something very different in his uncle's friend. He had a sense of acquisition.

"Do you find many changes here?" he asked agreeably.

"They find me," Fortescue suavely corrected him. "They come trooping up every street to meet me. They lie in wait for me all along the banks of that restless old river" —

"Mutation! mutation, sir!" Colonel Percy solemnly interrupted. The word and the intonation pleased him — so he said "Mutation" once more.

"It must exert a depressing influence," Horace Percy suggested.

"It exhilarates me!" cried Fortescue unexpectedly. He lightly fanned away the cigar-smoke from his handsome face, and he laughed a little. "It lets me know how the world goes thundering on through space. I have been thinking it a broken-down hack, and I come to America to find it a fresh young flyer with a prime track before it."

"The world moves, sir — the world moves. Especially the Western Hemisphere," said Colonel Percy. "Advancement — yes — arts and manufactures — very good — very good. But not *too* fast. Moderation. Moderation."

The odor of sanctity did not cling to Mr. Fortescue's metaphors, and the old gentleman was minded to reiterate circumspectly — "Not *too* fast — Moderation. Moderation."

Maurice Brennett had shown some impatience throughout this conversation — now it took the form of speech. "I fancy Mr. Fortescue flatters us," he said, rather incisively. "Or perhaps it is because he thought so slightingly of us when he was here before, that our few changes and our equivocal progress exhilarate him — or, it may be, he is reconciling himself, with the very genius of philosophy, to his sojourn among us."

"He needs no 'genius of philosophy' for that, I am very sure," said Colonel Percy, with healthy self-esteem. "He is singularly favored if he has not had more serious causes for unhappiness."

"I have happily survived them. I have a knack at living — other men are content to breathe," Fortescue boasted airily. "But I lay no claim to genius of any sort. Genius," — he continued, with quick discursiveness — "Genius is the perfect poise of the highest powers."

His manner vitalized the phrase, and the old man, whose kind habit it was to pat Intellect on the back, exclaimed — "Good! Very good! Epigrammatic."

He chipped out the syllables of this long word as if he found it very good, too.

"And I hope, my dear sir, your 'knack at living' may never fail you," he added, rubbing his hands and looking about him for approbation, for he fancied he had said a neat thing.

But his little joke limped by unnoticed. It suddenly occurred to him that the attention of the group seemed to irresistibly gravitate toward Fortescue. The others spoke only of him, and he was absorbed in himself. Horace Percy listened with responsive interest to his every word; Travis, who had joined the party, demonstrated a facility of acquiescence; and Maurice Brennett was watching him like a hawk. It was not Colonel Percy's habit to assist in magnifying the importance of other men, and to condescend to jests that are cavalierly overlooked; jealous of his own consequence, he was quick to perceive that his meaning had escaped the stranger's negligent attention.

"With me," Fortescue declared buoyantly, "the theory of failure and its practical demonstration run in parallel lines — never touching."

Then he turned with his grand air to Colonel Percy, — "Your good wishes for my future ought to have much influence in keeping them from converging," he said suavely.

The old gentleman acknowledged this tribute with a wrinkled smile, and he looked about him with portly pomposity, despite an uncomfortable inward monition that Fortescue was somehow, incomprehensibly, laughing at him.

To a man of his temperament this was peculiarly irritating. He was not ill-tempered, and he usually maintained a conscientious reverence for those behests of polite society which prevent one from walking rough-shod over his neighbor's sensibilities, but to him all others must bow down. He would go any lengths to bring you to your knees. Mr. Fortescue had withheld the requisite genuflection. It was with a distinct intention to discipline him that the old gentleman, affecting an amiable inadvertence, hastily anticipated his nephew's reply to a question which the stranger asked.

"Yes — yes — Horace has been out of town — or you would have met earlier. He has visited his plantations. He plants extensively now. He plants. By the way the old Paturin place has recently come into his possession. Paturin, — you remember?"

He looked at his interlocutor with a world of speculation in his eye.

Fortescue removed his cigar from his lips, turned a smiling face full upon the old gentleman, and responded, — "Paturin! — I think I remember. A fine body of land." Then he replaced his cigar and pulled away with coolest unconcern.

The old fellow stared. *He thought he remembered Paturin!* Colonel Percy himself would never forget the night — in the times of the heavy gambling on the Mississippi steamboats — when he had seen this man, then a young sprig, barely come to his majority, stake this same "fine body of land" and its growing crop of cotton, and lose on a reckless "two pair" against "three of a kind."

And now he thought he remembered Paturin!

Colonel Percy felt that there was an infinite impudence in this seeming indifference — or perhaps Fortescue was only unwilling that one should know how deep were the wounds made by this chance thrust—this reminder of his flung-away fortune. But it coerced a respect for the personal pride which he held like a sword between himself and too close an advance from a grossly inquisitive world.

After this Brennett seemed feverishly anxious to get away, and presently he and Fortescue left the others and walked together up the street.

Travis lingered only a few moments. As he overtook them he heard Brennett saying in a tense, sneering, half-suppressed voice: "What is the use of all this display— *ep-i-gram-mat-ic* wisdom! *It can't* be in character."

Fortescue said nothing, for at that instant the puzzled Travis joined them. As he walked abreast with them he noted in surprise the surly look in the faces of both men. He came at once to his sage conclusion.

"These intellectual fellows are too devilish jealous!" he said to himself. "How they do grudge each other their little innings!"

Perhaps Maurice Brennett's impressions of the scene might be most fully gauged by the fact that he, assisted by Mr. Fortescue or assisting him, spent the next few days in a laborious examination of sundry records on which the name of Fortescue appeared, and thenceforth this scion of the family so far overcame his pride and sensitiveness as to allude often and readily to various pieces of property which had passed from his hands, his memory being greatly refreshed by exhaustive lists obtained during his researches into the arcana of real estate.

Fortescue's reckless prodigality had convinced Travis, after some observation, that the project of buying the claim to the Graftenburg houses was feasible, but he was much surprised by the readiness and cheapness with which the purchase was effected.

Brennett deemed it expedient to add a contingent element to the transaction.

"We must make it to Fortescue's interest that the compromise shall actually go through," he said privately to Travis, "or it may be difficult to get him to bestir himself enough to effect it. The affair is obliged to be carried on in his name, and ostensibly by him, although we furnish the money for lawyer's fees and all that. But we can't show at all, you know. So it is best to give Fortescue only five thousand dollars now, and five thousand if we succeed in making the compromise. Hold out that prospect to Fortescue and it will keep him down to his work. He will exert himself to see the lawyers and have the thing pushed through at once."

On this basis the negotiation was consummated and, to Fortescue's lively satisfaction, five thousand dollars changed hands.

After he had left the room with the check in his pocket-book, Travis commented on the transaction. "That's the greediest man to gobble up a little dab of money I ever saw," he said to Brennett. "If I were in his place I'd plough for a living before I would sell my claim to a splendid property like that for such a pittance."

He thought it over in silence for a moment — then shook his wise head. "I can't understand it, Brennett. It gets away with me."

And Brennett said nothing.

For the remainder of the afternoon Travis pondered deeply at intervals upon this problem. It was a long time for any one subject to occupy his attention. Hours after the consultation, he remarked, apropos of nothing, "It's a conundrum, Brennett," and still later he broke a brooding silence with the exclamation, "Give it up!" On each occasion there was a swift expression of alarm among the anxious lines on Brennett's face — lines which it had not known a month ago. But the absorption gradually relaxed its hold upon Travis, and that evening, in the glare of gas-lights, the popping of corks, and the special Providence of filling a "bob-tail flush" at a critical juncture, the last lingering recollection of the "conundrum" slipped through his sieve of a mind according to the habit on which Brennett had relied.

Into the strong sweep of Fortescue's influence Horace Percy had drifted without resistance, for if he were Hotspur at all, he was Hotspur with those sturdy elements of obduracy and fierceness left out. His wilfulness needed only a curb to bring it to naught. He had no coarse proclivities, but he possessed an infinite leisure; he was malleable, impressionable, and reflected the moods of the man nearest his elbow. His chief restraints had hitherto lain in his intellectual tastes, and although he had sometimes affected the *rôle* of wild young blood, and enjoyed the flutter of anxiety his suddenly erratic habits occasioned among his relatives, he had found the *jeunesse dorée* were but as sounding brass — dull, commonplace fellows, as a rule, and ineffectual for mental attrition and congenial companionship. But the pyrotechnic qualities of Fortescue's mind dazzled and delighted him; the man personally impressed and interested him singularly; he even began to entertain an admiring friendship for him — in common with many of the same stamp, for Fortescue had his following. To fraternize with him, however, involved more or less a return to those wild scenes, of which the joyousness had hitherto seemed a trifle chimerical to the hesitant and fastidious Percy. Now they were suddenly invested with a strong actuality of interest and a potent fascination. Fortescue's tireless brilliancy, his rampant gayety, his indefatigable vitality and buoyant spirit were subtly imparted to his associates, and his zest of enjoyment, even thus warmed over, had a fine flavor. They delighted in those sensations with which he was wont to shatter the nerves of a too sensitive public. Enlivening stories of Horace's participation in these escapades sometimes reached his uncle's ears. When they were supplemented by vivaciously accurate accounts of his reckless expenditure of money and the sums he lost at cards, they almost broke Colonel Percy's heart. In the midst of these beguilements, however, his nephew was impeded by a threatened attack of pneumonia. "And in reason," said the pious old man, humbly submitting to Providence, "it's the very best thing that could happen to Horace."

The physician peremptorily forbade all exposure, and counselled the patient to keep his room. Horace considered this a lamentable waste of time, but it did not impair his cheerfulness, for he was not allowed to be lonely; his wild young friends daily congregated about him, to "keep up his spirits," which they did, noisily enough.

One afternoon, Maurice Brennett, still maintaining that anxious espionage upon Fortescue, deemed it expedient to affect an interest in the invalid. He found, as he had expected, this choice coterie of associates grouped about the sofa on which young Percy lay at length. Among them was Fortescue, — loud, hilarious, flushed with wine, immensely glad to see Brennett, immensely hospitable to Percy's guests, immensely entertained by Percy's illness, which he evidently considered a good practical joke. Brennett's entrance had interrupted a remonstrance from Travis, which, after the usual greetings, was resumed by that gentleman in his habitual languid drawl, and with an expostulatory gesture of his listless hand and arm, held out expressively as he lounged in the easy-chair on one side of the fireplace. "It is out of the question," he said, "to have all this noise and confusion in a sick man's room. We ought to stay away from here until Percy gets better."

Fortescue, to whom this was addressed, regarded him intently for a moment. Then dropping into the easy-chair opposite, with Travis's own look, with Travis's own languid manner, with Travis's own expostulatory wave of his cigar, held at arm's length in his right hand, with every inflection of Travis's voice, he repeated the words of the considerate remonstrance, and so marvellously perfect was the mimicry that a roar of astonished delight went up from the spectators. In the momentary sensation that ensued, not one of the careless fellows was observant enough to note that a glance of much significance flashed from Brennett's bright eyes into John Fortescue's laughing eyes; not one so quick as to detect the sudden paling of the flushed face as the laughing eyes caught the glance; for a little while there was an extreme gravity in the demeanor of the lively cynosure of the circle.

And as the days passed, this phase of their versatile friend's abilities was not again obtrusively presented.

During Horace's illness he was in a measure at the mercy of his uncle, who thought it his duty to take advantage of the opportunity which the seizure afforded to badger the young fellow. Colonel Percy ascribed the attack to the wine-bottle and the spring races. The physicians did not altogether concur in this opinion. They admitted that too much wine was bad, and too much races also. But these diversions do not of themselves tend to produce pneumonia; the faculty took a lower moral ground.

Colonel Percy began with the most important point.

"Horace," he said solemnly, "you are wasting a great deal of money. Why will you persist in gambling in this wicked way? Wicked — very wicked. This man Fortescue has a bad influence on you. He will ruin you, sir. He is ruining all the young fellows. I happen to know that you have been gambling heavily. And — losing!"

"Losing! Lost the last stiver. Poor as a church mouse," assented Horace easily. He was in his complacently iniquitous frame of mind to-day and enjoyed his uncle's uneasiness. "So poor because I will gamble. Will gamble because I am so wicked. Therefore I'm so wicked because I'm so poor. Moral — if you don't want to be wicked you must n't be poor. Q. E. D."

Colonel Percy listened to this with an intent brow, vaguely conscious that there was something wrong somewhere, but unable to "spot it." Then he sternly attempted to repress this levity.

"I speak for your good. Yes. Your conduct is unseemly. It has been remarked."

Which was true. Colonel Percy thought it was bad to be wicked, but to be remarked in wickedness was far worse. With a weighty manner and extreme emphasis he repeated — "It has been remarked, sir. Remarked. You have been *seen* fantastically tipsy," he cried, with a shrill rising inflection. "People laughed, sir! They *laughed!*"

Horace colored. The reproach struck home. He felt that there was cause for serious mortification in this. He cherished the pre-eminence with which his fortune had endowed him. He fostered notoriety — to be remarked was one of the dearest conditions of his life, but with envy and bated breath, and by no means as a target for the ridicule which his uncle's words implied.

As Colonel Percy talked on, Horace fell, as was his wont, under the influence of whoever was nearest his elbow. He began to repent. The idea of ridicule, deftly inserted, was more wholesome in its effects than prayers.

Its effects were unfortunately fleeting. When the old man was gone and his enlivening young friends returned, Horace, with a bewildering moral versatility, hedged on his contrition, and throughout his convalescence there was a fine display of those inconsistencies and vacillations of character for which he was famous.

About this time, however, he came under the domination of an influence which his uncle, in the innocence of his heart, welcomed.

Languid and enfeebled by illness, Percy had neither the nerve nor inclination to keep the gait at which Fortescue pursued pleasure, and thus gradually fell away from him. His society seemed to have lost, also, its attraction for Brennett, who hitherto, prompted apparently by friendship, had openly made earnest efforts to repress Fortescue's unseemly exuberance of notoriety. But, in despair, perhaps, he had relinquished them at last. Fortescue remained the most conspicuous figure of his conspicuous clique, and his hilarious drunken *bon mots* were all over New Orleans — people repeating them, reprehensively, as in duty bound, but with infinite relish, as the old Adam constrained them.

Between Brennett and Percy, thus distanced, there had long existed a friendship of that cool conventional sort which but for accident might have amounted only to acquaintance. Now it seemed suddenly to intensify and become an intimacy. Brennett was a man of keenly alert and educated faculties. In notable contrast with his chosen associates his life was well-ordered and his habits singularly correct. He had no hold on Percy through participation in the amusements which the young fellow had recently affected, but to Horace the companionship was grateful, for Brennett was one of those rare conversationalists who gently titillate the intelligence of an interlocutor so that he enjoys without effort or exhaustion. They found many subjects in common. They spent much time together in these spring days, and as the season advanced and the annual exodus began to be talked of, it was natural enough that Percy should invite his agreeable and unexceptionable friend to make him a visit at his country home. It was no less natural that Brennett should accept the invitation. And thus his schemes ramified.

CHAPTER X.

THE pulses of life throbbed languidly in Chattalla. Sometimes there was hardly a creature to be seen upon the Square — and then again the noontide sunshine would rest only on the figure of a belated countryman, drunk overnight, lying in the safe shadow of the Temple of Justice, and sleeping off the effects of "bust head," in the soft spring grass beneath the budding sycamore tree. Sometimes a wagon would rattle heavily across the stones; at long intervals the sound of chaffering would rise upon the air from "Jerusalem;" or perhaps the silence might be broken by the talk of a knot of gentlemen who brought chairs from the bank, and took up a position in the midst of the public pavement. If you should thread your way through this group, you would not overhear the discussion of news of the present day, local or foreign — you would catch such phrases as — "The enemy's artillery opened the ball,"— or, "Then we executed a brilliant flank movement." And you would go on realizing that all their interest lay in the past, and that they looked upon the future as only capable of furnishing a series of meagre and supplemental episodes.

It seemed to Estwicke afterward that one of these episodes, which roused Chattalla and diverted it momentarily from its occupation of contemplating its own history, was charged with the special purpose of effecting a breach between himself and General Vayne. It operated solely upon the peculiarities of their respective temperaments, for each had in the matter as slight concern as might be.

One morning Estwicke came down by rail from the barracks, and as he entered the lower cross-hall of the court-house he encountered General Vayne marching meditatively back and forth upon the brick-paved floor.

"I have been endeavoring, sir," said General Vayne, as he offered his hand, "to drill some raw recruits of recollections. I am a witness, you know, in that Jartree suit against the life insurance company — shabby, shabby affair! Do you know, sir," lowering his voice effectively, "that the pretext upon which they refuse to pay the loss is that Major Jartree died — by — his — own — hand!" Impressive pause. "They claim that the deed was done for the sake of securing the insurance money for his children!" Still more impressive pause. "That he *died*, sir, in the act of cheating and chousing. *My* friend, Major Jartree!"

He drew himself up to his full height, twirling his mustache fiercely with his left hand, and looking frowningly intent — much as he did when he led a charge at Shiloh or Monterey.

There was an expression of embarrassment on Estwicke's face; he was about to speak, but General Vayne, roused with affronted friendship, went swiftly on, —

"I am only to testify to the life-long integrity of Major Jartree — my limited knowledge of the minutiæ of this affair will permit me to go no further. But I am glad to enter the lists on any terms. I am glad to break a lance for those orphaned children! *Six* of them, Captain Estwicke — six of those helpless children, all under fifteen years of age! No father — mother a confirmed invalid — and their half-brothers both family-men struggling along on little tid-bits of salaries. But " — with a change of voice, and waving the whole matter into a diminishing distance with his expressive left hand, "the effort on the part of the company to avoid the obligation is utterly futile. It will only be painful to Major Jartree's friends and relatives to hear the puny, malicious attempts to tarnish his motives and character. *That* can't be done, sir, here in Chattalla, where the man was known and beloved and revered — *my* friend, Major Jartree! It is impossible for them to procure any reputable, credible testimony!"

"Perhaps you are unaware," said Estwicke, with a sudden hot flush, "that I am here to-day to testify in behalf of the insurance company."

General Vayne fell back a step.

"Most certainly, sir, I was unaware of it," he said, with slow emphasis. "And"—severely—"it seems to me you should before have stated the fact."

Now, General Vayne was the father of a daughter — otherwise Estwicke would have sharply retorted that he had found it impossible to get in a word edgewise. He trembled with the effort at repression, but still stood confronting the elder gentleman, and intimating by his expectant eye that he anticipated something more definite in the way of an apology.

In General Vayne's foolish, partisan indignation that the legal adversary of Major Jartree's orphans had any witness at all, and that he himself had been thus unwittingly and ludicrously hob-nobbing with the enemy, he would have been glad to put Estwicke off with something less than the full honors of war. But the young man's manner and attitude constrained him.

"In that case," he resumed stiffly, "I beg to withdraw anything offensive I may have said concerning the character of the testimony which the insurance company can command."

Here Estwicke should have dropped it.

"I did not have the opportunity," he persisted, however, imperiously resolved to place himself exactly right upon the record, "to intimate earlier my slight connection with the affair. I was interested and surprised by what you were saying."

And here General Vayne should have dropped it.

"And, if I may ask, what did I say to surprise you?" he demanded.

Combat was to Estwicke like the breath of his nostrils. Already restive under the many restraints imposed by the other's seniority and paternity, his aggressive manner was only imperfectly tempered as he replied: —

"If you may ask, I may answer. I was surprised that so serious a doubt should be entertained that Major Jartree killed himself."

"Doubt, sir! That he killed himself!" exclaimed General Vayne. "If I were warned of God in a vision I could not — I could not constrain myself to believe it! My friend" — his voice trembled — "Major Jartree!"

"And, Captain Estwicke," he added, after a momentary pause, "it will be very difficult to make a jury believe *that*, in the face of Major Jartree's character, which, fortunately, he left behind him, and which cannot be taken away even — from — a — dead — man."

"I shall not attempt to make a jury believe it," said Estwicke, irritated beyond bounds. "I shall only tell the jury, under oath, what I know."

General Vayne looked at him gravely.

"I beg your pardon once more. I supposed that you were here to prove some slight collateral point. I had no idea that you intended to *try* to make the jury believe that. Let me ask you, Captain Estwicke," he continued, in a sudden tremor for the result of the case, "how you, a stranger, happen to be so fully informed about this matter?"

So much had been said of questionable intent that Estwicke fancied an implication in this, too.

"I should answer that question more appropriately from the witness stand," he replied, altogether overtaken.

"Thank you!" cried General Vayne, fierily, "I am schooled!"

He was about to pass by, but Estwicke, already penitent, hastily added —

"I was at Bandusia Springs when he killed himself — I mean when he died."

"I perceive in you, sir, a very formidable witness against the widow and the orphan," said General Vayne, hotly.

"I assure you," returned Estwicke, losing every vestige of self-control, "other people have some rights under the law — even an insurance company — and the law accords them my testimony, such as it is."

"I wish you joy of your tilt in its behalf, and I have the honor to wish you also, sir, a very good morning." And General Vayne passed swiftly through the door and strode off down the pavement to the gate, twirling his long, gray mustache, and touching his hat with a military salute to the men he met, who greeted him in like manner.

There were ten windows in the Circuit Court room, all of them furnished with great, green shutters, which stood, night and day, broadly flaring. This gave them from within a bare and unnaturally glaring aspect, and might have suggested, to a mind enervated and rendered morbid by the sophistication of shades and inside blinds, a painful resemblance to eyes lidless and lashless. In the summer-time, when the grimy and cobwebbed sashes were thrown up, the thick leaves of the sycamore close at hand, with here the flash of the dew and there the flutter of a wing, afforded a pretty make-shift for upholstery, but to-day only the budding branches touched the glass and occasionally rapped sharply upon it as if to call to order the assemblage within.

Besides the Bar, many of the unprofessional "quality" of Chattalla were present, and a considerable number of heavy country fellows from the outlying districts of the county, clad in brown jeans and stolidly eying the town folks, lounged on the benches or strolled aimlessly in and out of the room. Close to the wall, on the left, sat rows of the litigation-loving negroes, whose habit it is to frequent the trial of all causes, great or small. Admirers of oratory are these, and never a word is lost upon them. The jury held their heads attentively askew, for already the plaintiff's *prima facie* case had been made out, and depositions were being read on the other side. Then Estwicke was called, and as he took his conspicuous place on the stand an expectant silence ensued.

The glare of the ten windows was full upon his expressive, irregular features, and his dark red hair, clipped close about his finely shaped head. His whiskers and mustache seemed to take a lighter tinge. There was a slight frown upon his face, and a grave, almost anxious, intentness in his brown eyes belied the cool, impassive manner with which he awaited the questions.

The first of these were comparatively unimportant, and elicited ready replies. They were put by the defendant's senior counsel, a muscular, wiry, hatchet-faced man of the name of Kendricks, a stranger at this bar, and bearing in his garb and manner the stamp of a metropolis. He was a practitioner of some note in the city of Marston, and Temple Meredith had at first regarded with self-gratulation the fact of being associated with him in this case. It was calculated, Meredith thought, to impress the public with a sense of his increasing professional importance, since it could not be generally known that the influence of a kinsman, who was a director in the insurance company, had caused that corporation to secure also the young fellow's valuable services. And in fact his services were valuable. He had done most of the drudgery in preparing the case, he had studied it carefully, drawn the papers, discovered important testimony, and armed himself to the teeth with precedent. But now that it had come on for trial, and was before the public, Kendricks had resumed his position as principal performer, and left the young man, ambitious of distinction, to saw away on the second fiddle with what complacence he might. Meredith maintained his habitual serenity of aspect, but, after the manner of such young shoots who desire to be century oaks in a fortnight, he felt ill-used. It never occurred to him that this state of silent obscurity was exactly the same which Kendricks had graced some twenty years before.

Presently a sudden break occurred in the examination.

"State anything that Major Jartree may have said to you on the subject of suicide."

The witness hesitated, turned his hat in his hand, and glanced down at it, conscious of General Vayne's fierce eyes fixed upon him — conscious of no others. A flush rose into his face — and then he looked up. He was sensible of an angry contempt for himself that he had sought to shirk any man's gaze, that there should be any man whose displeasure he deprecated — and deprecated for a selfish reason. And in this instant he caught the expression of faces that had a far more unnerving effect — that smote upon his heart. The dead man's two sons sat before him — shabby-genteel young drudges, with joyless, troubled eyes, in which he read the terrible anxiety that possesses men who hold character dear, when character is called in question. And he remembered, too, the widow and the six orphans whose little all was in jeopardy.

He chafed under the sense of these influences. "Have I a conscience?" he asked himself. "Do I realize the obligations of an oath?"

In the effort to sustain his equilibrium he was unaware how much of the indifference, which he sought to foster in his mind and heart, was expressed in his manner as he replied, "Major Jartree often spoke to me of suicide. He alluded to it as 'the solution of a problem.'"

General Vayne threw himself back impatiently in his chair, which creaked beneath the shifting of his heavy weight. There was a cruel, blanching dismay in the faces of the dead man's sons. They looked at each other in painful doubt and bewilderment, and then they looked back in increasing surprise at the witness.

This to the crowd seemed almost conclusive. The depositions of the physicians which had been read proved only that Major Jartree had for some time, under advice, used morphine, and had taken an overdose. From their showing, it might have been an accident. This testimony seemed to indicate a deliberate intention.

Estwicke was requested to give the particulars, so far as his memory might serve, of all that Major Jartree had said alluding to suicide, and the circumstances under which these conversations took place.

And as he complied, the impression he created was one which his slightest friend might regret. His glance was both hard and careless. Now and then he turned, with an idle gesture, his soft hat which he held folded in his hand. His manner seemed the exponent of a callous nature —

the very tones of his voice indicated a peculiarly frivolous insensibility to the painful and even tragic elements involved in the recital. For it began to be very evident that a bankrupt, in broken health, in great depression of spirit, in frantic anxiety for his children's future and the support of an invalid wife, the dead man had sacrificed his honesty, his conscience, his life, for a pittance, and sacrificed it in vain. He had talked too much in his loneliness and his sorrows to a friendly young stranger whom he had met at the "Springs," whither his sons had sent him for a few weeks to recuperate his health and divert his mind — they felt every day even yet the hard pinching of the economies which that extravagance had entailed upon them. Though Estwicke gave every detail so lightly, as he recounted the scenes, they seemed to pass visibly before the jury. Even the least imaginative among them had a vivid mental picture of the long, mysterious, wooded Cumberland spurs, and the grim gray cliff projected against a red sunset sky, and heard the dead man's shrill tones, breaking into the still evening air, as he rose, and with uplifted hand protested, — "A man's life is his own, Captain Estwicke, — shall he not say when it shall end!" And again there was a conversation in the freshness of the morning as they sat in the observatory, which hung over the precipice and quivered and shuddered with the wind, and here he had calculated the depth below, and argued with his companion whether it were certain death to fall. And once they drank together the sparkling chalybeate water that bubbled out from a cleft in a crag. "I wish you health, my young friend," he had said. "You are at the entrance of the great stage. I hope you have a fine *rôle* to play, and a good stock company of friends for support, and a great ovation and glorification awaiting you. I am but a supernumerary at best, and nearer the exit than you think. Instead of this health-giving water I should drink some deadly drug. And then you would see with what grace I can make my bow to an audience which has not troubled itself overmuch about me, and about which I shall trouble myself no more."

General Vayne rose and walked heavily out of the room. He went down the stairs, leaning ponderously on the balustrade, and joined Mr. Ridgeway who chanced to be aimlessly strolling about the porch.

"Sir," said General Vayne, facing round upon his friend in the flickering shadow of the leafless sycamore boughs, "sir, the quality of sympathy is the one quality which lifts the human animal above the beasts that perish. The man who lacks it, lacks his soul."

After a pause he continued impressively. "It is a quality, sir, which ennobles a beggar and adorns a prince."

Then he fell suddenly from his rounded periods into an inconsequent heap, so to speak, of indignation.

"I — tell — you — what — it — is — sir," — he said in that effective diminuendo — "this belated invasion — this post-mortem invasion, as one might call it, is" —

He checked himself; he would not speak disparagingly of a man behind his back, — not even of the post-mortem invader, his own familiar home-made Yankee who invaded his native soil.

For a time the two elderly gentlemen sat on the front steps in silence. Then General Vayne rose and paced up and down the brick-floored hall, struggling with an inclination to return to the court-room and hear the testimony that was so repugnant to him. Finally the impulse prevailed. When he went back he found that Estwicke was under cross-examination. This was very skilfully conducted, but elicited nothing of value, except that he had heard other men who had never committed suicide say many like things, and that he had considered these of no special import until after Major Jartree's death. There were no contradictions, no admissions, no involutions. He was the ideal witness, bold, succinct, and as transparent as crystal. As he went down from the stand, Meredith, with the *camaraderie* of youth, indicated by a gesture of invitation, a vacant chair at his side. Estwicke hesitated; then, saying to himself that he would not truckle, he would not seem to avoid them, he sat down by the defendant's lawyers, although he thought as he did so that this was an overt act of perfect accord which he might well spare himself, and he felt as if he and they were conspirators in some dark deed against the widow and the orphans.

The plaintiff's rebutting testimony was now to be taken, and General Vayne was the first witness called.

"Will you state," said the counsel, "what was Major Jartree's character for integrity."

"Sir," exclaimed General Vayne, while the tears rushed to his enthusiastic eyes, and he made an agitated gesture as if he would clasp his missing right hand — clasping only the empty air, "I would answer for his integrity with my life — with — my — life!"

There was throughout the room an electric current of painful sympathy. The jury were surprised, thrilled, touched. The hatchet-faced Kendricks was on his feet in an instant with an objection.

"Could I say more — or less?" cried the witness, suddenly, forestalling the plaintiff's counsel, "knowing him as I did — *my* friend, Major Jartree! Only the voice of the stranger is raised against him!"

All eyes were turned toward Estwicke. He was a-tingle in every fibre, his face grew hot and scarlet, the veins in his temples were blue and swollen; he made a movement as if he were about to rise.

"Steady — steady!" said the placid and debonair Meredith in an undertone, laying a staying hand on Estwicke's shoulder.

The contentious Kendricks was in his element. "I appeal to your Honor," he vociferated, "to protect my witness"— Estwicke gasped —"to protect my witness against these aspersions intended to prejudice the jury against the conclusive testimony he has given."

"Aspersions!" exclaimed General Vayne, leaning forward suddenly toward the plaintiff's lawyers. "*Did* he say *aspersions?*"

There was a jostling rush forward to obtain a better view of the actors in the little drama, and the constantly contracting crowd was shaded off by a line of black faces enlivened by glittering ivories and the whites of astonished rolling eyes. A clamor of voices had arisen, and above all dominated the sheriff's stentorian "Silence in court!"

"I'll commit somebody presently," said the judge impersonally. He had a wooden face, an impassive manner, and a brier-root pipe which he smoked imperturbably throughout the proceedings. He was a man of few words but of prompt action; at the sound of his inexpressive voice the tumult was stilled instantly.

"Will your Honor be so good as to admonish the witness that reflections on those who preceded him are not evidence and are inadmissible."

"The witness must comport himself with all due regard to this court and counsel," said the judge. Then the examination was resumed.

"What was Major Jartree's habit of conversation?"

"He often spoke figuratively. He might have been easily misunderstood by a man of different mental calibre — a literal-minded man."

"Will your Honor instruct the witness to confine himself to the necessary replies," exclaimed Kendricks, again on his feet. "The witness does not answer questions. He is only seeking to utilize Captain Estwicke's testimony, which he has heard, to make an argument. I see that we ought to have had all these witnesses put under the rule."

"Too late, now," interpolated the judge, dryly.

"Instead of answering questions," pursued Kendricks, "the witness is trying to persuade the jury that all Major Jartree said to Captain Estwicke were merely flowers of rhetoric which"—with a fine sneer—"his limited mental capacity prevented him from comprehending."

"Counsel may sit down," said the impassive judge, who had weathered many a storm like this.

Kendricks sat down in — paradoxically — a towering rage, and the plaintiff's lawyer proceeded.

"What was Major Jartree's temperament?"

The witness looked inquiringly.

"State whether he was kindly disposed, or otherwise, and anything you may know of his character."

"Kind, sir? He had the kindest heart that ever beat! He was humane, and gentle, and generous! He was imbued with a fine char-r-ity." Here the witness demonstrated his own char-r-ity by pausing impressively to scowl at Estwicke. "He saw men, not as they were, but as they sought to be. He revered his fellow-creature. He beheld in man the majesty of his Maker's image!"

"I object," cried Kendricks hastily. For there was a change ominous to his client's interests in the expression of the jurymen. They had all known and been "mighty sorry" for Major Jartree, who was an amiable but useless old gentleman, and nobody's enemy but his own. They recognized him in all this, but somehow he loomed before them in impressive proportions as General Vayne lent them his moral magnifying glass. "If the court please, this is not evidence," persisted Kendricks.

"Keep strictly to the point," said the judge.

"I will, your Honor," returned the witness earnestly.

"Was he a religious man?"

"He was a sincere and humble Christian," said General Vayne conclusively — in his own way he was a pious man himself.

"Can you state anything which would intimate his possible horror of the crime of suicide?"

"Sir, he entertained a deep reverence for the sanctity of life. He took ample cognizance of that stupendous right to exist which dignifies the meanest worm of the earth. I once heard him say to a grandchild who was torturing an insect — 'My dear, the beetle is your brother. Spare him!'"

He repeated this with a noble gesture of intercession and a fine oratorical effect. He fixed his magnetic eyes on the jury who were subtly agitated by an illogical responsive fervor, and then with a sudden wild burst of indignation he exclaimed: —

"And they ask us to believe that this man, of all men, held himself, whom God had so nobly endowed, as slighter than the beetle — and took his life and falsified his character, so graciously won, to cheat an insurance company. It is monstrous — monstrous! *My* friend! Major Jartree!"

"Stop! *Stop!* STOP!" Kendricks had roared in a steadily increasing crescendo, but throughout these vociferations General Vayne had kept steadily on, regarding them only as a strategic movement of the enemy designed to divert his attention.

"Your Honor, I insist — I *demand* that you admonish

this witness as to his duty, and require him to conform to it."

"The witness *must* answer questions, and say nothing further," said the judge emphatically.

The witness turned his flushed, enthusiastic face toward the plaintiff's lawyers as an invitation to come again. They were taking heart of grace. It is not always safe to trust the appearance of a jury, but those twelve good and lawful men were beginning to assume the aspect of a row of intent and eager partisans. An influence more potent than law or right reason swayed them. The witness had fast hold of their heart-strings, and their pulses quickened under his touch.

"What was the character of Major Jartree's mind?"

"He possessed a highly cultivated understanding, sir. His power of discrimination between right and wrong was as solid as the heart of that tree, and as perfectly adjusted as the hair-trigger of your pistol, sir."

"What was his habit in the matter of prudence or rashness?"

"He was cool and deliberate. He possessed remarkable foresight. I will instance the fact that he foresaw, from the beginning, the result of the Late War"—which on the day of the surrender had been a great surprise to General Vayne.

"You are not here to instance facts," exclaimed Kendricks pettishly.

To this General Vayne paid no manner of attention, but went on eagerly.

"If he were capable of such a deed, for such a purpose — the mere supposition is abhorrent — he could but have perceived that it would of necessity defeat itself."

"I desire to ask of your Honor," said Kendricks, once more on his feet, and utterly losing control of his temper, "whether throughout the testimony of this witness I am to be subjected to the ignominy of this bravado, and my client's interests to a flagrant injustice? It is plain that the witness does not desire to give evidence. He only seeks to insinuate prejudice and to foster misapprehension in the minds of the jury."

General Vayne rose slowly from the chair. The movement at such a moment was unprecedented and unexpected, and there was a breathless pause of surprise and doubt. He was so pre-eminently a calm man that he never found it necessary to subject his intentions to the scrutiny and question imperative with men of impulse. His gesture was appropriately deliberate as he reached up to the judge's desk and grasped the heavy glass inkstand that stood there. The next moment it was hurled wildly at the head of the defendant's counsel, impartially distributing its contents on the irreproachable shirt-bosoms of the "quality" of Chattalla, and endangering in its defective aim the row of negroes, high up on the benches, who dodged as one man. The wind of its flight, as it crashed harmless against the wall, nearly took off a darkey's ear, and impressed with his peril, and holding the threatened member in his cautious hand, he vociferated — "I tell ye now, dey'd better leff de ole gen'al alone!"

Kendricks had — instinctively, perhaps — thrust his arm behind him. It was a significant motion. The next moment something steely and sinister gleamed in his hand. But quick as he was, he was hardly quick enough. The pistol was cocked, but not levelled, when General Vayne rushed upon him. There was a swift, muscular movement of that dextrous left arm, and the learned counsel, hit fair and full between the eyes, was sprawling upon the floor, the revolver discharging in his fall, and the bullet skipping lightsomely through the little that was left of the crowd. An eager curiosity as to the subsequent proceedings rallied the audience, and it was reenforced, in a solid phalanx, by the Grand Jury, that had been in session in the opposite room, and was roused from its absorptions by the exhilarating note of the pistol.

The judge sat astounded upon the bench. "Why, bless my soul, General!" he exclaimed weakly. And then once more, "Bless my soul!"

He gave, however, a sign of return to judicial consciousness in imposing a fine of fifty dollars upon General Vayne for contempt of court; and to the lovers of sensation it seemed that the Grand Jury was providentially close at hand, for it went back to its den and indicted the stranger for carrying concealed weapons.

"Mr. Sheriff," said the judge, "adjourn the court till two o'clock."

"Oyez! Oyez! Oyez!" quavered Mr. Sheriff, greatly distraught. "The honorable Circuit Court stands adjourned till two of the clock!"

General Vayne's friends had hustled him out of the room. He was in the deepest humiliation. The want of dignity in his demonstration smote upon him sorely. That *he* should have so far forgotten himself! That *he* should lift his hand against his fellow-man — without a pistol in it!

When his colleague had left the room the defendant's junior counsel walked to the other door and waylaid a plethoric, eager, unwieldy old man who was hastening after General Vayne.

"Let me detain you a moment," said Meredith politely. "Mr. Ridgeway, I think?"

The old gentleman, facing about, solemnly acknowledged it.

"'This is a terrible affair, Mr. Ridgeway, and for General Vayne's own sake it must not be allowed to stand as it is. As you are a friend of his, you must help me to get an apology from him."

The old gentleman seemed on the verge of apoplexy. He became scarlet in the face as he stood unsteadily before his junior. He spluttered and gasped in his excitement; his eager words struggled for precedence, and ran over each other — "Anapology? — 'napology, sir? Anapology for being shot at!"

"The pistol was discharged when Mr. Kendricks was knocked down," said Meredith. "Do you think it is fair to conclude that he would have fired it?"

"Wha — what was he doing with it, then?" spluttered the old gentleman sarcastically.

"Don't you admit the possibility that he drew it to intimidate General Vayne — he could not stand still and be struck, and he could not strike a maimed man. You don't reflect, Mr. Ridgeway, that General Vayne will occupy the intolerable position of taking advantage of that circumstance. Of course Mr. Kendricks can do nothing but submit to the indignity."

The old gentleman tugged meditatively at his tuft of beard, as if it had some cerebral connection and he sought thus to stimulate mental activity.

As the lawyer was accustomed to present only one side of a question, and Mr. Ridgeway to see only one side, neither took any notice of Mr. Kendricks's "intolerable position," one ignoring it from intention and the other from fatuity. And at this moment, that gentleman, walking the narrow bounds of his room at the hotel, was absorbed in agonizing deprecation of public opinion, which he knew would not take into account a hurled inkstand in a case in which a pistol had been drawn on an unarmed and maimed man.

In a sudden flutter of anxiety, Mr. Ridgeway acceded, with apoplectic haste, to Meredith's suggestion, and the ill-assorted couple crossed the square to one of the lawyer's offices, where General Vayne sat with a friend, who, upon recognizing Meredith, rose and left the room, marvelling greatly as to his mission.

"General Vayne," said Meredith, who had previously met the elder gentleman, "I do not come from Mr. Kendricks; understand that. But I think some disinterested person should say to you, both on his account and your own, that you mistook altogether his intention. If you had been calm, you would have realized that his manner of urging his objection was a mere matter of course; it was his duty to his client's interest to seek to injure your testimony."

"Calm, sir, calm!" exclaimed General Vayne, his bald head purple. "I assure you, sir, I was as calm as I am at this moment."

"It is absurd, General," said Mr. Ridgeway, eagerly, "to attribute to a sane man an intention of seriously reflecting upon you. Your friends cannot sufficiently regret that under this delusion you should have permitted yourself to insult a gentleman " — .

"And a gentleman in the discharge of a purely professional duty," added the wily young diplomatist.

General Vayne sprang up and began to walk back and forth the length of the apartment, nervously pulling his mustache.

"And in the presence of a motley throng," said the elder peacemaker.

"Bringing a court of justice into contempt," said the lawyer.

"And offering a spectacle of insubordination to the men of your command, who hold you as an exemplar," pursued Mr. Ridgeway.

The unsuspecting subject of all this craft groaned aloud.

"Inflicting a public humiliation, and personal injury, and pecuniary loss upon a man who only sought to do his duty to his client," said Meredith.

The simple-hearted gentleman paused in his rapid striding to and fro, and with that agitated gesture, as if he would clasp his missing hand, he turned credulous eyes first on one of the tacticians, then on the other.

"And a stranger in the town!" exclaimed Mr. Ridgeway, capping the climax.

"I — I — will write to him," declared General Vayne, altogether overwhelmed. He turned to the table, and placed pen, ink, and paper with that adroit left hand. "I — I — am afraid I have been very hasty — very wrong — I will write." Then, suddenly, "No, I will not write. The affront was offered in the presence of a large assemblage " — this was his way of dignifying that motley little crowd; "I will apologize publicly, sir, publicly."

He looked about him wildly for his hat, caught it up, and strode with his buoyant step into the sunshine, twirling his gray mustache, and glancing keenly about for the object of his search.

The other two had risen at the same instant, and as they were about to follow him out of the door, the young lawyer, equally surprised and elated by the readiness with which peace had been patched up, attempted to exchange a leer of congratulation with his red-faced coadjutor. The demonstration was received with an expression of blank inquiry.

"Why, God bless me!" thought young America, feeling much like a child caught making faces, and mastering the situation with an effort, "here's another!"

Kendricks had already emerged from his room at the hotel. It had required some nerve to face Chattalla again, alive, as he knew it must be, with its enjoyment of the "fight free for all," but he did not want the "cursed little town" to say he was hiding, and with this view he was strolling listlessly about the public square. There General Vayne met him. Admiring Chattalla could only see from a distance the dumb show of an oratorical apology, and catch, now and then, the echo of a rotund period. It seemed, however, that the thing was very handsomely done, and handsomely received, too; for this unexpected turn of affairs had solved the lawyer's dilemma, which had offered the equally impracticable alternatives of challenging a one-armed man, or submitting to the ignominy of a blow. His relief gave his manner an unwonted geniality, and as they parted, Chattalla, looking after them, said that this was no doubt the best solution, although the whole affair, from the inkstand to the apology, was painfully "irregular." Then knots of men fell to talking about the propriety of blows, and apologies, under "The Code."

It was a long day to Estwicke, and fraught with many anxieties, but late in the afternoon, as he pressed with the crowd out of the court-house yard, they all seemed merged in the canvassing of his position in regard to General Vayne, and how far it might affect the future. He had inwardly resented the allusion to himself in the court-room, and he was not a man to tamely submit to an affront. But how was it possible to openly resent it from one old enough to be his father, whose hospitality he had often accepted, and with whose family he was on terms of cordial friendship? Then, too, impartially viewed, the ground of offence was untenable. He had been called a stranger, which was true, and it had been intimated that he might have misunderstood General Vayne's friend. Ought he, in justice to himself, to allow this to bar all further intercourse between them; to go to General Vayne's house no more; to relinquish, in effect, his hope of winning the woman he loved, and every dear prospect of the future?

The question was summarily settled. As he crossed the square he passed General Vayne. The elder gentleman returned his bow with a courtesy as fierce and as punctilious as if they faced each other at twelve paces. Estwicke went on, his blood on fire, swearing a mighty oath that he would take what cognizance he could of his own dignity, and that, whatever sacrifices might be involved, he would not go again to the house of a man who had offered him a public affront, confirming its deliberate intention by his manner afterward, which intimated a feeling approaching enmity.

CHAPTER XI.

THE lawyer whom Miss St. Pierre was destined to consult had no prevision of his coming client. Such prevision might have induced some exhilaration of spirit, for after court was adjourned on the day of the "shindy," as Meredith characterized it — the affair always figured in General Vayne's subsequent meditations as "that deplorable encounter"— the young man, strolling down Main Street, was rather dismayed by the prospect of the long evening before him; now that the abnormal excitements of the day were over he was beginning to be impressed with the facilities of Chattalla for unlimited dulness. He felt it, therefore, as something in the nature of a rescue when he suddenly heard his name called, and, turning, saw a carriage, which had stopped near the sidewalk, a face that he knew framed in the window, and a delicate gray glove beckoning to him with much cordiality of gesture. He threw away his cigar and hastened to shake hands with Mrs. Percy.

"Why did n't you let me know that you were here? Why have n't you been out to see me?" she exclaimed, graciously. For she made a special point of cultivating such of her pliable son's acquaintances as were not given over to the iniquitous beguilements of the wine bottle and the spring races. Besides, in the dreary interval which she spent in the country between her winters in New Orleans and her summers at the White Sulphur, she prized "company" only as a woman who is fond of society, but suffers a periodic bucolic eclipse, can prize it. She carried her forty-eight years lightly,— the style of her black-velvet dress and bonnet betokened that she accorded much attention to the mandates of fashion, and her religious friends objected with disparaging piety that she was a worldly-minded woman. She had a fresh complexion, dark hair, a Roman nose, bright gray eyes, and a charming smile. She bent this full upon him as she added, "When did you reach Chattalla?"

"Eight o'clock this morning," said Meredith, answering all three questions at once.

"Ah, then that explains it. I forgive you on condition of future good behavior. But you must come out and dine with us this afternoon. Jump in. I won't take any refusal."

"You won't have the opportunity, I assure you," said Meredith, briskly stepping into the carriage.

Thus it was he chanced to meet Miss St. Pierre, who was still Mrs. Percy's guest.

She introduced him graciously to the young girl who sat beside her. "I am so glad you happened to be here while I still have Miss St. Pierre with me. I take great pleasure in making my two *most* charming young friends known to each other," she added, with that habit of blandishment which was not so patently insincere as to detract from the pleasure its exercise afforded to those in her good books.

Her two most charming young friends smiled rather inanely at each other in default of an appropriate response. And it presently occurred to Meredith that the other charming young friend was habitually in default in this respect. She did not, as he phrased it, "talk back," and although he admired the acquiescent gentleness of her voice in her monosyllabic replies, and her blonde prettiness, enhanced by its sombre crape setting, his interest in her died out naturally enough as he grew absorbed in the spirited dialogue with Mrs. Percy, who did "talk back." It was soon revivified, however, and by an odd circumstance — a very odd circumstance it seemed to him — which came about in the course of conversation.

"And by the way," said Mrs. Percy, after a time, "tell me what brought you to Chattalla — if it was not to see me?"

"Nothing half so pleasant — professional business."

"Ah!" said Mrs. Percy, shaking her head with a melancholy gesture, the effect of which was impaired to some degree by the frivolous flutter it occasioned in the jet-tipped plumes on the top of her bonnet. "If Horace would only devote himself, as you do, to some serious solid pursuit! I tell him you are an example for him. If he would only enter the profession too!"

"There's so much room for him!" cried Meredith, with a laugh. "Tell him that, too, — from me."

Mrs. Percy waved her fan in remonstrant dissent. "Young men used to say that kind of thing when I was a girl — away back in the middle ages. You young pessimists have n't a patent on that sort of railing. Well, I hope the court will keep you here for a good while."

Antoinette suddenly fixed her eyes upon him. Speaking of her own accord for the first time, she asked gravely, as if the matter had a vital significance, —

"Are *you* a lawyer, Mr. Meredith?"

This personal inquiry from a stranger was so abrupt and unexpected that Meredith stared for an instant — then could not forbear a smile. To justify the smile, he replied with an attempt at pleasantry. "I can't deny the soft impeachment." After this the conversation flowed on in orthodox fashion. The incident did not leave his thoughts, however. He could not determine to what he might attribute this interest. She had put the question in so serious a manner. She had waited for the reply with eager attention. It flattered him, and it piqued his curiosity. " Why did she ask ? " he marvelled. " What does it matter to her whether I am a judge or a hod-carrier ? "

Ever and anon as he sat opposite, he glanced furtively at her. She seemed absorbed now — meditative. He wondered what she could be thinking about. He had no idea it was anything so solid as business.

She had not been stricken by the personal interest which his vanity was fain to ascribe to her, but she was very favorably impressed with his bright, clever face, and his air of decision and imperturbable serenity; these endowments aided the fact that he was a lawyer, which suggested the idea that she might have him to investigate the title to her property, and also to decide what had best be done to discover the owner of the locket she had found.

She had driven into Chattalla to-day with Mrs. Percy, intending to acquaint her with these perplexities, and under her chaperonage to consult some lawyer of the town. But Mrs. Percy had talked so much! — she and her particular friends were victims of that dissipation known among country ladies as " Spending the Day," and in these feminine caucuses they became singularly well-informed as to the affairs of other people; when she observed the large crowd about the square, which indicated that the circuit court was in session, she gave Antoinette so minute a detail of all the litigation, actual and incipient, in which mutual acquaintances were involved, that at last the girl was fairly frightened from the intended confidence, appreciating how disastrous it would be to have people speculating about an hypothetical flaw in her title, when in all probability there was no Fortescue living to lay claim to her property, and perceiving distinctly that whatever she told Mrs. Percy would, however unintentionally, be finally transmitted to the county. Even the question of the locket was so intimately connected with these interests that it was manifestly unwise to excite a useless romantic curiosity in the mystery encircling it, until she could advise with a lawyer as to its value as proof of Fortescue's death. So she said nothing, and finally, when the horses' heads were turned homeward, she had been absorbed in disappointment until they had chanced to meet Meredith, and the fact that he was a lawyer had been elicited. At her age she had had necessarily little enough experience of the world, and that little was drawn from its superficial and smiling phases of life in society and boarding-schools. She knew nothing whatever of its sterner aspects and commercial habitudes. Conventional as she was in every look, tone, and gesture, it did not for a moment occur to her that the course she now had in contemplation was *outré* in any respect; she did not recognize the impropriety of consulting a gentleman professionally who was out on a holiday and in the midst of a visit at a friend's house; she had no appreciation of the recklessness of her project, and gave no heed to the fact that she had never heard his name until an hour ago, and knew nothing of him or his reputation at the bar. Now and then she glanced at him as she sat opposite, and each hurried survey strengthened her purpose. She said to herself that he had an intellectual face, and sagaciously concluded that whatever there was to know in the law Mr. Temple Meredith had probably found it out. As to his youth — the reproach and shame of the neophytes of his profession, a reproach and shame which they can only live down by slow degrees — she never once thought of his youth. Such as she have scant regard for the value of experience. Her only anxiety was the fear that an opportunity to consult him would not be presented.

When they reached Mrs. Percy's place the sun was going down behind the heavy woods which, at this distance westward from the town, still stood untouched. The air was languorous and full of vernal suggestions — but for the bare boughs that encompassed the house, a large modern brick structure faced with stone, one might have believed that spring had come. The dark masses of evergreens about the grounds were edged with a most vivid and delicate emerald tint. Here and there the eye caught the blaze of some brilliant hot-house plant already set out in the open air. The windows of the parlor stood wide to the breeze, and within as well as without were everywhere evidences of much worldly prosperity. The whole scene was a wonderful contrast to the desolate barren that lay ten miles away and north of Chattalla, and to the dilapidated cannon-shattered house that stood forlorn and alone in its midst.

They found in the parlor Mrs. Percy's mother, a platitudinarian meek old lady, with a mouse-like manner, and always more or less agitated by an intermittent intention of repressing a pair of too airily fluttering diaphanous cap-strings. She had been additionally perturbed by the lateness of their return, for it was long past the dinner hour, and she feared some accident had befallen them. Here, too, awaiting them, was old Mr. Ridgeway, who had stopped on his way home from town, eager and excited about the prospective route of a new turnpike that was to be built through these broad acres of woodland, and determined that Mrs. Percy's influence as a stockholder in the company should be used with discretion, which in his opinion was synonymous with his interest, for he owned the adjoining tract. He was easily enough persuaded to stay to dinner, which was presently announced, and throughout the meal he monopolized the conversation — talking turnpike steadily on, without hindrance or pause. It was perhaps in the hope of effecting some diversion that Mrs. Percy, instead of returning to the parlor when they had risen from the table, led the way out upon the front veranda. The hope was vain; the party was hardly established here in rustic chairs before a square of light was projected from each of the windows, as the servant placed the lamps in the parlor; old Mr. Ridgeway sprang up with a buoyancy scarcely to be expected in a man of his size, produced from his pocket a map of the county, and insisted that the two elder ladies should go within and have the evidence of their own eyes as to the triumphs of turnpikeage which he proposed.

Meredith watched the trio through the open window for a moment — the visitor gesticulatory and given over to long exhortations; Mrs. Percy indifferent and as likely to favor one side as the other; and old Mrs. Lorent, scrutinizing the map with so close an attention that her fluttering capstrings were brought in dangerous proximity to the lamp-chimney. Then he realized all at once that he was left to the mercy of the catechistical young lady. He looked at her narrowly as she sat near him in the mingled light of the moon and the glow that fell through the open windows. She seemed thoughtful. Her eyes were downcast. Her face was very grave.

Suddenly she glanced up. "Mr. Meredith," she said, "as you are a lawyer it has occurred to me that I might ask you to examine the title of some property I have in Graftenburg — I have been told that the title is defective."

The surprise in his face which he could not control made her aware how far she had departed from established usage. She hardly gave him time for his murmured — "I shall be very happy." She continued hastily —

"Perhaps this is not the customary way of managing such things. I'm sure I don't know. I've had no experience in business affairs. This property only recently came into my possession. Before, I had nothing." She had lost her equilibrium and was blushing painfully. "I suppose I seem odd enough to die!" she concluded desperately.

This poor young lady considered oddity one of the worst forms of wickedness, and she was conscious of appearing very queer indeed in Temple Meredith's eyes. In her confusion and mortification she was on the brink of tears. He hastened to reassure her.

"I will do everything that is possible in the matter," he said earnestly. "Now, what is the difficulty about the title?"

"I don't know how to express these things intelligibly — as men do," said the conventional Miss St. Pierre, looking at him with appealing eyes, her cheeks crimson, her lips unsteady. "I shall have to tell it in my own fashion — you must try to understand it."

"I have no doubt you will make it plain enough," he replied in a matter-of-course manner, as if the whole confidence were a routine affair.

But he was thinking in great enjoyment that this was indeed an innovation upon the regular professional consultation. Instead of the prosaic mid-day atmosphere of his law-office in Marston, the din of the streets, the burly office furniture, the frowning assemblage of law-books, they were encompassed by a romantic blue twilight, pierced through and through with silver shafts from the moon. A whippoorwill's plaint was rising from the dark forest. There were delicate shadows of budding vines traced on the floor of the veranda. And what an infinite remove from all his experience of the genus client was this fair-haired, dark-robed young girl, blushing and faltering, and almost in tears because she could not explain a matter of business "like a man."

His father had early warned him never to undertake business without a retainer. Meredith remembered in secret and unfilial glee this golden rule of practice, and laid himself heavy odds that his client would not know the meaning of the term were it demanded of her.

As she detailed the story her composure returned, and it became more easily maintained when she observed the change in his face as his covert amusement, of which she had been subtly aware, gave way to a grave interest and much surprise. There was a pause when she had concluded. He silently revolved what had been said.

."Although finding the locket in an empty grave on the battlefield is not positive proof, it is certainly presumptive evidence of the man's death," he remarked at length. "Still he may be alive. It is possible that he lost the locket, or it may have been stolen from him."

"Or he may have given it away," she suggested.

"Not likely," the lawyer replied. "It is evidently a woman's gift to him, valuable chiefly from association. That fact indicates his presence on the spot. The battlefield" — he repeated, meditatively. "Do you know certainly that he was in either army?"

"I can't say. I know very little of him beyond his relationship to me, and I never saw him."

"You can think of no way by which he or his heirs can be discovered, or the fact of his death proved?"

"None at all. He was a wild, reckless, wandering

man. And he was singularly alone in the world, having no relatives of his father's family, and of his mother's connections I am the nearest, although the relationship is very distant."

There was another silence. The wind rustled in the vines and stirred her fair hair; the shifting moonbeams trembled on the floor.

"Perhaps it would be well for you to look at a paper which Mr. Travis sent me," she said, in a business-like voice. "It is an extract from the record."

His lips quivered slightly.

"Oh, ought I to say an 'abstract' of the record?" she cried. "How should I know!"

"It would be dreadful if you knew!" Meredith protested, with a laugh. "But let me see the 'extract.'"

She laughed too a little, but cast a deprecatory glance upon him as she rose and swept past him through the long window into the parlor, where she searched a little inlaid trinket of a writing-desk for the document which was incongruous enough with its dainty receptacle.

Mrs. Percy, still infinitely bored, sitting by the table at the other end of the room, followed her motions with wistful eyes.

"Somebody's photograph she is going to show him, I suppose," thought this victim of the Turnpike Company.

As Antoinette came back the young man rose and received the roll of surly-looking legal cap with a bow and smile which might have been a fit acknowledgment if she had given him a rose instead. Then he leaned against the window-frame and began to flutter the pages, the handwriting being distinct enough to his young eyes even at that distance from the lamp.

"It is not a photograph," said Mrs. Percy, watching them from within; "it must be sheet-music, or more likely a copy of verses."

Antoinette had dropped again into her little rustic arm-chair; she watched him intently while he read, altogether unaware that now and then, as he turned the pages, he was vividly conscious of her upturned, childish face, and her appealing eyes. She herself had found the paper hard reading, and she rather wondered that he should whisk over the leaves so lightly, seeming to take in only a point here and there. But with the lawyer's sixth sense, acquired by the habit of manipulating facts enveloped, mummy-like, in the infinite swathings of technical verbiage, he had easily separated all that was important from the rest.

"Well," he said, as he handed it back to her, "I have extracted something from this, although I hope you won't accuse me of having abstracted anything."

She was surprised at the good nature with which she regarded his harping on that trifling mistake.

"If an 'extract' from a poem, why not from the record?" she argued.

"Why not?" he rejoined, with a laugh.

She, too, smiled as she leaned her elbow on the arm of her chair, propping her flushed cheek with the stiff roll of legal cap, that was doubtless surprised to find itself in such pretty company.

Meredith had grown grave, reflective. "I think," he said, still lounging against the window-frame and checking off each point he made by tapping his hand with her fan, which he had picked up from the floor, "I think it more than probable that Fortescue's remedy is barred by the statute. Mrs. Perrier bought this property in April, 1857, immediately after the determination of Clendenning's estate *per autre vie*. And then, of course, Fortescue's right of action had accrued. The law in Tennessee allows for the institution of proceedings to recover real estate seven years next after the right of action has accrued. But on account of the disorder and confusion caused by the war, a period of something more than five years — from the sixth day of May, 1861, to the first day of January, 1867 — has been prescribed, during which no statute of limitations can be held to have operated. Now, you see, Mrs. Perrier held the property under a deed duly registered, claiming it as her own throughout the seven years originally limited, and the period allowed for the war. Unless Fortescue or his heir can set up some disability, there is no show for him now."

"If — if — if he were disabled in any way, would there be a — a — 'show' for him?" she asked earnestly.

He was holding her fan to his lips, and looking at her over it with laughing eyes.

"Oh, now *I know* that I have said something dreadfully ignorant," she cried in deprecation.

"You can't imagine how it shocks me," he protested.

"Of course," she argued, "if I knew all the law that there is, I shouldn't apply to you."

"There's a compliment in that," declared Meredith. "You didn't intend it for me, but there is no law that I know of to prevent me from appropriating it."

She glanced away, laughing in confusion, and then the learned counsellor, flirting the fan, proceeded, —

"Now, I'll tell you all about the disability. There are certain persons against whom the prescription does not run — minors; married women; persons 'beyond the seas,' which, in Tennessee, means, 'without the limits of the United States;' persons *non compos mentis;* and also, in some of the States, persons who are imprisoned, — all are excepted by the law if, when their right first accrued, they were laboring under any one of these disabilities, in which case they are allowed three years next after the removal of the disability to bring their action. Now, it is possible that Fortescue or his heir may have been under one of these disabilities, and may yet appear and make a fight for the property; but I think it exceedingly improbable."

She remained silent and meditative for a few moments. Then she repeated, in a thoughtful voice, like a child learning a lesson, "minors, married women, persons 'beyond the seas,' lunatics, and convicts. That's a nice company! Did it ever occur to you," she added, with the rising inflection of a laugh, and an archness that was unexpected and uncharacteristic, "did it ever occur to you that the law seems to consider married women persons to whom the fullest sympathy should be accorded and exceptional privileges allowed, in common with other grievously afflicted humanity, those who have suffered loss of mind, for instance, or imprisonment?"

"The law is a cynic," said Meredith as he stepped out into the moonlight.

And there he sat in its gentle radiance, discoursing mellifluously of the statute of limitations, of seisin, of disseisin in fact and by election, of tenancy at will and at sufferance, and cognate "curious and cunning learnings of the law"— emphasizing all his remarks with the fan, but never lapsing from an almost judicial gravity, influenced by a desire that she should understand the subject in all its bearings.

As she listened, she thought him a prodigy of legal erudition, and could not sufficiently applaud her own acumen and tact which had led her to place her interests in his hands. She felt altogether at ease now. He possessed, besides all his superior mental endowments, an extreme caution, — a quality which she held in high esteem, and which, as a general thing, she exercised. She deduced this from the fact that he had remarked parenthetically that he was glad to have seen the abstract, but that upon his return to Marston, he would go to Graftenburg where he would examine the record itself.

Then too he gave her a warning.

"Let me advise you, Miss St. Pierre, to say nothing to your friends about this supposed defect in the title of the property." As she had confided so readily in him he thought her nature was effusive, and that she needed a check. "That would be very impolitic, for if the title should prove to be perfect, the value of the property would be injured by the doubt in the minds of unprofessional people. It is very difficult to eradicate that kind of impression."

"Oh, I will not. I have not mentioned the matter to any one but you."

There was a convincing earnestness in her eyes as she raised them. Her child-like reliance upon an utter stranger was very beguiling. Alas, for this wise young counsellor!

He drifted back presently to his disquisition, and the moonlight shimmered about him, and the bird's melancholy monody rose fitfully from the deep shadows of the forest, and in the pauses they could hear the river flow, and when his eyes met the girl's, for all his learning, they lingered.

And now there was a stir within; the elders were coming out upon the veranda, and all too soon the professional consultation was ended.

When the young man returned to Marston, he mentioned rather pridefully to his father that during his absence he had had some business put into his hands, involving real estate in Graftenburg, which would require him to go to that city shortly for the purpose of examining the records.

"I am glad of it," said the old gentleman, gratified by this confirmation of his theory that if you don't help a young lawyer too much, he will help himself. "I'm glad of it. Don't grudge time and attention. Real estate is a very different style of business from that *cause célèbre* of yours — old Krieger and his two glandered mules."

His son laughed. "I dare say old Krieger's mules were as important to him as the real estate is to this client."

"All right — if you are disposed to hang your legal laurels on the long ears of those interesting animals, I have only to say — prosperity attend you," retorted the old gentleman, waggishly.

A few days later the young man did run down to Graftenburg, but he proceeded by indirection, setting out for that city *viâ* the Chattalla branch railroad, which in the nature of things, leads no further than Chattalla. He spent much time during the early part of his sojourn, *in transitu* between the hotel of the village and Mrs. Percy's place. His constant requisition of a certain swift trotter from the principal livery stable awakened in its proprietor a great admiration of his acumen in horseflesh, supplemented by no little curiosity and speculation.

"It's my belief," he said, as a result of much cogitation, "that that young chap — and he knows a good horse when he sees him — is courtin' somebody in this neighborhood."

He looked after the rapidly revolving wheels that bore his patron away, and shook his head sagely.

Not only in the village did Meredith's conduct provoke comment.

"It strikes me," said Mrs. Percy, privately to her mother, "that Mr. Meredith's deficiency in the matter of geography is positively painful. The poor young man seems utterly ignorant that Chattalla is not on the direct road between Marston and Graftenburg. He told me last evening that he had only stopped on his way!"

She found little difficulty in persuading him to subject himself no longer to the discomforts of the little hotel in the village, and after this he was established in Horace Percy's room on very much the footing of a son of the house, and with all his friend's effects at command — his books to read, his horse to ride, his boat to row. Some concession, however, was made to the absent. Meredith beguiled half an hour of his leisure one day by writing to Horace, describing the usurpation of his prerogatives, and politely inviting him to remain in New Orleans.

The elders of the household were readily propitiated. Mrs. Lorent found the guest, in her platitudinarian phrase, "a very worthy young man." Mrs. Percy often sighed and sadly shook her bedecked head, protesting that she would tell Horace what an example his friend was. And old Mr. Lorent, her father, who was a mere wreck physically, but with political opinions as fresh and vigorous as when he cast his first vote in 1820, declared that he had not seen the young fellow's equal for fifty years, and that his views on specie payment would have graced the days of "Old Bullion."

All this praise did not tend to impair the position he held in Antoinette's esteem. It fact it only served to confirm her own opinion.

They were often together, wandering through the grounds or along the bank of the river, while the warm vernal breeze stirred the trees, and the sunshine dripped, like some golden fluid, from one budding bough to another. The air tasted like wine. Wings were sweeping across the sky — and it was blue! Oh, perfect spring-days *sub tegmine fagi!* Oh, love and youth! Oh, Damon, no longer playing on an oaten pipe, which is comparatively meaningless, but with case-learning and precedent, with subtle distinctions and clever deductions. Oh, modern shepherd, whose silly sheep are sublimated in learned parchments! Oh, dear delights of seisin and disseisin, made plain as might be to pretty Nisa, who no longer cruelly disdains as of yore but is reduced to admiration of science, of its erudite professor, of the great future stretching out before him. And, oh, that great future! — that infinite possibility which stretches before every young man. How is it that, when youth goes, it goes too? And then your great future lies in your past. Your world has flattened out a little; the holy pool is stagnant, for the wing of your aspiration troubles the waters only once in a lifetime, and only once can you heal your sorrows and consecrate your purposes. After that you become critical — you measure your powers — you doubt — your hands fall. Then stock the holy pool with fish, my friend, and get your living out of it.

And yet this modern Damon had his woes and, perhaps for the lack of the oaten pipe, they were silent. Only within himself he argued dextrously whether it would be becoming to notify Nisa that she had acquired a new title — an indefeasible title to his heart — and her rights could never be barred by any statute of limitations whatever. But he had known her so short a time — only two weeks and a half. Still, he submitted, he had seen so much of her — their knowledge of each other would amount to full six months of ordinary acquaintance, prosecuted through a call now and then, and an occasional waltz at a German. On the other hand, such an avowal so soon after their first meeting might seem to her an impertinence. He ran over in his mind all the experience of his friends that had come to his knowledge — of those who were married, those who were engaged, and those who had ever sought to be. He, so ready with authorities, could not now cite one case in point — could not quote one dictum bearing even remotely on the subject. There was no precedent whatever — it would be a very informal proceeding. It was doubtless better to have all the pleadings in due form.

This man of words, who needed so few now, was depressed in spirit and rather wistful on the day preceding his departure for Graftenburg.

"This time to-morrow I shall not be with you when you come out to look at the sunset," he said, as they stood together on the front veranda. "I shall see it from the car windows, — it will be a great red and yellow daub skurrying by, flecked with cinders and smirched with smoke. And the fields of winter wheat — all of a crude green — will reel out from the woods somewhere, and the trees will go staggering about the landscape, and all nature will seem a coarse, drunken thing. And I shall realize that I am a man of towns and artificial life, and such as that is not for me." He pointed with Horace Percy's light riding whip at the calm and gracious splendor of the western skies, and then he fell to flicking his boots.

As if he cared for the sunset except that she looked at it!

The clouds were still aflame; long lines of crimson light flashed down the river alternating with its steely gleam; the brown boles of the trees on the opposite bank could still be distinguished. But the moonrise had followed hard upon the setting of the sun and a vagueness was coming into this tender harmony of coloring — not jarringly, but slipping through it with all soft and sweet accord.

"I'll write to you from Graftenburg about that matter of the record," he said presently, brightening with the thought.

"You are very kind," she murmured.

"And when I next come to Chattalla we'll talk it all over again."

There was certainly nothing more to talk over, and he had no further business at Chattalla, but as he stood silent for a moment he was seriously questioning how soon — how very soon — could he play truant to his other engagements.

"Possibly on the — no, certainly on the 28th of June I shall be here again."

And on this understanding they separated.

"Temple!" exclaimed old Mr. Meredith, tartly, as his son came suddenly into the office one day, "you stayed in Graftenburg long enough to commit the records to memory. I was afraid I should be obliged to send Bryant to New York in your place. Not that you know any more law than he does," he added disparagingly. "God knows it's Hobson's choice!"

And so Temple Meredith went to New York on business for his father.

It was only a short time after his departure that Antoinette received from a notable and highly reputable firm of lawyers in Graftenburg a letter which ran thus: —

MADAM: — We write to inform you that in accordance with the instructions of our client, Mr. John D. Fortescue, we will at an early day bring suit for the recovery of the property in this city now held by you under color of title by the will of the late Mrs. Perrier.

Mr. Fortescue directs us to say that he will resort to this course with great reluctance; rather than do so he would make a liberal settlement with you. If, after consideration of the matter, you are disposed to offer any terms, we shall be happy to submit them to Mr. Fortescue.

Very respectfully yours,
WYNDHAM & ORRIS.

She read and re-read this letter, and then thought it over in much perturbation. That singular circumstance — the discovery of the locket in an empty grave — made it seem as if Fortescue had strangely come from the dead to dispossess her. Although Meredith had assured her that she had no positive proof of his death, the belief had previously become so rooted in her mind that it was difficult to eradicate it. She determined that she would be reasonable now and harbor no more fantasies. She would see things as they really were, not distorted, through a childish love of mystery. She began to think that from the first she had unjustly suspected Mr. Travis's motives; for this threatened attack upon the property was a fulfilment of his warnings. The only apparent discrepancy — the length of time which had elapsed since the determination of the estate *per autre vie* — could probably be explained when Fortescue's lawyers should confer with hers; perhaps he had been under one of those disabilities of which Temple Meredith had spoken, and had thus escaped the bar that would otherwise prevent him from recovering the property.

Yet even while resolving to banish from her mind her fantastic suspicions, she was vaguely conscious of a plot in the air, and, struggle as she might, this vague consciousness hampered the decision she sought to base on the bare facts before her, and still influenced her action. She did not answer the lawyer's letter. She inclosed it to Temple Meredith, supposing that he was still in Marston, with a request that he would give it his attention and obtain Mr. Fortescue's present address, in order that the locket might be returned. Her instinct was to keep them all at a distance; she would treat with them only through Meredith.

When this letter arrived in Marston, it was handed to

his father with a number of others. "Hey! What's that — Temple's mail?" the old gentleman asked, as he thrust his pen behind his ear.

A couple of wedding cards fell upon the floor from one of the open envelopes in his hand. He stooped with difficulty to regain them, and when he had risen to his portly perpendicular, he was red in the face and testy in temper.

"Weddings, and parties, and such follies!" he ejaculated scornfully; for he had come to think all was folly that did not tend to litigation or issue therefrom. "No way for a young man to get on. Wasting time; fritter, fritter" —

As he shuffled the envelopes, he paused to look attentively at the blurred and unintelligible postmark of Antoinette's letter, from which the stamp had chanced to be lost. He drew his own inference from its delicate exterior and graceful, feminine chirography, and righteously separated it from those envelopes of formidable aspect which unmistakably indicated business correspondence. These he promptly forwarded to his son, while Antoinette's letter was relegated to a place among the wedding cards and flimsy little notes treating of impending Germans and private theatricals.

"I'll keep these invitations and such trash till he comes; he'll be here in a week. He won't want to be bothered with them now, for they can't do him any good there, — nor anywhere else."

He placed them methodically together, and pigeonholed them in the darkest corner of his desk, to await Temple's return.

It was long delayed by unforeseen complications of the business which had carried him to New York, and old Mr. Meredith, forwarding from time to time his son's correspondence, had utterly forgotten the little notes in his desk.

Antoinette, in great surprise, waited vainly for an answer. Twice, during the weeks that ensued, she began to write to Meredith again; twice she burned her letter, fearful, in her inopportune caution, that her interference would work mischief, that her impatience might harry him into precipitate and thoughtless action. She was checked, too, by a sense of something unbecoming in her persistence; it might seem as if she had scant confidence in his judgment, and desired to call him to account, to dictate and superintend him in the matter. And surely he knew best, she argued, whether the delay was injurious or an advantage. She had committed everything to his guidance, and it was for him to act, not her. In some indignation she thought that he might have sent her a line to allay her anxiety; but, on the other hand, he could hardly be expected to realize how anxious she was. He might be making investigations important to her interests, and wished to reply only when he had reached a decision, or had something definite to say. She had become sharply conscious of her inexperience in the ways of the world, and admitted to consideration the possibility that men of business might be more deliberate in matters of importance than she had supposed.

She sought to divert her mind as much as possible from this perplexing absorption, and to await patiently further developments; but this was difficult in the dull routine of country life. After she had returned to General Vayne's plantation, however, more frivolous interests asserted a claim to her attention. She found that great events were impending; the whole household was in a state of gratified expectancy; the boys were noisy and hilarious; there was festivity intimated in the very waving of Mrs. Kirby's curls; only Marcia seemed a little languid, and somehow unaccountably and constantly disappointed.

"We are getting ready, my dear, for Thursday, the ninth — Edgar's birthday," said Mrs. Kirby. "Marcia always lets him have his own way on that day; yes, and he desires to give a fishing party. Lucky, was n't it," she added, with an expression of deep slyness, "that he had a whim to invite some grown people, too? — makes it so much more pleasant for *us*, you know."

Then she turned beamingly to her brother.

"And *you* ought, Francis, to invite formally all whom Edgar has asked. Suppose you write the notes now. Yes; no time like the present."

General Vayne obediently seated himself, and, pen in hand, awaited further instructions.

"Let me see," continued the old lady, meditatively, "there were Mr. and Mrs. Ridgeway, and their grandchildren — don't forget the children."

General Vayne's pen, with splutter and splash, flourished across the page, and the Ridgeways were invited in all due form.

"And Captain Estwicke," lined out Mrs. Kirby, who knew nothing of the disagreement.

General Vayne's pen paused in mid-air. To be sure, he disliked — nay, he heartily detested — Estwicke, and desired no further intercourse with him. But in a manner he had been already asked, and the "sacred laws of hospitality" were involved in so reiterating the invitation that it would be possible for him to accept or refuse, at his own pleasure.

Splutter, scrawl, splash once more.

There is an infinite sarcasm in a double-faced fact. It is perhaps an apt illustration of this that Estwicke should receive a note, which left General Vayne in this mood, as a covert apology; that he should flinch under its supposed generosity; that he should scourge himself, as having grossly refused to concede aught to the heat of partisanship, when the character of a man's friend was at stake and his orphans in danger of beggary; that he should upbraid himself as a churl, who would take no cognizance of the gracious cordiality and kindliness he had enjoyed until it was extended again.

In this propitiatory and humble frame of mind, uncharacteristic enough, he, too, was eagerly expectant of the great day.

While all these unconscious factors in his schemes were thus giving themselves up to the anticipation of frivolous diversion, Maurice Brennett was like a worm in the fire. He could not imagine why Fortescue's lawyers should have heard nothing whatever from Miss St. Pierre in response to their effort to promote a settlement. As day after day passed without result, he at length felt it necessary to take a hand in the game himself.

Some time earlier than this, Fortescue had concluded to go to Tennessee, for the purpose of a more comprehensive consultation with his lawyers than could be readily compassed by correspondence. Brennett had urged this plan, and when at last it was adopted, he told Travis that he intended to accompany Fortescue.

"Ten to one," he said, "the fellow won't see the lawyers at all, unless there is somebody along to keep him up to the mark. He will be gambling and drinking, and forget why he went there at all."

When Travis stopped in Graftenburg, on his way to the Louisville races, he was greatly dismayed to learn from Brennett that some ill-feeling had here been developed between him and Fortescue. Agitated by the prospect of internal dissension at such a crisis, Travis reproached Brennett with this patent imprudence.

"For the sake," he said, "of a pitiful little three thousand dollars," — he always spoke contemptuously of comparatively small sums of money, and with bated breath and deep respect of large, — "for the sake of a pitiful little three thousand dollars you jeopardize all our chances. If you incense that fellow against you, he may ruin our prospects yet; he may go back on our contract, and bring suit for the Graftenburg property on his own hook. We couldn't chirp if he should, because our agreement is champertous, you know. Why did you lend him money if you didn't expect to stand to lose?"

For Brennett, it seemed, had loaned Fortescue three thousand dollars, dividing the debt for the sake of a more speedy collection, and taking six notes for five hundred dollars each, thus bringing it within the expeditious jurisdiction of a justice of the peace. When they fell due, and the money was not forthcoming, there were some hot words about the matter. Brennett — in a ridiculous pet, as it seemed to Travis, for there was nothing to be gained — sued, got judgment, issued executions, which were levied upon Fortescue's interest in the Graftenburg property, and, until the next term of the circuit court, could proceed no further.

"Perhaps I was wrong," Brennett admitted. "Still, I have thought of a way to utilize the affair."

"I should like to know how," said Travis, "if it were only for curiosity."

"Well," said Brennett, meditatively, "I am going up there in the country with Percy. I should like to get the machinery of this proposed compromise into running order, and, if I could discover what the hitch is there, I might start the rest. I may meet Miss St. Pierre. If I tell her that I am a creditor of Fortescue's, and have therefore a personal interest in promoting a settlement, it might be admissible for me to talk the matter over with her. I could find out why she makes no move in the affair. I might be able to facilitate — even to effect a compromise."

"That's a first-rate idea, Brennett. Such a head for expedients as you have! But it is soft in places. Lending money to Fortescue — of all the men in the world! And I never heard before of your lending money."

It might not have occurred to a more clever brain than Travis's that there was literally no "value received" for these notes that John Fortescue gave to Maurice Brennett only two weeks ago, but dated thirty days earlier, on which a justice of the peace in Graftenburg solemnly rendered judgment, and executions were issued and levied.

Still Travis harbored some vague uneasiness.

"Has Fortescue started back to New Orleans?" he asked.

"He is there by this time," replied Brennett.

"Look here, Brennett, we ought to keep on that fellow's blind side. Was he friendly with you when he set out?"

"Oh, friendly enough," rejoined Brennett, carelessly.

Brennett's "head for expedients" presently evolved the idea that it might be productive of good results to open a correspondence with Miss St. Pierre before a personal interview. It would be a less awkward method of introducing the subject than by word of mouth. His letter simply stated the fact that he held judgments against Mr. Fortescue for the sum of three thousand dollars, and had levied executions upon his interest in the Graftenburg property now in her possession. Hearing, however, that a negotiation for a settlement between her and Mr. Fortescue was pending, he wrote to notify her that he claimed payment out of any fund which in such settlement might become due to Mr. Fortescue and with the view of avoiding further litigation.

This letter occasioned Antoinette far less disquietude than the one from the lawyers. She was only annoyed that Mr. Fortescue's creditors should be writing to *her*. She did not reply, for she did not know how much, or how little, or what it would be judicious to say. She merely made a mental note of the name signed and laid the letter aside to be enclosed to Temple Meredith, when she should have received a response to her former communication which she expected by every mail.

And still it did not come, and Maurice Brennett's letter continued unanswered.

He could not sufficiently congratulate himself that his plans were complete for an invasion of the enemy's country.

CHAPTER XII.

THE sky looked down so tenderly, so tenderly. And the haunted thickets were all a-bloom. Gentle grasses had crept to the verge of the open, empty graves, and trailing through them was the mystic purple passion-flower. Delicately tinted wild roses had clambered into the funereal cedar, hiding its sorrow with the splendors of a new spring. All along the green perspective the elder shook out its snowy banners.

Restful places were these — where only the unquiet ghosts were wont to walk. Here the dove was on her nest. The mocking-bird's melody thrilled through the solitude. All the timid and helpless wild things found their refuge among the phantoms; there were rabbits, and squirrels, and quail. No fear of man in these sequestered spots unbroken by the ploughshare still, untrodden by mortal foot.

A luxuriant growth of bear-grass fringed the banks of the river as it flowed through the battle-field. The reflection of the tall, stately stems, hung about with myriads of snowy bell-like blossoms, embellished the margin of the bright water for miles. And the water was very bright to-day — full of concentric silver circlets, and golden sunshine, and a blue sky brought down to earth and made sweetly familiar. It seemed that the two skiffs, freighted with Edgar's birthday guests, could but glide swiftly through so limpid a medium, and they skimmed along as if propelling themselves with their unfeathered wings.

"We shall meet Mr. Percy at the Coteatoy Bluffs, — Horace Percy," said Mrs. Kirby with animation. "He reached Chattalla yesterday — yes — in the afternoon. He took great pains," she continued, laughing slyly, "to let us know he had returned. He drove over last evening — yes — he said he was fishing for an invitation to fish."

She waved her curls and smiled blandly. "Like a match-making mother," thought Estwicke furiously.

With jealous quickness he turned his eyes on Marcia. No rush of emotion had sent the color to her cheeks now — only the faintly roseate tinge, that dwelt there when her heart was calm, merged delicately and imperceptibly into the warm whiteness of her brow and throat. She had thrown off her hat. The sunbeams mingled with that perennial golden glinting in her brown hair. The pliant grace of her figure embellished the simple lawn dress which she wore, such as she always wore these warm days, — it was pure white, with a dainty lace-like pattern traced upon it in black stripes; one dress differed from another only in the arrangement of many fluted ruffles, that gave it a petalled appearance — "double," as the gardeners say; it was like a flower, moreover, in its exquisite freshness — it seemed to Estwicke to have bloomed only this morning.

"He was a very successful angler," said Mrs. Kirby, — "caught two invitations, in fact. He tells us that he has a friend staying with him — a Mr. Brennett — and that he is presumptuous enough to hope that together they can fill the gap made by my brother's absence. Yes, my brother was called to Marston on business — very suddenly — will be gone several weeks — too bad — too bad!"

Here and there, as they rowed, they could catch a

glimpse of the battle-field — the long lines of fortifications rising in billowy green sweeps from the level expanse. In mid-stream were the stone piers of the old turnpike bridge. As the boat was passing, Estwicke glanced up and up the piles of masonry, austere and sternly suggestive, despite the soft matutinal influences; despite the mosses and vines that come always with their clinging grace to dull the sharp edges of ruin; despite a nest in a niche and a brooding bird.

Well, the sentries tramped over this water once! Only the sunshine guards the wreck of a bridge now. And here blood was shed. There were flames in the night to cover a mad retreat and impede a swift and fierce pursuit. And now only Marcia's joyous laughter, and the fresh, sweet voices of the children in the other skiff, and the melodious dip of oars, and the restful peace of the springtide. And all that is gone; is forgotten. And better so! A moment more and the ruined piers were behind them.

And now they were among the shadows; they had reached the forests at last, and a bend in the river brought them suddenly in sight of the Coteatoy Bluffs and of a skiff drifting in the deep glooms below. Brennett, idly dipping his oars now and then, was cynically watching Percy, who was standing, his dark eyes turned eagerly upon the approaching boats, his fresh complexion all the fresher for a sudden accession of color, his delicate black mustache scarcely hiding a quiver of excitement on his lips. His white linen suit rendered his tall, lithe figure and every gesture, as he fanned himself with his hat, very distinct upon the olive green and brownish shadows about him, and instantly the children in the nearest skiff set up a shrill acclaim of recognition and salutation. Mrs. Kirby waved her curls and nodded benignly to him. Marcia was blushing and smiling. Mrs. Ridgeway flourished her handkerchief.

"Why, God bless me," spluttered old Mr. Ridgeway, "how well the boy is looking."

Estwicke suddenly felt alien — friendless. This man was coming back among people who had known him from his infancy; they all called him "Horace." His intimacy with them had its root in habitudes that dated back two generations. They all liked him, and indeed it would be strange if a dull old stock of a country neighborhood, such as this, were insensible of the charm of a gay, vivacious young worldling grafted upon it, brilliant with foreign influences, and vigorous with a new growth. His careful art in conserving his popularity had been observed only sufficiently to give rise to the local report that he had political aspirations, and to lead to harmless solicitations from "many voters." He fought shy of these, gratified, but unambitious of the heavy cares of legislation; his coyness was held as proof of precocious statesmanship, of latent designs awaiting development, and gave him the reputation of being "deep."

It did not escape Estwicke's fierce scrutiny that when the newcomers had run their boat close alongside, Percy's notice of the other members of the party was the merest mechanical courtesy, and his eyes were loath to turn away from Marcia's face. But the meeting involved the prosaic necessity of introducing his friend, and it followed hard upon this moment of sentimental apotheosis.

That moment had its peculiar interest for others. Maurice Brennett fixed his piercing eyes upon Miss Vayne with questioning intentness, until her name was pronounced, when it died out as suddenly as it had sprung up. But he looked hard at Miss St. Pierre as he was presented to her, and now his attention did not flag. It struck Estwicke's whimsical imagination with a fleeting wonder that a hawk could bow in so conventional a manner and look so like a gentleman. For he had at once recognized the man, and that strong likeness to the feathered rascal which he had first observed over the card-table in Meredith's room. Brennett, too, recognized him, but in a cursory and superficial manner that hardly impinged for an instant upon his deeper absorption.

"May I beg a place in your boat for Mr. Brennett?" said Percy, claiming Mrs. Kirby's indulgence. "I am sure it would be much more agreeable for him there."

"Oh, certainly," said Mrs. Kirby, "and you must come too."

"Both would be too heavy in addition to your party. I think I had better stay at anchor here."

"I hope that through your agency Chattalla has produced a fine impression on Mr. Brennett — yes — *impressed* him," said Mrs. Kirby, beaming out of her old black bonnet.

"Oh, I have done my duty as cicerone. I have been trying all the morning to find a lion or two about the place to show him."

"How lucky you are!" cried Marcia, joyously. "You have found a whole menagerie!"

"It will not be so easy for you to get away from the lions," said Mrs. Kirby, eagerly desirous of removing any constraint which the informality of their invitation might have occasioned.

From the readiness with which Percy adapted himself to the situation, it might be inferred that no man had had so little fear of lions since the days of Daniel. By reason of the proximity of the boats, it was easy for him to lean across the intervening water and talk to Marcia — in a half-suppressed tone, as if he were desirous not to offend the delicate susceptibilities of the fish. Naturally, as she turned to reply, she had, in a degree, the air of ignoring Estwicke, who, when he relinquished his oar, had seated himself beside her. It was only after some little time that she became aware of her remissness; then she made an effort to draw him into the conversation. But he had suddenly grown unresponsive — almost formal. Although he kept a careful restraint upon his words and manner, that he might make no overt sign of indignation, he resented the fact that she should have put a slight upon him for Percy's sake; her afterthought made scant amends. Besides, he argued, her absorbed interest in Percy was significant; so far as he himself was concerned it ought to be definitive. Why should he hope against hope? He remained seated beside her, but he fell to angling presently, and seldom spoke unless directly addressed.

When Brennett stepped from one skiff to the other, the only vacant seat was beside Miss St. Pierre. As he took it he was still looking hard at her with speculating uncertainty and surprise. He had been altogether unprepared for this passive young lady with her infantile — not to say expressionless countenance. Travis's character-sketch, in which the predominating traits were quick intelligence and tenacity of purpose, might well apply to Miss Vayne. He hardly felt satisfied as to their identity until he once more heard them addressed by their respective names. Then he again bent his keen eyes upon Antoinette's quiescent face. Its unsuggestiveness operated momentarily as a check upon him. To judge from it she was made up of all gentle and negative qualities. He had a swift fear that he would not find here any traits of character sufficiently definite and developed to furnish him a basis for a plan of action, an impetus for that lagging project, the compromise. "Surely," he said to himself in irritation, "no other man ever had so unpromising material to work upon, — a dolt, like Travis; a runaway horse, like Fortescue; and this nonentity, this utter blank!" And looking more like a hawk than ever, for his life he could see nothing further.

He declined the offer of a rod — he was always an unsuccessful angler, he said, and the two were thrown upon the resource of conversation to beguile the tedium of the next hour or so.

It began in this way.

"You don't fish, Miss St. Pierre. May I ask why?"

This inquiry was propounded with a searching glance. He waited for her reply with an attention which seemed to attach to it a disproportionate importance.

"I don't care for fishing," she said. "It always seems to me a cruel sport."

"Cruel? Ah, well, perhaps. But I confess I had not thought of that. I can't regard a fish as a hero who fights for his home and his life and dies a martyr. For gustatory reasons I hope I never shall. That reflection would not improve his flavor."

She only smiled as a rejoinder. Her peculiar talent for forcing the burden of the conversation on her interlocutor, whoever he might be, was somewhat conspicuous in the pause that ensued.

He pulled at his mustache with a preoccupied air. Even her casual silence was noteworthy — so important were the interests at stake, and so utterly destitute was he of any idea as to how he had best proceed.

"What sort of fish are in this river?" he asked. Apparently he was talking only for the sake of conversation.

"They are not valued highly, I believe," she replied.

"That is why it seems especially cruel to catch them — when no one cares particularly for them."

"Ah! that lets in the light. Even a sensibility so delicate has its practical element. If they were valuable you would not think it cruel to catch them; if they were valuable it might seem cruel of them not to come up and be caught. Is that your meaning?"

He had anticipated that she would be confused because of this misinterpretation, and would perhaps protest. She laughed a little, opening and shutting her black fan, and then she began to listlessly fan herself.

"I have always heard that a woman's moral intuition is more reliable than a man's conscientious perception. I like to be supplied with those infallible feminine convictions. I appreciate their value. I shall add that maxim of yours to my treasures, — 'Don't be cruel unless it's worth while.'"

He said this as if it were humorously intended, but there was a peculiarly irritating, though slight, suggestion of sarcasm in the tones of his voice. She did not seem, however, to apprehend it. She smiled placidly as her calm, unspeaking eyes rested on the swift current and its shimmering silver circlets, that whirled and whirled interfulgent, the blue sky above and the reflected blue sky below.

"She controls her temper," he said to himself; "or, perhaps," he added dubiously, "she has no temper to control."

Once more he looked at her speculatively, and he felt that he made no progress.

He tried another policy.

"I hope you never attempt to put your Tennessee friends out of conceit with their little river," he said presently, glancing disparagingly about. "Do you claim to be remarkably knowing in the matter of rivers because you live upon the banks of the Mississippi?"

She was not ready at repartee, and was at a loss for an answer to a question like this. But he was looking straight at her, and she must speak.

"No-o," she hesitated, at a venture.

"That is right," he rejoined, lightly. "It is what I should have expected of you. For I remember now that old French motto of the St. Xantaine family, which, freely translated, might be made to read — 'Deal gently with people who don't own a Big River.'"

There was a change now; her color intensified, it rose to the roots of her fair hair and crept down the shadowy black crape about her throat; a surprised pleasure looked out brightly from her eyes; her lips curved suddenly in a pretty smile.

"That is a very free translation," she said, laughing.

"Can a translator be expected to do more than give the spirit of the original?"

He spoke carelessly, but his face expressed a grave, almost breathless interest. Here, certainly, was something definite at last. Who believed more faithfully than she that the St. Xantaines had no need of the homage of Maurice Brennett, or of any other man. And yet she was flattered — infinitely flattered — by this slight tribute to the family, charged with an adequate recognition of its antiquity. It was hardly to be expected that in the consummate adroitness with which he had flung this seemingly casual remark into the conversation she should discover an astute intention. But her manner of receiving it augured great weakness. "And yet this trait of family pride is something intense," he said to himself.

He was silent for a time, absorbed in bootless surprise that, propitiated as she must have been — as he could hardly have believed possible — by the gift of the heirloom, she should suddenly have developed that distrust of Travis which he had detected in her letters. His swift mind rushed upon its conclusion. "She was influenced against him afterward by some outside cause — a strong cause, certainly. What was it?"

He had no inclination, however, to speculate vaguely about the wrecked scheme of the exchange of property. He only wished to steer his course so as to avoid that sunken rock which had demolished his first project. What was it?

In this momentary lapse of observation, something escaped him. She was looking at him; kindly. At the instant of his introduction she had recognized his name as that of the man whose letter she had never answered, and who held an interest similar to Fortescue's in her property; so fraught with perplexity had this whole subject become that she felt at first an unreasonable prejudice against him on this score. Now, however, she was beginning to be agreeably impressed by his manner, and more by his face, expressive as it was of a subtle power and some deep meaning — too deep, she knew intuitively, for her fathoming. She fell to wondering who he was, and why she had never heard of him in New Orleans, and what he did with himself in the world.

Presently he resumed: "And what do you think of Tennessee cotton, Miss St. Pierre? Does it seem a caricature of the plant when you remember the big fields, almost breast high even at this time of the year, along Bayou Gloire?"

"Oh, Bayou Gloire! How familiar that sounds!" she cried. "Are you from that part of the State?"

"No — I am not from Louisiana. My experience along Bayou Gloire has been only as an angler — ah, I forget your tender sensibilities! To reassure you, I will say that I committed few murders — the skill was lacking. I used to go with Mr. Travis — who, as you know, is an expert sportsman and truculent to a degree. By the way, when did you see him last?"

There was a pause. Surely she had no need to guard her words. But all that had come from Travis's visit — the proposed exchange of property, the first suggestion of an outstanding title, the significance which finding the locket in an empty grave seemed then to possess — invested the very mention of it with a certain importance, which, however, she felt was undue, and very foolish.

She had a sense, that made her angry with herself, of closely skirting many secrets as she said,

"It has been some time now since I have seen him."

The pause and this simple reply gave him food for reflection.

"How reticent she must be where anything touches her interests," was his conclusion. "'Some time'— that might mean three weeks, or three months, or three years. She has no reason, I should judge, not to state explicitly when it was. She is instinctively, constitutionally cautious and reticent."

The approach, accidental though it had seemed, to these subjects, which had given her so much disquietude, had the effect of putting her on her guard. She noted, with a sudden surprise, the keenly observant expression of his bright eyes. She had an unpleasant fancy that there was something sinister in their brilliancy; she began to feel like a creature undergoing vivisection, whose sufferings might be aggravated by the knowledge that they were not for the benefit of humanity or of science, but for the personal advantage of the operator. She did not entirely understand her own motive, but the leading idea in her mind was to interrupt his study of her pause and her words, and above all, and before all, to change the look he bent upon her. Yet even while she spoke she was arguing within herself as to why she should fear his analysis or his look.

"Have you known Mr. Travis long?" she asked.

"For many years," he returned. "We were at college together. I have a number of friends among your connections and relatives. It makes me feel as if I had met you before. You will permit me that little hallucination of acquaintance?"

She smiled upon him in sudden reassurance. How absurd, she said to herself, that she should imagine that this man weighed her words and watched her face with some intent and secret motive! What purpose could he serve?

"I have often heard you spoken of among them. Perhaps you know that you are a favorite subject of conversation with Mrs. Bradley. The last time I saw her she was talking of you to a more distant relative of yours,— Mr. Fortescue."

Once more she experienced a quick revulsion of feeling. It seemed to her that, considering their mutual position toward John Fortescue in the impending litigation, this mention of him was hardly appropriate. Somehow she was definitely aware of an intention here. She recognized the address which had thus innocuously thrown him into the conversation, and she felt instinctively that more was to come. She deprecated it. She would have avoided it if she could. She had a vague idea of trying to draw some one else into the conversation, but a glance at the other members of the party demonstrated how futile such an effort would be. Mr. Ridgeway was assisting Mrs. Kirby, in the midst of whispered excitement, to land a fish. Beyond these bulky old people could be seen Mrs. Ridgeway's broad shoulders in a state of abnormal activity, as she animatedly wound and unwound a snarl of fish-line. At the other end of the boat was Marcia, listening to Horace Percy, and now and then turning to appeal to Estwicke, whose evident absorption in their talk — although he was saying little — as well as the distance, precluded Antoinette's hope of appropriately claiming his attention.

Brennett's low voice, subdued in deference to the requirements of the anglers, and inaudible except to her, diverted her from her indefinite, hazy project.

"Did you ever meet Mr. Fortescue?" he asked; "but no; you must have been too young. I remember now that he said he has not been to New Orleans before for many years."

"I have never met him," she replied gravely.

"You have missed something," he said, with a half suppressed, sardonic laugh. "A man with the world in a sling — like Fortescue — is worth knowing. He goes everywhere, he sees everything, he knows everybody. The interest of his debts brings him a handsome income. The rights of other people are nullified, so far as he is concerned, by a self-arrogated prerogative that is almost royal. And he considers himself a king — a king among fools, and levies a heavy tribute, as I know to my cost. And that reminds me," he added, turning to her suddenly, "that you never answered my letter."

In the momentary confusion which this outburst induced, she was at first sensible only of the rudeness and bad taste which it involved, and she appreciated keenly the very evident fact that Maurice Brennett had been bred to know how reprehensible rudeness and bad taste are. The next instant the nebulous suspicions afloat in her mind — the suspicions which the lawyers' letter and Brennett's had failed to disperse — suddenly crystallized. There was no adequate reason for it, but all at once she believed that the man calling himself Fortescue was an impostor, and that the locket, with that name in it, which she had found in an empty grave on the battle-field, belonged to a soldier long ago dead. And here was the impostor's chosen coadjutor! This, and this only, would give him a motive to weigh her words; this, and this only, would set him to watch her face. She felt sure that for some reason, some unconjecturable reason, she personally had become important to the success of their scheme. There was something he wanted to find out from her; she was to be their unconscious ally against her own interests. She began to try to remember what she had said, and what it might mean to him. But she could not think, — a chilly trepidation was overpowering her, — vague, unreasonable; she only knew that she feared him.

"I was sorry to trouble you with a letter on business," he continued. "And I am aware that among the important absorptions of a young lady's correspondence such dull matters must wait. But I have at length begun to despair of my turn."

"My lawyer will give you an answer," she replied tremulously.

She hardly noticed that they had quitted the shade of the Coteatoy Bluffs, and were pulling steadily up the stream toward a shelving bank, where the party proposed to take lunch. The continuous chatter, in the usual tone of voice now, of the other occupants of the boat fell unheeded upon her ears. As she mentally canvassed the situation, she was mechanically drawing her black gloves back and forth in her soft, white hands, and now and then toying nervously with the buttons. This sign of agitation did not escape his attention as he sat beside her, his hat drawn down over his brow to shield his eyes from the glare of the sunlight and its reflection on the water. As the skiff was run upon the bank, he stepped out and offered to assist her. She gave him her hand with, he fancied, some slight reluctance. He felt that it trembled and was cold. "She is nervous and timorous beyond the natural timidity of her sex, and somehow or other she is afraid of *me*," he said to himself, surprised.

The way was stony and rough; here and there the roots of a tree protruded. In one of these Antoinette caught her foot and almost fell. Brennett and Estwicke each offered his arm at the same moment, but she affected not to see Brennett and accepted Estwicke's proffer. Only once she spoke to him.

"Take me to Mrs. Kirby," she said. "I think she has a vinaigrette, and I've signalized the occasion by getting up a headache."

"Perhaps it is the effect of the sun," said Estwicke. "Suppose you rest here in the shade while I go for the vinaigrette."

"No — no — I'll go with you," she insisted eagerly.

As they walked on together she was silent, and Estwicke, too, seemed abstracted. But the influence of his familiar presence reassured her to some degree. The soft green shadows were grateful after the glare on the river; a bird was singing somewhere; the wind stirred. She was among her friends — she let her hand rest heavily on Estwicke's arm as they strolled slowly along beneath the overhanging boughs — why should she entertain a fear so vague that she could not put it into words? If all that she suspected were true, who could be endangered but Brennett and his accomplice? It was only necessary to be cautious so that no money might be lost by their finesse.

She recovered her composure more easily from a certain self-gratulation which she began to experience just now. How fortunate it was, she thought, that she had not written again to Temple Meredith and possibly influenced him to unwise and premature action. Perhaps he, too, had detected something abnormal in the circumstances surrounding these two men, and intended to speak only when he had merged his suspicions in certainty. She resolved that she would not write again — she would not hamper him with an insistent letter at a juncture like this. As the facts gradually developed they seemed more and more to justify caution, and certainly this demonstration ought to convince her that it was not she who had suffered by the delay. She would wait patiently, and Maurice Brennett might wait also.

They presently overtook Mrs. Kirby, and when Antoinette made known her wants the old lady offered the vinaigrette with disconnected exclamations of sympathy. She seemed to specially deprecate this seizure. "Try to shake it off, my dear," she said, in an earnest aside. "You won't be able to talk to Mr. Brennett. I was *so* glad he came — yes. Horace Percy says he is such an agreeable, intellectual man — and you are so fond of books! And we have so little company in the country for you."

Mrs. Kirby was of opinion that men are born into this world for the single purpose of falling willing victims to the fascinations of young ladies. It really was a pity that Antoinette's headache should interfere with her opportunity of enslaving so agreeable and intellectual a victim, especially as dear Antoinette — such a sweet girl, too — was not usually interesting to gentlemen. Captain

Estwicke had evidently not been particularly attracted, and Mr. Travis had come no more. But already Mr. Brennett seemed greatly impressed. In the boat she had noticed how deeply he was absorbed in the conversation.

"Oh, it's a fearful bore to talk to him," cried Antoinette fervently.

Mrs. Kirby looked at her in disappointment and grave reprobation. Here was all the material for a charming romance, except the good-will of the lady.

Still, when Brennett joined them, Mrs. Kirby hopefully welcomed him; more than once afterward she observed that, as he half-reclined on the grass near them, lazily supporting himself on one elbow, he cast a swift glance of covert attention upon the young girl. It augured a deepening interest, and was an infinite accession to the sentimental old lady's satisfaction. How should she divine that he was only saying to himself, again and again — "Reticent and cautious — extremely timid and proud — and what can I make of this?"

He sought to renew his conversation with her, and Mrs. Kirby would have been very glad to give him a clear field. But Antoinette was so monosyllabic and absent-minded that, ascribing her lassitude to her headache, the old lady tried to make amends. The talk fell naturally upon mutual acquaintances in Graftenburg. Gradually she became animated and retrospective. She gave him, with great particularity, the "maiden names" of the mothers and grandmothers of his friends, and various collateral relationships fell tributary into the sweeping current of reminiscence; dates ran riot upon it, and the sails of many a memory-treasured romance spread themselves to the breeze. The graces of Maurice Brennett's intellect were chiefly displayed in the brilliancy with which he listened.

Although he bore himself thus creditably, the little matters which so engrossed Mrs. Kirby fatigued him beyond measure. Sometimes the whinnying laughter of the coltish Vayne boys broke sharply on the air, and as his eyes mechanically followed the sound, he found a momentary diversion in the spectacle presented by them and their juvenile friends — all grouped suggestively close to the hamper — the smallest, Edgar, treated now like a hero among them, and now sadly badgered, according to the ups and downs of a bigger world. It was even a relief — absurd as that might seem — to catch a few words of old Mr. Ridgeway's eager apoplectic discourse, on a wide range of subjects intermediary between the plan of atonement and the policy of the nation, with which Estwicke, hard by, was regaled along with the sandwiches.

For Estwicke no longer remained beside Marcia, and thus assisted at the conversational triumphs of his rival — it was Percy's habit to talk much, and much about himself, recounting glib little stories in which, without coarsely bragging, he dexterously contrived to appear always as an enviable figure. She maintained a responsive animation, and when Estwicke had strolled away to the other group her laugh still reached him. It was a very charming laugh. He did not doubt its mirthfulness. The picture was suggestive as Percy sat beside her on the bole of a great tree, fallen in a late wind-storm, the leaves still green on the boughs that clustered about them. This day was as an idyl to them, Estwicke said to himself — and as for him and his heavy heart, and his misplaced love, and his cold torpor of despair, these were merely the requisite contrasting elements in the perfect poem.

And now the sun was sinking, and the pleasure party was afloat again and speeding down the river, — past the

Coteatoy Bluffs; past the National Cemetery, with its vast array of mounds marshalled about the flagstaff, with its monument in the midst, and at intervals field-pieces and piles of balls. And now past another cemetery, its ghastlier simulacrum — where no monument rises, no flag waves, — with only the splendors of the evening sky above it, and the glancing wings of the homeward bound birds. Here are the piers of the old bridge; and here is the green enamelled stretch of the battle-field. The scent of clover is on the air; the cry of quail rises from the grass.

The sky is crimson and the water is crimson, and they land in the midst of the red sunset.

CHAPTER XIII.

THERE was a golden moon in the purple dusk, and the world was sweet one night. Delicate odors drifted along the imperceptible current of the air from the lilies that grew in the fissures of the bomb-riven stones which had once upheld the sunken terraces. A mocking-bird, perched somewhere on the shattered cupola, was singing as if he were a conscientious contractor, pledged to supply the earth with music. The creamy, gold-centreed roses that clambered up the pillars of the portico caught the dew and glistened. One could look out at the cruel old battle-field only through their charmed vistas. There was no wind, and the shadows that thronged the haunted thickets, and lined the redoubts, and lurked in the rifle-pits, were motionless.

When Brennett and Percy reached the house this evening, a week, perhaps, after the fishing party, they found the family seated upon the long, broad portico for the enjoyment of the fresh air. It was not Brennett's first visit. Since the day of the excursion he had been here once by invitation, and had called once. Except for the most unmeaning conventionalities, he had not spoken to Antoinette, and she was genuinely astonished that he had made no overture to recur to the subject of conversation which he had seemed persistently anxious to pursue on the occasion of their first meeting. This evening, immediately after the greetings, he took a chair near her and a little apart from the others. It might have been accident; she thought it design.

And yet, when he turned and spoke to her, nothing could be more commonplace than his words and manner; more in accord with this world's ways; more antagonistic to the suspicion of plots and such fantastic vagaries with which she had lately been prone to invest all prosaic events.

"There is the recompense for the loss of the trees; you can't get an adequate idea of the moonlight anywhere else," he said, looking out at it, as it lay in a splendid vastness upon the vast plain. "In towns you have it cut into parallelograms and triangles. You may demonstrate a theorem at every street corner. In the woods, the shadows are paramount. At sea, the water asserts itself; it has its reflections, and its motion, and its suggestions of glancing color. Here, the still earth takes the moonlight like a benediction. And you can be still, too, and perhaps blessed. How is that, Miss St. Pierre? Do you feel its influence? Does the world fall away? Are you ready to renounce the artificialities?"

A fit rejoinder did not present itself. Her belief that Brennett was involved in some plot against her interests, and her eager scrutiny to detect a purpose in all he said, preoccupied her faculties, and she was conscious of seeming flatly unresponsive, as she replied, with a little laugh, "No–o, I hardly think I am ready to renounce the artificialities."

"That is an essentially feminine conclusion," he returned lightly. "Women are all for — not the artificialities, no, I will say, for — progress. They have no sympathy with that yearning for the more primitive modes of life, which sends a man to the woods, to 'rough it' with his dog and gun. When a woman sighs for nature, the beautiful and true, she wants it *en fête champêtre*. She predicates upon nature a parasol. And there must be cavaliers and claret cup."

Evidently the man had no purpose in his speech. Her interest in the subject suddenly became more genuine.

"But for our influence, then," she said, "our civilizing influence, man might still be in the wilderness. Is that your theory?"

"Perhaps."

"It is well that somebody is progressive."

"But am I right? Are women progressive? Are *you* progressive?"

"Oh, yes; very."

"So I should judge. And that is why it seems to me strange that you have not replied to the letter written by Mr. Fortescue's lawyers."

He was looking hard at her. His eyes gleamed, two brilliant points of light, in the dusky shade of the vines which hung above him. At a little distance were the other members of the party in the full moonlight, their black shadows impishly foreshortened, but sharply defined upon the great blocks of limestone that floored the portico. With their every gesture these silhouettes moved in a silently exaggerated excitement, and there were many gestures, for the group was merry and animated. Edgar was standing between his sister and aunt, and Percy was drawing from him a naïvely enthusiastic account of the wonders he had seen at the circus yesterday. The little boy's shrill treble rang loud above the other laughing voices, and all together overpowered the low tones of the two who sat apart. Antoinette glanced absently at this vivacious quartette, then at the silent, bobbing, elfish caricature behind it, convulsed with noiseless merriment, and once more at Brennett. He was still gazing at her. She caught her breath with a quick start, and the blood rushed to her face. For there was a sarcastic expression in his eyes, a peculiar intonation in his voice, as he laughed a little, significantly. What was the import of the tone and look she could not divine; she did not pause to analyze them, nor to consider her reply. She was angered suddenly and beyond endurance, and she spoke upon the impulse of the moment.

"And it seems to me *not* a little strange, Mr. Brennett, that you should, uninvited, persistently question me about my own affairs. If ever I should want your advice, I shall venture to ask for it. Until then may I beg that you do not interfere in matters with which you have no concern."

There was a flash of astonishment in his eyes, and a grave constraint in the change of his face. She knew, the moment after she had spoken, that she had been guilty, not only of bad manners, but of great folly, in permitting herself to fly into a passion without a sufficient provocation. What so intangible as a tone, what ground of offence so untenable! And had the man no "concern" in the matter? And yet, for all her confusion and regret, she felt that his surprise was cleverly simulated, and that he had wished to produce the result he had so effectually done, — to make her angry, provoke her to an outbreak, and put her in the wrong.

"I cannot sufficiently reprobate my rudeness," he said. "Let me assure you it was unintentional. It did not occur to me that the mention of the subject was amiss. I did not suppose that you would consider me an officious intermeddler, as I have a pecuniary interest involved, being Mr. Fortescue's creditor. I took the liberty, you may remember, of writing to you to that effect some time ago. I thought I might perhaps talk the matter over with you and learn your intention in regard to the proposed adjustment. Naturally, I am anxious that it should be speedily effected, so that I can collect a very bad debt. I don't say all this to justify myself — only in some small degree as an excuse. I can find no words to ask your pardon."

He was leaning forward with an extreme earnestness of manner. One hand lay on the balustrade; the other, holding his hat, was upon his knee. His eager, deprecatory face was plainly shown in the moonlight. She dropped her eyes, a deep flush burned on her cheeks; the shadow of a belated humming-bird, still fluttering high among the roses, wavered now across her fair hair and now across the long black folds of her dress.

She was fully aware that this was a solemn sham, but with a curious doubleness she saw the hardship of the position in which he had adroitly placed himself as if it were real. With her stern ideas of right she could not let matters thus remain. For what proof — what proof had she with which to assail his statement. He must have the benefit of the doubt.

"Mr. Brennett," she began, "I can't accept your apology — for I must offer mine. I was not warranted in what I said — I "—

"Oh, I beg of you " — he interrupted, with a gesture of insistence.

"If you please, I should like to ask you a question about this claim of Mr. Fortescue's," she resumed, thinking this less awkward than a forced transition to other topics, and besides shrewdly wishing to secure some advantage since the subject had been broached.

"If I can give you any information I shall be very happy."

"I should like to know why Mr. Fortescue failed to

press his claim against my half-sister, Mrs. Perrier. He has permitted it to lie idle a long time."

She paused for an instant, endeavoring to find fit and intelligible expressions for her ideas. Then, with a recollection of one of Temple Meredith's phrasings, she went on.

"The length of time that has elapsed since the determination of the estate *per autre vie* is more than sufficient to bar his claim. I can't understand upon what pretext he intends to attack the property now."

"It is easily enough explained," said Brennett. "He was abroad at the time of the determination of the estate *per autre vie*. He was not aware of it himself until just before his return last March. The fact of this absence makes it possible for him to recover now, for, as you may perhaps know, the statute expressly excepts persons who are 'without the limits of the United States.' So, you see, he has three years from last March to institute proceedings for the recovery of the property. The law allows three years next after the removal of the disability."

Antoinette was silent, and for a moment he was silent too. She was canvassing what he had said — reasonable, credible enough, but for one discrepancy — a fatal discrepancy. For how could it be, if Fortescue remained abroad since '57, that that locket, a woman's gift, with his name and hers engraved in it, was lost on the battlefield; that it was found in an empty grave from which a soldier, killed in the great struggle, had been afterward removed. This was some strange imposture. She was sure of it.

His voice recalled her attention. He had returned to the subject of the statute of limitations. At first it seemed to her that he was disposed to talk discursively. "In Tennessee," he said, "for rather more than five years and a half — during the war and some time afterward — the operation of the statute of limitations was intermitted. Well, pending this intermission, when, by reason of the suspension of the courts, he could by no possibility have instituted suit, Mr. Fortescue returned to this country, entered the army, was badly wounded at this battle out here, and "—

She started so violently that he suddenly stopped speaking and looked at her in surprise. He gave her no time to recover. He asked a curt question which necessitated an instant reply. "Did you never hear that he was wounded at this battle?"

"Yes — no" — she faltered. "I know little about him," she went on, striving to muster her composure. "He is a very distant relative. I have never seen him, and have rarely heard him mentioned."

"You seemed surprised. What did I say to surprise you?" asked Brennett quickly.

She answered precipitately, still startled and confused.

"I was surprised that you should say he was wounded here — so near to us now. I was — I was — a little nervous," she concluded, inconsequently.

Brennett laughed carelessly, as if the matter involved only a young lady's morbidly delicate sensibilities.

"You must be very nervous, indeed, to shudder at the idea that a man was wounded near this place so many years ago. Reassure yourself, Miss St. Pierre, by remembering how many were killed."

Still his eyes were intent upon the shifting expressions on her face. There was no imposture, she was thinking now. The finding of that trinket was accounted for so readily — so naturally. Her secret was rendered of no avail when this man knew and mentioned the fact that Fortescue had borne a part in the great conflict. What was more probable than that he had lost the locket when he was wounded? She had always fancied that the bit of watch-chain by which it was suspended had been cut smoothly off by a bullet, but the wound was not of necessity mortal. Now she realized how simple and likely a thing it was that the locket had fallen unnoticed, and that afterward, as the earth was shovelled away, it slipped into a soldier's grave, where, among the clods and withered leaves, it had since lain undisturbed. She said to herself that she must discard the idea that Brennett had deftly constructed an ingenious plot, and that this locket was the clue to its weak point. She had a sense of loss, for she had relied upon it as a masked battery, certain in some way to demolish the imposture she had so strongly suspected.

As her wandering glance came back from the west, where Fort Despair and the haunted thickets rose starkly up, silent and lonely in the white moonlight, she became conscious that he was still watching her, and she detected in his face a certain speculation. She wondered at his surprise as he had wondered at hers.

"Why does he find it so strange?" she thought.

"There are depths here still unsounded," Brennett argued within himself. "The lead-line has not reached the bottom."

"As I was saying," he continued, "Fortescue was wounded and captured. He remained in prison until the surrender, when he went immediately to France, and did not come back to this country until March, 1871. Under ordinary circumstances, even a temporary return would operate as a removal of the disability, but the suspension was prescribed in view of an abnormal state of affairs, and he has three years from the time he landed last March in which to bring suit."

Fortescue certainly seemed to command the situation. Her recollections of Meredith's exposition in regard to the state of the title only confirmed her in this conclusion. It was with some vague idea of appearing undismayed by these formidable representations that she said, —

"But suppose the court should decide that the return during the suspension did operate as a removal of the disability?"

"Such a decision would be contrary both to the spirit and letter of the enactment. How could the man bring an action at law when no courts were held, and the whole country was filled with contending armies? Such a decision would be very unjust, and law, you know, is not only 'the perfection of reason,' but justice besides. Then there is precedent in his favor. His counsel think his case very strong. You see, I have posted myself, having an interest involved, and hearing from him that a proposal to adjust the matter amicably was under consideration. His lawyers were averse to making the proposition. They endeavored to dissuade him. No one else with such a case would think of a compromise. But you know with a man like Fortescue argument is futile and common sense thrown away."

"I don't know, for I don't know Mr. Fortescue at all."

"I remember now that you told me that before. *I* know him, though. But *I* made no effort to dissuade him. If I could I wouldn't."

He laughed after a moment's reflection; then turned his head and glanced about him.

"It is a lapse, certainly, from the eternal fitness of things, that in the presence of this moonlight and these roses a man should find nothing better to talk to you about than his paltry three thousand dollars, and your property, and Mr. Fortescue's claim."

Perhaps she had no realizing sense of this incongruity. She pursued the subject with grave intentness.

"Why wouldn't you advise him against a settlement if you and his lawyers think it impolitic."

"Because I am not a disinterested man, Miss St. Pierre. He owes me money. I shall get it sooner if you and he can come to terms, than at the end of a lawsuit."

She said nothing, and after a little he resumed, —

"Honestly, it is the best solution for all concerned. He prefers ready money now to the property after long litigation. I want his debt paid. And you have a large estate in jeopardy — as good as lost if you go into court. And then you have, besides the financial interests, a matter of feeling involved."

"A matter of feeling!" she exclaimed.

He turned his eyes upon her with a vague doubt in his face.

"Well," he said, "one person cannot judge for another, but it seems to me it would be more — more — politic, it would be wiser — to give Fortescue what he will take and get him out of the country, for the sake of the past — you know — of your family. There's no way of — of — muzzling *him*, you know."

"What — what — do you mean?" she asked, her heart beating fast, her color fluctuating.

"I hope — I hope — I haven't offended you," he said with great eagerness. "The allusion escaped me in viewing the question from all its standpoints."

"What do you mean?" she asked again.

"I only meant a caution. Fortescue is a drunkard. He has no remorse, nor pity, nor shame. And drunken men tell secrets. They got him out of the country once to hush him up. And this affair has brought him back.

He ought to be induced to go again, and to go forever. But now there is no one who cares — except you."

"I! why should I care?"

He looked at her with an expression of sudden comprehension.

"Why," he exclaimed, "you don't know?"

"No," she faltered, shaken with a wild terror.

"Well, then, let it go! I thought you surely knew. But it is better as it is, perhaps."

She was trembling in every fibre, her lips were parted, and her breath came fast. There was a cruel dismay and horror in her blanching face.

"Take care," he said hastily. "Those people will observe your agitation. You don't want everybody speculating, you know. Suppose we walk to the end of the portico for a moment. It will give you an opportunity to recover your self-control."

She rose in silence. As he removed to one side the chair which stood in her way, he turned his head toward the others of the party. "We are going to get some of the Cloth-of-gold roses, Mrs. Kirby," he said. Then the two walked together down to the end of the portico. The sentimental old lady looked rather wistfully at Antoinette standing silent and motionless in the moonlight, her black skirt trailing in sombre contrast upon the white floor, and observed Mr. Brennett's deferential care in trimming the thorns from the stems of the flowers before handing them to her. The tableau addressed itself strongly to Mrs. Kirby's imagination, and the hypothetical romance she sought to foster had her best wishes.

"It is singularly unfortunate," Brennett was saying in low tones, "that I should have chanced to broach that subject, so calculated to disturb your peace of mind. But let it be as it was before I spoke. Remain in ignorance.

You will be happier." He still had the flowers and his penknife in his hand. He raised his head slightly, and she caught his swift glance. Somehow she fancied he looked to see how she was taking it.

"You are very right," she said, still in a tremor. "I have no desire to know. Pray don't mention it again."

His face was half averted, but she detected in it a suggestion of disappointment. And as she turned her fast-filling eyes to the moonlit vastness of the battle-field, all blurred and swaying before her, she began to understand the situation.

This was what the newspapers called "black-mail."

She had read of such dastardly things, but they had hardly seemed possible. This man and his coadjutor, Fortescue, had concocted together some frightful lie that would force money from her. She had given up at last the theory of an imposture. She now believed their purpose grew out of the fact that Fortescue's case was in some way fatally defective and could not stand in court. Should she defy them, they might find an appropriate sequel to their scheme in breaking rock in the State Prison. For she remembered having heard once an incident bearing upon a certain fierce Tennessee statute, by which an effort to extort money by threatening to impute to another an offence or crime is made a felony, and is punished by five years' imprisonment in the penitentiary. This man was playing a desperate game,— more desperate, perhaps, than he knew. For one moment she felt that she could not forego this revenge. To compass it she could pursue them to the ends of the earth. Then her characteristic caution returned, with its complex elements of pusillanimity and a just regard of consequences. This lie involved some one near and dear to her,— her father, her mother, or how could it be efficacious with her? And how could she combat it? They had died in her early infancy. She had never known them. But Fortescue had known them. Would his word be more credible as to them in public estimation, or hers? That anything disgraceful to them was true, she did not believe for an instant. But if a specious lie were promulgated and not disproved, it would be true to the world. A heavy sense of responsibility had descended upon her. It was not for herself alone that she must act; it was for those who were dead, and who could not speak.

If only she had some advice! She began to cast about in her mind as to whom she might apply. There was only General Vayne. On his good faith and his friendship she knew she could rely. But he was a man without policy or prudence; his life throughout had given evidence of this fact, and the mere recollection of that fantastically rash episode at the court-house so short a time ago was enough to deter her. The story would be elicited, and if General Vayne should look upon it only as an iniquitous attempt to extort money from her,— a helpless woman, and his daughter's guest,— proved or unproved, Maurice Brennett would never get out of the town alive. Then there would be a great commotion, and the wicked fabrication would come out.

She determined that never, if it could be prevented, should that lie be divulged. Never should it be put into words. Money was no object, and it could not be again, except as it might be used to keep down that black calumny which could not be refuted now. She would compromise,— she would give up anything, everything, when Temple Meredith should come to carry out her wishes. He had said that he would be here on the 28th of June, and it was not so far away. She was aware that her position, weak as it was, had its strong point. That cruel lie would not be made public so long as they hoped to effect a compromise through its agency, held *in terrorem* over her. Thus she could safely postpone taking action.

Brennett's finesse was a weapon of which every edge cut, but he could form no idea of the depth of the wounds left by its keen strokes this time. She had been startled, agitated at first. That was only natural, and of no special import. Now she had recovered her composure; and her calmly inexpressive face, as they walked down the portico to rejoin the others, gave him no indication of the effect of what he had said, and no augury as to how it would influence the future. He could not pursue the subject. Her reply had effectually closed it. He could only wait, and wait in doubt.

After the visitors were gone, the home-circle sat some time longer in the moonlight. Mrs. Kirby noticed that Antoinette was silent and abstracted, and when they had at last risen to go within, she still listlessly lingered outside. The old lady, chancing to turn at the door, saw her at a moment when she thought herself unobserved; it was with a gesture of disdainful rejection that she was throwing her flowers away, the fresh and beautiful roses which Maurice Brennett had cut for her.

They fell upon the bomb-riven pavement, and there the next day, when the sun was hot, they withered.

CHAPTER XIV.

AND the next day before the sun was hot, his schemes too showed signs of wilting.

This was a wonderful day; the sky had withdrawn itself to an infinite altitude; a few fleecy white clouds raced with their shadows across the wide expanse of the battle-field; the green wheat shoaled and surged ceaselessly with elusive silvery undulations. On the great earthworks the plums hung ripe and red, amid a tangled profusion of blackberries and a mass of flowering vines. With their redundant, leafy growth of young trees, the redoubts loomed up in abnormal proportions. It was not easy for Maurice Brennett to distinguish, even with his field-glass, the height of the parapet in the midst of the heavy foliage. But until he reached the river he was glancing about listlessly enough, for it was only an evanescent curiosity which he had chanced to express concerning the country and its history, and which had induced Percy to offer to drive with him over the battle-field, and show all its points of interest.

The river was haunted by the odor of ferns; its rhythmic murmured monody was altogether overborne by the voices of Percy and a young acquaintance whom he had encountered on the ferry-boat, and who stood, while *in transitu*, with one boot upon the hub of the buggy-wheel and persistently talked "horse." The conversation grated on Brennett's preoccupied mood, and, feigning an accession of interest in the scene before him, he alighted from the vehicle, that he might bring his glass to bear upon the massive isolated columns of masonry — the piers of the old turnpike bridge — which rose suggestive and drear in the midst of the shining current.

Toole noticed the gesture.

"The bredge got burned up in the war, Squair," he observed companionably, nodding his great unkempt, tawny head, on the back of which an old straw hat was precariously perched.

Brennett lowered the glass and looked coldly at the officious speaker. Then he turned his shoulder with a studied air of inattention, and once more lifted the glass to his eyes.

His manner might have repressed another man in a similarly low station, but Toole, in his good nature, was rather obtuse, and continued with easy *camaraderie*, for he held himself the equal in all essentials of the "Squair," or any other man.

"I tell ye it sots a-body sorter catawampus plumb till now ter git ter studyin' 'bout'n that thar job. 'T war the reskiest thing I ever seen done; it beat my time! An off'cer fired that thar bredge with his own hands, an' that kem about powerful cur'ous, 'kase the off'cers ginerally gits the glory whilst the men gits the resk. But I never look at them old piers 'thout thinkin' 'bout that feller. He was ez plucky ez the nex' one, an' the finest-built man ye ever seen. He looked sorter stavin' somehows, an' wild, an' fiery, an' he hed sech eyes in his head that when he fixed 'em on a-body, ye jes' knowed ye was bound ter mosey, ef he hed tole ye ter mosey. I hed seen him wunst afore, a-ridin' along o' Gen'al Crespeau in one o' his raids up this ruver; he was on the Gen'al's staff."

A strange thing had happened. The glass in Brennett's hand was trembling; his color had changed; he had slowly reversed his position and was gazing intently at Toole.

"The looks o' that thar man is fairly welded in my mind. I s'pose it's account o' what he done hyar. We hed been a-scrimmagin' some up thar on Beargrass Creek, an' hed been cut up cornsider'ble, an' treated ginerally with perslimness, 'kase thar war n't none sca'cely of us. An' jes' ez it was cleverly dark, we kem a-dustin', hickelty pickelty, acrost this hyar old bredge, — on the run, I tell ye! They hed some fraish cavalry in pursuit, what hed n't been in the fight, an' ef they could hev made out ter foller us acrost the ruver jes' then, they 'd a-scooped the whole bilin' of us. We hed the pruttiest sorter chance o' bein' cut off from the main body, 'kase our horses was too dead beat ter travel another foot, an' our ammunition hed in an' about gin out. That thar old bredge hed been sorter perpared aforehand ter burn in case of a retreat. The boys hed piled bresh up under the floorin' an' along the sides, an' hed poured out some ile thar, but we never thunk ez how the Yanks war a-goin' ter be so close a-hint us, an' our time so short. Waal, when the order was gin ter fire it, some durned artillery o' theirn that hed got in battery up thar on Boker's Knob, they seen the move, an' they begun ter fling shell an' shot a good piece this side o' the ruver ter hender us from gittin' at the bredge. An' they hed some sharp-shooters thar that kem inter the game, an' they made it look like hell broke loose round thar fur about two minits. We never hed no fire balls nor nothink' ter throw ez was sartain ter sot the bredge a-burnin'. The men ordered thar jes' hed ter trot down under them yellin' shells an' singin' minies, an' kindle up the bresh with a torch, same ez ef it was a wood fire in a chimbly. Waal, they never got thar; some was killed, an' some was wounded, an' some jes' turned around an' dusted! An' hyar come that cavalry on the other side, — ye could 'a heard them fraish horses o' theirn a-lopin', ef ye hed been ever so fur off, it 'peared like. In two minits more we 'd 'a hed 'em 'mongst us, an' our horses was too dead beat ter travel another foot. Thar war n't no time for orders nor nothink else. The fust I knowed this hyar man — a mighty suddint man he was — he jes' sprung out 'n the dark somewhar like ez ef he 'd been flung from a cannon's mouth. He rode! rode like a streak o' light! He went a-spurrin' down ter the bredge with a torch in his hand flamin' out like a big, red feather. An' when he shot by me his eyes was blazin' in his head, an' his teeth was set close — Lord! how he looked! An' did n't them sharp-shooters pay him most pertic'lar attention when he hed got a-nigh that bredge. That torch made him a fair target fur 'em. His horse was shot under him jes' about thar," he paused, and pointed with his pipe-stem. "When I seen that light sink I thought we was goners. But it did n't set him back none. He was up agin in a minit — an' walk! you never seen a man walk like that. Light on his feet! for all he was so tall an' heavy. He walked, sir, same as a kildee! He hed the furder e-end o' that bredge a-roarin' in a second. He fired it in fifty places. He stood so long on that middle pier, I thought he 'd be burned alive. All the men was shoutin' ter him ter come back. He got off 'thout a hair of his head bein' teched, I hearn. 'T was a meracle — a plumb meracle. Everybody that seen it said so. Why the nex' day I swum the ruver ter swap a few lies with them Yankee pickets that we hed struck up an acquaintance with acrost the water, an' ter beg a chaw o' terbacco, an' smoke a pipe or two, sorter sociable like, an' they was jes' a-talkin' 'bout that thar man an' how he acted. They said they 'd like ter git a-holt o' him fur a minit or two jes' ter see what he was made out 'n. I tole 'em ez how thar sharp-shooters hed better load up with silver 'stead o' lead nex' time they got a show at that thar kildee o' ourn. His life 'peared ter be witched. But law! 't war n't more 'n a week arterward when I seen him on the groun' thar a-nigh Fort Despair, stone dead; he was killed in the big battle, shot through the lungs and the head, and half crushed by the carcass o' his horse. I could n't holp bein' sorry ez the war hed n't kerried off somebody ez was less account, an' lef' Major Fortescue. That was his name — John Fortescue."

He turned his slow eyes on his interlocutor, and laughed a little at his own foolish sentimentality about a man he had never known.

Brennett precipitately raised the glass to his face; perhaps its expression was not to be trusted even to the slow perceptions of this unspeculative bumpkin. His hand grew rigid with the effort of his will to still its muscles. But his breath was short; his lip was quivering and white.

He might not have attained even this degree of self-control had not the vivacious talk and laughter of the young men in the buggy convinced him that Percy had heard nothing. But any day, on their way to or from Chattalla, the ferry-man might rehearse the story. He might even tell it to Miss St. Pierre. He was familiar and garrulous, and his avocation kept him upon the highway; otherwise it would hardly be possible that he could have ready speech of people in their social station.

It was only an accident — no design — that Brennett turned the powerful glass upon that great flower-decked redoubt, called Fort Despair in the years gone by. He had no sense of what he saw. All his faculties were bent inward. He was striving to rally his courage, his tact, his invention, but he could only remember helplessly how near success had seemed, how deeply for its sake he had involved himself; he could only repeat again and again that the man lived on the highway — he lived on the highway, and in his very avocation he had a constant reminder of the burning of the bridge, else there would be no need of a ferry-boat.

Brennett scarcely heard Toole's voice still drawling on :

"An' it's a cur'us thing 'bout 'n that off'cer; what d' ye think happened hyar one night las' winter? Bless God, ef I did n't 'low fur a spell ez I hed seen his ghost! fur a fack, I did! Thar war a gentleman that kem from Gen'al Vayne's house, an' jes' afore he rid down onto the ferry" —

Toole had broken off abruptly, — oddly enough at the moment that the field-glass was directed upon Fort Despair. And as Brennett became suddenly aware of this, he was also conscious that his motions were furtively watched. He lowered the glass and looked curiously at the ferry-man, who drew down his hat and averted his face. His hold had grown light upon the rope. There was a visible tremor along the sturdy muscles of his bare, sun-embrowned arms. The color had deserted his tanned face, leaving it sickly and sallow. He seemed all at once to have grown gaunt.

Question as he might, the wily schemer felt baffled. He had no abstract interest in humanity; his keen and insidious knowledge of human nature and motives had been acquired by strictly utilitarian processes. Had this man not loomed up formidable, with his aimless reminiscence, Brennett would not have given him and his idiosyncrasies so much as a contemptuous curse. But he saw in him now his destruction or his prey.

He had received a subtle intimation that the change in Toole's manner had some connection with the field-glass. And here was a mystery. This was an illiterate country lout, with no knowledge of the science of optics or the properties of concave and convex lenses. Brennett understood at last, and it struck him so suddenly that it took his breath away; Toole had been a soldier, and was aware of the long range of this implement as he was aware of the long range of a rifle. And after so many years, was Fort Despair, with its embrasures empty except for the nestlings, with its crown of flowers, with its summer songs, a terror to him still?

The sense of power restored Brennett. When he lifted the glass and casually surveyed first the piers, then the far-reaching perspective of the river, he even had room for a calculating cruelty of pleasure in Toole's long-drawn sigh of relief. But Toole was forgotten when the glass was again suddenly turned upon the redoubt. Among the scarlet trumpet-blossoms and the wind-tossed fruit-trees on the parapet the shadows were fitful; but one was motionless — the similitude of a man? — nay, the substance. Far, far away the ploughs were running; only a meditative cow stood here and there in the wide strip of uncultivated land that lay, — a series of out-cropping ledges and brambly tangles, — between the rifle-pits of the old picket-line and the banks of the river. He was out of reach of human sight; he had baffled the law and human vengeance; conjecture had forgotten him; and still he was within the compass of human ingenuity. The field-glass was so powerful; the wits behind it were so sharp. And surely it seemed a strange thing that a full-grown man, a man in poor garments, should be basking idly like a lizard on the red clay parapet, while all the crop was "in the grass," and cotton-scraping wages were rising with the thermometer. He was moving at last, — moving slowly. Could it be that the fluttering of a red bandanna handkerchief with which the ferry-man mopped his brow was a signal?

The figure, — a tall, erect figure, — skulked stealthily along the parapet. Once it paused and turned; yes, it was turning its face toward the river. But was the glass so perfect? Brennett asked himself abruptly. It blurred; it mingled. Was there a breath upon it, — the wing of a moth, — fallen pollen from a passing bee? Was some damnable trifle to snatch from him this moment, — this meagre moment that he craved, — of more value than ten years of his life! The next instant his sardonic laughter set the air a-shiver. The fault lay in God's handiwork. The blurrings, the distortions, were in the man's face! Ah! the good glass!

"I have come late to Fort Despair," Brennett said to himself, as he watched the figure drop down gradually out of sight, "but not too late for a heavy onslaught yet."

A tumult of exultation surged within him. The ferry-man, with all his brain a-fire, with his heart bursting, with his liberty, it might be, at stake, could not see what he knew was lurking there, — could not be sure what, with that marvellously extended faculty of vision, the stranger saw.

Brennett was laughing still as he turned to the brawny fellow who, pallid and gasping, feebly tugged at the rope.

"There," he said, pointing with his field-glass to the great, blooming redoubt, "is the reason that in the country a man's greed for gain is blunted."

Toole stared at him in amaze and said nothing.

"Luxury is so easy to come by. A graceless lout like that, lying there in the sun on the parapet of Fort Despair, would n't bestir himself for a million. And I'm not so sure he's wrong. He hears the river sing. The wind keeps him company. Now and then a ripe plum falls in his reach. If a snake comes, he makes great shift to throw a stone, and dozes. The sun mints gold for him all day. Give up this wealth for a ploughman's wages, or the fourth of a scanty crop on somebody's acres exhausted with fifty years of cotton-growing? Not he!"

The boat was moving smoothly once more. The cords on the brawny arms stood out with renewed effort. Toole felt as if he were laying hold again on life. A long, strong breath of relief was swelling his lungs. The hot tears of pity for himself stood in his eyes.

"What a pore fool I be," he thought compassionately. "I seen from the fust ez the man hed a field-glass, an' was a-swingin' it round the country. An' I mus' git so catawampus fur nothink! An' he air a stranger hyar, an' dunno Graffy when he see him. Ef it hed been anybody else, though!" He trembled again at the idea.

"Not he!" pursued Brennett. "He looks at you as you pull this heavy boat back and forth, for money and the hope of ease some day, and I am afraid he laughs. Perhaps he laughs, too, at Mr. Percy, who professes to be a man of leisure, and who works very hard, often against great odds, to amuse himself. He doesn't know me, I dare say; if he did, I am sure he would laugh at me."

"What be your work?" asked Toole inquisitively.

"I might accurately define it as 'tempting Providence,'" said Brennett.

Toole was a trifle dubious.

"I reckon we're all in that trade," he rejoined piously.

Brennett frowned in sudden irritation; he had used the words as preliminary to an exposition of the peculiar and excessive risks and anxieties of speculating in cotton futures. Inadvertently they were too true. "Well, crack that nut," he muttered contemptuously.

They were nearing the land, and his purpose was served. He had succeeded in allaying Toole's fears and absorbing his attention. Percy would never hear that recital of military experience, if Maurice Brennett were the man he took himself for.

He was about to return to the buggy, but checked himself with an after-thought. It went against the grain, but it was best to be civil.

"I'll explain my operations in the line of 'tempting Providence' some day as I cross again," he said agreeably. And, as he stepped into the buggy, Percy gathered up the lines and drove slowly along the steep bank, leaving Toole looking placidly after them, marvelling at his folly in having caused himself so poignant an anguish of fright.

But they did not continue their drive over the battle-field to-day. Brennett remembered abruptly that there were some important papers to be sent him by express, and which were already due. Thus it was that before the elusive, amethystine, matutinal haze had lifted from the landscape, leaving it a trifle crude of color, they were in Chattalla. The dew still gleamed on the leaves of the sycamore in the court-house yard; the blue-jays chattered, and quarrelled, and fairly fought in the court-house windows; the grass was high and rank. An old darkey with a scythe was listlessly mowing it in the intervals of recounting a miraculous story to two small white boys, who hung spell-bound upon his every word. A knot of lawyers sat and talked amicably on the court-house steps, nothing suggesting the prospective conflicts of the day save here and there a roll of legal cap. One of them, a young sprig, was trying to train a dog to smoke a pipe.

Some hill-country fellows lay in the grass, or stood about under the tree, having jogged in before day to attend to business in court. They bantered each other; now and then their jolly laughter rang out. A peaceful scene — almost pastoral.

Brennett and Percy gravitated naturally toward it, for the package of papers had not yet arrived at the express office; the sun was growing hot on the paving-stones of the Square, and the dust was rising. They lounged through the gate, which clanged noisily behind them as they made their way to the steps. Percy was not sorry when Brennett strolled off alone, for he had been silent, or monosyllabic, throughout the drive, and his host craved livelier companionship.

Brennett had no affinity with the lower strata of society — no good-natured leniency for ignorance, uncouthness, and shiftless poverty; that he should seek to join the rough fellows under the tree, as they joked the sheriff who was canvassing among them for re-election, was in itself so uncharacteristic a thing that he felt all the awkwardness incident to being out of one's sphere as he hazarded the remark —

"The warmest day of the season, gentlemen."

"That's so," they assented politely.

His eye was glittering, excited. The delicately arched nostrils of his sharp, hooked nose were quivering; the intricate lines between his eyebrows were so dark that they seemed to have been cleverly traced there with a bit of charcoal; the gracious sunshine that dripped through the leaves fell, as he took off his hat and fanned himself with it, on those gray glimmers which should not have come so early in his close-clipped hair.

"Fine prospect for fruit," he said, addressing himself especially to the sheriff, a tall, well-knit man, wearing a brown linen suit, the trousers thrust into the long legs of a pair of heavy boots, which were ornamented with large spurs.

"Very fine," assented the officer.

"I suppose you ship great quantities from this county?"

"No, scarcely any."

"No — no," drawled a robust young fellow with a florid face, black hair, and wide, black eyes, who was lying luxuriously in the grass; "ship cotton. That's the dinctum. Cotton's money — mebbe more — mebbe less; but cotton's money *every time!*"

"Good local market for fruit, then?" persisted Brennett.

"Why, no," said the sheriff; "because pretty much everybody in town has got a good big garden-spot of his own, and fruit-trees and vines in plenty; we ain't scrimped for room, you see. Fruit's dirt cheap here."

"I supposed that it would command a fine price, as I saw a man gathering even the volunteer fruit growing on one of those old redoubts not far from the river."

"A-law!" mumbled a toothless sexagenarian, "them places air a-roamin' with the haunts. An' wunst thar was wusser sights yit ter be seen thar; they was soakin' with blood. Leastways, Fort Despair was. I never know'd thar was a critter in the county ez would tech fruit that grow'd out 'n that sile."

"Fort Despair — that is the name," said Brennett, laughing a little; "it is near the river — in a line with the ferryman's house."

For some reason which Brennett could not divine, the other men glanced down, a trifle uneasily, at the young fellow in the grass. His face was smitten by some strong emotion; he lay quite still, his wide, black eyes, suddenly full of an untranslated meaning, turned absently up to the sky.

"And," thought Brennett, "to talk of ignorance!" That these men, these louts, should have something in their minds which it might ruin *him* not to know! He experienced an unreasoning anger that their lives should be less transparent than they seemed; that he should grope blindly among them; that, at this crisis, he should be hampered by those complex elements of hidden sensitiveness, and heart-history, and mental drama, which consonantly make up life in worthier spheres. Under the influence of this irritation, he grew all at once bold and fluent. "I dare say," he remarked, with a laugh, "the volunteer fruit is the ferryman's orchard. I noticed him signal with a red handkerchief, as we were crossing the river, to the man gathering plums on the fort." He had replaced his hat; he was filliping the ash from the cigar in his hand; he was turning away. "Very odd — the face of that man on the fort — very odd."

A grip like a vise fell upon his arm. He was suddenly shaken — shocked. He looked down at the sheriff's hand.

"Take it off," he said, between his set teeth, "or, by the Lord, I'll cut it off."

"How was the man's face odd?" gasped the officer, in the breathless interval of roaring to a negro boy to bring his horse.

He had scarcely relaxed his hold, but Brennett accommodated himself to it, remembering the crisis.

"I can't say exactly," he replied, trembling a little; "some curious facial distortion — he mowed like an idiot."

The grip slid from his arm.

"A marked man in a thousand!" exclaimed the officer.

"But you ought to know that stealing a little fruit is only technically a misdemeanor; there would surely be no prosecutor for such a trespass as that," remarked the innocent Mr. Brennett.

"Trespass! This is murder," said the sheriff gravely. He took a warrant from his pocket and handed it to a deputy, who galloped off at a tremendous rate of speed across the stony Square.

Brennett changed color. He had not supposed it so serious as this. Still it did not touch him.

The young man, at whom they had all looked doubtfully upon the mention of the ferryman, still lay on the grass, his head supported on his arms. He had grown pale; the shadows flickered over his face; his eyes were dilated as if they saw more or less than was before them.

"It hev come at last," he cried passionately, "I knew 't would. But it ain't brung no comfort. All the law in the land can't set my brother's plough a-runnin', and let his mother hear him singin' at his work. It can't gin him back a minit ter think on the Lord afore he went so suddint ter jedgment. It can't hender the grass from a-growin' on his grave, an' his folks from furgittin' him. I feel him slippin', slippin' away day arter day; an' afore his fish-traps is rotten, an' his gun bar'l is rusty, he'll be clar gone — the very thought of him — off'n the face o' the yearth! An' somebody else will live up all them years of time the Lord medjured out fur his space in the worl'." He turned his face upon his elbow and said no more.

The men who had crowded up to the scene of excitement shrank away from him after this outburst. But it gave Brennett an instant to recover himself. And he recovered himself with a sharp pang of disappointment. Of what avail was all this to him — *he* had no purpose to serve by the incarceration of the man who mowed like an idiot among the florescent splendors of Fort Despair.

He looked at the prosecutor, prone upon the ground. He looked at the sheriff. The official had arranged with a deputy to open court — he was about to mount. Had he taken no note of that significant statement concerning the ferryman's signalling red handkerchief? There was only a moment for Brennett, or all his finesse might yet be in vain — even now an officer was riding, like the wind, miles away. His haste and anxiety to assure himself that his craft had taken effect, impaired for a moment his judgment.

"I suppose I shall not be wanted here," he said, "unless a warrant is sworn out against Toole as accessory after the fact."

The sheriff cast upon him a swift glance of suspicion and disapproval.

"Toole will be taken," he said tartly, "according to the law which allows a sheriff, knowing a felony has been perpetrated, and having good ground for suspicion, to make an arrest without a warrant. You'll be needed to testify on the committing trial." Then he mounted and rode away.

"Blest," he said, "if that soft-spoken dandy chap ain't trying to learn Joe Bates his business! Mighty keen for Tom not to be left out in the cold, sure. Holds some kind of grudge against the pore fellow, I reckon."

The incidents of the day had jarred terribly upon Percy, making dissonant havoc among the *scherzo* harmonies, of which his life was composed. He had hastily joined Brennett upon observing the excitement in the crowd, and in helpless amaze discovered that his friend was the mainspring of the commotion.

"Damn it, Brennett," he cried fretfully, as the sheriff

rode off, leaving them alone, "your eyes are too sharp. I saw nothing when we were crossing the river. You can't expect me to stay here and hear your testimony. I'll go to the hotel and wait for you there. If you want me you can send for me. I would 'nt see Graffy or Toole either, for a million, though I dare say nothing very horrible will come of it. Rumor goes that the shooting was self-defence. But these things shock me, — they make me ill."

Percy was a punctilious host. This grating, disagreeable accident, as he construed it, had thoroughly disgusted him with his friend; yet he looked deprecatingly at Brennett, while avowing an intention of deserting him, a stranger in the town, and a guest, in the unpleasant episode of testifying in a criminal case. If Brennett had urged an objection he would have repressed his finical delicacy, and sat out the proceedings.

The rejoinder surprised him beyond measure. Brennett seemed to have taken no notice of the breach of hospitality. "Self-defence," he repeated. "Then it may not be impossible to procure bail."

"Drop it, Brennett, drop the unsavory subject. I shall dream of jails, and pining prisoners, and bolts and bars, for a week. Poor Toole — it's hard on an active fellow like that."

"You would not go on his bail-bond?" asked Brennett, with a look singularly like an expression of apprehension.

"Not unless I want to be beat out of several thousand dollars the quickest in this world — those men are in a panic — no obligation would have any weight with them. Can't you drop the subject?" Percy added frowningly. "Are we to stand here and gloat over the details all day."

He looked angrily and doubtfully at his friend. Was Brennett coarse enough to enjoy an excitement like this? Did he relish his *rôle* in the painful and pitiful little drama? Did he have no natural, unreasoning, foolish, humane regret, that he should be the chosen instrument of vengeance, to work justice, perhaps, but woe, and horror, and despair, in those humble lives? His face was thoughtful, his eyes downcast; he seemed revolving some mighty mental puzzle; he hardly noticed Percy, and for the first time it struck the young fellow that he did not altogether understand this man. "I wish you were in New Orleans, where I found you!" Percy thought with inhospitable discontent.

"I am going, Brennett," he added aloud. "You'll know where to send for me if you want me."

"All right," said the other.

As Percy turned hastily away he almost fell over the man lying in the grass.

"Ah, I beg your pardon," he said.

The man lifted the arm he had thrown over his face. Percy recognized the prosecutor and went on with a shudder.

He did not leave the hotel again during the day; he had no idea how it had passed, for, as he and his friend drove out of the town close upon twilight, he asked no question. The first intimation of the result was given him when they reached the river — it lay broad and red beneath the broad red sky; the ferry-boat, a dark blotch upon its brilliance, close in to the bank, pulsed with the crimson current. But the craft was a useless thing to-day, for no one was there. Percy glanced up at the weather-beaten log-cabin, the poor and humble neighbor of the flaunting and splendid redoubt.

"No good in calling," said Brennett, with a short, satiric laugh. "He won't hear you. We shall have to try the ford. It is six miles higher up the river, somebody told me."

"The nearest safe ford is ten miles higher," said Percy, as he turned the horses.

"It won't last long," Brennett remarked cheerfully. "The superintendent has been telegraphed — so I am told — and has replied that another ferryman will be here to-morrow."

Their new route took them in front of the little weather-beaten house. There was a "washing" still hanging, late though it was, on the clothes line; a group of huddled children, with a pale fright on their faces, stood in the door; a baby, in a tattered red dress, sat on the floor and bleated fitfully; a woman, with yellow hair, that hung loose about her shoulders and fluttered in the wind, was walking back and forth, ceaselessly, tearlessly, striking her hands together as she walked, saying no word, making no moan.

Percy hastily averted his eyes. He gave the off-horse a stinging cut with the whip, and the dreary little house and its splendid neighbor were in the fainting, fading distance.

CHAPTER XV.

IT was fine "growing weather" for the cotton, and in these hot days the Midas-touch of the sun had turned the wheat-fields to gold. From their midst the verdure-crowned earthworks rose like some gigantic basso-rilievo in green enamel. A fierce thunder-shower one afternoon had laid the dust and beaten the soft dirt-road, that swept in serpentine curves through the peaceful battle-field, into the ideal road for equestrians. Marcia, with one of her brothers, found a wonderful exhilaration in a smooth, swift dash through the freshness and perfume of the red sunset. They drew rein only when they had reached the boundary of their father's land and were about to turn their horses' heads homeward. She made some haste to do this, for where the plantation road struck into the turnpike she saw Estwicke riding along in the direction of the barracks. He had evidently not intended to call at General Vayne's on the way—but now his hand hesitated on the rein, and she indignantly deprecated that a chance meeting should force him into an attention which he had not contemplated. He had been there only once since the fishing excursion, making a short and formal call. She had not understood his stiff manner, and it induced a responsive constraint.

"Oh, no, Dick," she said urgently to her urchin escort, who at this moment expressed an inopportune desire to ride down to the river to see whether a boy who was fishing on the bank had caught anything, "I can't wait, and you must take me home."

Estwicke had put the whip to his horse and galloped up in time to hear Dick's protest. "Let me take your place," he said agreeably. Then to Marcia — "I suppose you will grant me the right of way through these fields with you."

She assented with an effort at smiling ease. But she was so habitually sincere that the slightest duplicity was deeply marked by contrast on her face and loudly advertised itself a fraud. This evident artificiality furnished Estwicke with a subject of meditation, and for a few moments both were silent as they rode on together, leaving Dick far behind on the bank of the river.

Estwicke was summarily roused from his preoccupation.

"Isn't that a dangerous horse for you to ride?" he asked, with the vicarious fright of a lover, as Hotspur shied suddenly.

Now, if any other lady had been mounted upon this animal, Estwicke would doubtless have considered him sufficiently gentle, for although young and a trifle freakish, he was evidently of a mild and tractable disposition, and well enough trained. Horse and rider each embellished the other. Estwicke had a vivid realization that in her black habit and hat she was handsomer than ever, and he was forced to admit that she rode with consummate grace and skill. Nevertheless he fully expected to see her thrown; his heart was in his mouth; a cold chill shot through every fibre; his hand was ready to catch the rein. He was irritated to observe that she was flattered by what he had said, and he divined that she thought it augured special virtues of horsewomanship to hold in subjection so insurgent and dangerous a spirit.

"Oh, yes," she exclaimed, with her wonted tone and manner, "Hotspur is w-i-i-ld as he can be! You ought just to see him in one of his tantrums! He threw me last week, but it is n't often that he can get me out of the saddle."

Estwicke was aghast at this "often." He could not altogether restrain his feeling.

"It surprises me," he said, with more truth than tact, "that General Vayne should allow his only daughter to risk herself on a vicious brute like that."

She flushed with some anger. She was half disposed to retort that General Vayne was popularly supposed to be able to manage his family affairs without assistance — only by an effort she withheld this thrust.

"His only daughter," she quoted, laughing. "If he had five or six I suppose you would think him justifiable in letting some of them break their necks. It never occurred to me before that the reason papa thinks so much of me is because there are so few of me."

"I wish he would n't let you ride that horse," persisted Estwicke gravely.

"Oh, if you think Hotspur is wild now, I don't know what you would have said about him last summer. He had been out to pasture — he had n't *seen* a saddle for months. Papa would n't let me mount him then. He was so frisky I did n't see how I should ever get him quiet. The men would n't plough with him, for he was so fretful; papa was away most of the time, and therefore could n't ride him. So Mr. Percy took him home and rode him every day for two weeks."

This turn to the conversation touched other feelings. Their sensitiveness was manifested in the rejoinder, "Obliging Mr. Percy!" uttered with unmistakable sarcasm.

Again her flush deepened to an angry glow. "He is always obliging," she said — " and — amiable."

Estwicke was minded to turn his horse and gallop away, leaving Hotspur to kill her if he would. Somehow he could not go; he remained, but he remained to retort.

"No doubt!" he exclaimed bitterly. "And in recognition of his grace of character, I suppose, you named your horse — 'Hotspur.'"

He was a soldier and a brave man. But he was flinching with abject terror the moment after he spoke. She wheeled her horse, and as she faced him suddenly, her beautiful eyes full of surprise, she demanded aggressively—

"Now what was that?"

"Nothing — nothing. Don't ask me to repeat it," Estwicke pleaded.

"I must know," she rejoined. "I think I understood you, but I am not certain. May I ask you to do me the favor of repeating and explaining."

This was said with an elaborate show of politeness, but it savored rather of the punctilio of the duello than of kindly Christian courtesy.

He hesitated and quailed before his formidable adversary. Now that he was called upon to put into words the theory over which he had brooded through the dark hours of sleepless nights, he began to realize how fantastic it was. Somehow he could find no words foolish enough to fit it. But he must answer.

"Miss Vayne," he said helplessly, laying his hand upon Hotspur's forelock, "let me off. Let me off — just this time."

"I want to know what you said," she replied sternly.

Estwicke felt that it was futile to temporize.

"Well," he began in great abasement, "the horse is named Hotspur, you know."

A pause ensued. Her eyes widened. "Yes, I know," she interpolated by way of giving his confession a much needed impetus.

"And Percy's name is Percy," continued Estwicke, painfully aware of seeming to drivel. The astonishment in her face nerved him to try to brace this impalpable fabric of the imagination with an historical back-bone.

"And you know there's that fellow from Northumberland — Percy — don't you know? — Harry Percy — Hotspur."

Her softly scornful laughter cut him as cruelly as a knife might have done. The color in her cheeks mounted to the roots of her hair. "I do homage to your ingenuity," she exclaimed with a sarcasm intended to be withering. "It is equally creditable to your heart and head! I have the pleasure of hoping that your speculations about me, and my horse, and my motives have served to amuse you for an idle half hour or so."

She looked him full in the eyes as she spoke, with her head erect, and a proud resentment eloquently expressed in her face. Then she shook the reins, and her horse sprang away like an unleashed hound.

She evidently wished to be rid of Estwicke. But he could not let her go now. He kept his horse side by side with hers, and as they came with a rush past Fort Despair he laid his hand upon Hotspur's rein, and checked the impetuous gallop. She turned her head with an angry impatience. There were hot tears in her eyes. They should not fall — they would never fall. But there they were — and he had seen them.

"I must speak to you," he said beseechingly. "If you are angry it will break my heart. Tell me you are not. Forgive me if you were."

A moment ago she was vowing that he should never

hear her speak another word. Now she determined to throw off the whole affair lightly; she would not allow him and Percy, and her horse's name as connected with them, to seem matters of such importance. But she could not tell him she was not angry; she would not say she forgave him.

"You certainly stand in wholesome awe of my displeasure," she returned, with a forced laugh. "It is a fearful thing, I know, but it has killed no one as yet."

"It will kill me," Estwicke protested, with inopportune fervor; "for no one loves you — no one can ever love you — as I do."

Her eyes flashed. "Captain Estwicke," she exclaimed hotly, "let my horse go."

"One moment — just hear me for one moment. You will do me a cruel injustice if you refuse to listen now. Since Percy came, even long before he came, that fancy about the horse's name has tortured me night and day. I have loved you all my life, it seems to me, for I never lived until I loved you. I have given you all my heart. It's nothing to give, since you don't care for it; but it's all I have. And I want, in return, one word of forgiveness — one word."

Her face was turned away; he could only see the downward sweep of her eyelashes and the delicate curve of her crimson cheek. He leaned forward wistfully, with his hand still on her horse's rein, and all his fiery heart in his eyes. She slowly turned her head yet further, and still he saw only those gentle suggestions of the beauty of that averted face.

"It is hard on me!" he broke out despairingly, after a moment. "I have so sedulously repressed my feelings. I have stood guard over every word I uttered — so afraid of speaking too soon or at an inopportune moment. I have eaten out my heart by slow degrees; and now — now — I have angered you beyond endurance, and you cannot forgive me."

Still not a word.

"I've got what I deserve, though," he continued bitterly, after another pause, in which there were quick changes of expression on his face. "It is a sort of stern justice that I should find you unrelenting — *you*, on whom I have no claim; for I have been hard, and cruel, and unresponsive when there was the strongest claim upon me."

"I don't believe it," she said suddenly.

"Oh, God bless you for that," he exclaimed, clasping one of the little gauntleted hands.

She had not intended to speak; she had not intended to forgive him at all. She drew her hand from his grasp, but slowly and gently.

"Don't you forgive me now?" he persisted. "You couldn't have said that, if you didn't forgive me."

Her face was still averted. "Well — perhaps."

"Then look at me — just once."

She did not turn her head; she still sat motionless.

"Tell me," he said, retaining his grasp upon her horse's rein, "is there some one whom you like better than me? Does he keep us apart?"

"I don't want to stand here any longer," she exclaimed suddenly, turning her flushed and embarrassed face toward the great, grim house in the midst of the plain, the reflected sunset gorgeously emblazoned on its shattered windows.

He still held the horse. "Is it Percy?" She made a gesture of impatience.

"Then don't you care for me a little — just a little, you know?"

"That's just what I don't know." She laughed, but the next moment she was flushing, and trembling, and ready to cry.

"Then, some day — some day, soon, may I tell you again that I love you, and hear what you have to say to me then?"

"I can't stay here any longer," she declared evasively.

As they rode slowly along, Estwicke looked at her and sighed. "That day," he said, "you know the day I mean, I must tell you something more — the great trouble and haunting sorrow of my life. Something painful and cruel to tell."

"Then don't tell it to me," she replied gently.

"I was in fault throughout," he continued. "I was hard, and cowardly, and ungenerous, and petty-minded. Oh, I don't know anybody who would have done as I did."

She said nothing, but there was a stony incredulity expressed in her face.

"I am afraid to tell you — to jeopardize every hope. Yet I cannot endure that you should think me different from what I am. Sometimes, when fellows are friendly and make much of me, I feel like a fraud. I wonder what they would have done in my place, and I wonder what they would think of me if they knew all. But I don't care for them. With you it's different. I can't deceive you. You ought to know how I might come out if anything should happen to try me hard. I will tell you, and let you judge."

"You need tell me nothing!" she cried impetuously. "I can trust you without it."

"If I only deserved this!" he exclaimed. "But if you can believe in me against my own word, can't you care for me — even a little?"

She rode on silently.

He leaned forward and once more clasped her hand.

"Or rather, dearest, let me take it for granted."

"For the sake of argument," she assented doubtfully.

And the sun went down over Fort Despair, and in all the east there was no moon. The long-waning brightness had fled from the battle-field; it lay now dim, and drear, and colorless, beneath the vast, vague sky. The fort was beleaguered by a multitude of shadows. The wind brought strange voices from out the haunted thickets. A shiver ran through the flowers and grasses that hung above the yawning, empty graves. A bugle's resonance was thrilling along the air. The still evening palpitated with the throb of the drum. The tread of martial feet shook the ground. And all unheeding — here where the battle was fought — youth, and love, and life rode bravely through the spectred twilight.

CHAPTER XVI.

THERE was a flag flying over Chattalla; the "old flag," thus called in contradistinction to another, that had once flashed across the clouds here and was gone like a meteor. The Square was filled with an eager and intent crowd of recently re-enfranchised and intelligent voters; the grass in the court-house yard was trampled by many jostling feet; a rude platform had risen among the dappling shadows, and the figure there, with its imposing dignity and impressive attitude, might realize to the imagination a Roman senator. His fine voice filled the wide spaces of the sunlit air; the glance of his earnest eyes kindled a responsive enthusiasm; a magnetic thrill quivered through his audience. Only Maurice Brennett, of all the fellow-citizens whom General Vayne harangued, was analytic enough to find him a study, and sufficiently discriminating to perceive how very amusing he was. He hurled back, with infinite gusto, insinuations against his party — his people. He visibly joyed in his elocutionary bitterness. He stormily counselled mildness, calmness, conservatism, above all, consistency. His apostrophe to the flag that waved above them was oddly accented by an unconscious convulsive gesture, as if he would clasp his missing right hand. "It was to Us," he said, "the symbol of a hard-won Victory, of a generous Peace, and of Freedom in the largest sense known to the universe." The fervor of his sincerity caught in the crowd, and flamed out in cheers for the old flag for the first time in ten years. Despite the wild incongruities of his patriotism, there was so splendid a display of oratory here and there, that Brennett's cynical face was more than once smitten with sudden gravity. His faculty for the utilitarian fixed upon this gift. "If that man," he said to Percy, "had even a modicum of common sense he could do anything — anything."

But presently his lips were curving again, for General Vayne was vaunting the great Volunteer State, and the language was depleted of adjectives. He alluded to her hosts of "Fighting Tennesseans," and called upon the heights of Monterey, upon Old Hickory's "mile-long line" at New Orleans, upon the "Battle of the Horseshoe," upon their blood that deluged Shiloh, the bare hills engirdling Nashville, the wide wastes around Murfreesboro', to tell of their valor. Then he proceeded to do this himself — in so eloquent, so fiery, so tender a strain that it brought the remnant of his brigade to the front with the old rebel charging yell, which set the great bell in the court-house tower to shivering.

He stated that he was no candidate for any office whatever within the gift of the people, and had no interest save theirs at heart; in short, he represented himself as a sort of self-organized tutelary deity of the party, appearing before them only in support of its principles. "You all know *me*," he said, with some pardonable pride, as they manifested their appreciation of the purity of his motives. "I stand upon my native heath, and" — effective diminuendo — "my name is Macgregor!"

In the thunder of applause that followed his peroration, a grizzled, elderly wight turned, with grave, breathless interest, to Percy.

"What makes the old Gen'al say he stands on his

naked heels an' his name's Grigory?" he asked swiftly. "I didn't know old Frank Vayne's middle name was Grigory."

Could there be a more felicitous anti-climax! Brennett fell back against the iron fence, laughing with sardonic delight. He had intended to humor the little-great man's self-valuation by pressing up with the town and country magnates, to join in shaking severely the orator's hand, with congratulations on the "powerful effort," as the phrase went. But he saw, with surprise, that General Vayne was pushing through the crowd toward him, waving off the effusive demonstrations of his friends with a calm self-sufficiency that was curiously independent of vanity. His face was flushed; there was an anxious gleam in his eyes; he fixed them eagerly on Mr. Ridgeway, who chanced to be standing close by, and although he shook hands with Brennett it was evidently the elder gentleman with whom he wished to confer — about no private matter, apparently, for he began without preamble, —

"A great surprise, sir. Lamentable — lamentable! I had heard nothing of it until his messenger met me at the depot. I had promised to speak at once, so I sent you a line from there. We can arrange it now?" He stroked his gray mustache, and looked alertly expectant.

Mr. Ridgeway took a firm stand, metaphorically and literally. He steadied his unwieldy bulk on his two ponderous legs, turned his argumentative spectacles on his friend, and spluttered emphatically, —

"You are not able to lose that money, General, and I'm sure I'm not."

"Lose money, sir?"

"He'd *bolt*, sir; if that man, Toole, were bailed, he'd bolt."

Maurice Brennett's face was suddenly petrified — its

cynical laugh upon it. But, with those distended muscles hardened and rigid, his bright eyes narrowed, his teeth gleaming through his parted lips, there was marvellously little joviality suggested. The two important old cocks were hardly as provocative of mirth as he had thought them an instant ago. He retained barely power enough to look, breathlessly, from one to the other.

"Permit me, sir," said General Vayne loftily, "to differ with you. I will not entertain the suspicion. That man served four years in my brigade." He looked triumphantly at his interlocutor. The logical inference was too plain. The man could n't bolt.

Mr. Ridgeway nodded his big head and his big Panama hat very much to one side. "I know all that, and I should be his friend now if he had behaved better in this affair."

"Patent your art, my dear sir, 'friendship made easy,'" cried General Vayne satirically. "Drop your friends when they don't 'behave better!'"

"General," said Mr. Ridgeway, with excellent temper, "I don't want you to throw your money like soapsuds into a sinkhole; and I don't want to throw mine there either."

"No man — be he gentle or simple — shall ever seek help from me and I withhold this hand," cried General Vayne impetuously. He raised his only hand and struck it violently against the iron fence. "Do you know, sir," he continued solemnly, "that man's wife lies at the point of death, prostrated by the shock of his arrest and smitten with paralysis. There has not been a dollar in that house for weeks — and no flour, no meal, no meat; those children — Lord knows how many — have subsisted by *begging!* Begging from the neighbors! The turnpike company is only awaiting the moment of her dissolution to turn that family out upon the road. The man's occupation is gone, and he has all those starving children to provide for."

"A good reason for bolting, if there were no other." Maurice Brennett had suddenly found his voice, for Mr. Ridgeway's face was a study of agonized indecision. Perhaps all might yet remain as it was.

General Vayne turned slowly, with a haughty stare in his intent eyes, as he fiercely twirled his mustache.

"Under your favor, sir," he said, loftily, "a good reason for *not* bolting, if there were no other."

Percy pressed Brennett's shoulder with his own as a warning to forbear, for his friend was naturally associated with himself in General Vayne's mind, and he took politic care that all such association should be pleasant.

"I beg your pardon," said Brennett — he was breathing more freely — "I had only heard that the man is a low fellow and abetted in this transaction. A terrible affair, I'm told; shocked the community."

"It did, — it did," spluttered Mr. Ridgeway. "The law must be upheld, or the country won't be fit to live in."

"I regard the law of the land, gentlemen, as the will of God," said General Vayne sweepingly. "And — it — allows — this — man — the — privilege — of *bail*."

There was no answer to this. Even the wordy and intellectual Maurice Brennett had not a syllable of replication. He looked at General Vayne with a wonderful sharpening of those rapacious suggestions in his eyes. Old Mr. Ridgeway, with an air of absence of mind, brought out his handkerchief and harrowed with it the furrows and creases of his fat face.

"I regret to have troubled you, sir," said General Vayne, turning with elaborate courtesy to Mr. Ridgeway. "I took the liberty of asking your co-operation simply because I knew that the law requires two sureties on a bail-bond."

He hesitated a moment, then, drawing himself to his full height, he said, with a fierce humility that was strikingly like pride: "In the s-h-shattered condition of my fortune I sometimes hardly know how I stand with the usurers, but I believe my estate will bear a mortgage for two thousand dollars more, and I will borrow the money and give it to the man to deposit in lieu of bail."

A sudden idea flashed upon Percy. He was so in the habit of putting his own money in a safe place that this method of propitiation had not before occurred to him.

"If you will permit me, General," he said, with a charming air of deference and modesty, "*I* should be pleased to go on the bail-bond with you."

General Vayne cast on him a glance of approval. "I thank you, sir," he said. "But if there is any money to be lost here, I shall lose it. I bid you good day, gentlemen." He waved his hand ceremoniously, turned, strode up the pavement, and disappeared within the court-house.

Mr. Ridgeway's lungs lay far inland in a fat country. A huge sigh laboriously travelled up from them, and he took off his hat and rubbed his handkerchief around and around on his bald, shining, moist pate.

Men who speculate upon contingencies have a fine opportunity for realizing how purblind and finite is the vaunted faculty called foresight, and how infinitely intricate is that mechanism known as the ordering of events.

"That such a man as General Vayne should bestir himself for a cracker like Toole!" Brennett exclaimed aloud, in the abandonment of his despair.

He lingered long in the village that morning, watching in helpless excitement the uncontrollable course of the events which he himself had set in motion. His finesse had only resulted in making Toole the most prominent figure in public view, for General Vayne told on every street-corner the pathetic story of the wife's untimely death and the homeless children's destitution. A subscription for their benefit was headed by his own name, and his large ideals and inflated way of looking at things were abundantly manifest when he appealed to the ex-soldiers of Chattalla in behalf of the tow-headed brats out on the turnpike, as the children of a veteran who had stood his ground in a hundred battles; when he spoke of the illiterate lout of a drunken ferry-man as his "brave Companion in Arms." Other names followed fast; there was something enthusing in a glimpse through that foolish magnifying glass. Toole had never had so much money at once as when he tramped silently out of the town and along the dusty, white turnpike till miles lay behind him, and at last the dark little log-cabin, that was to be no longer his home came in sight. Hardly in sight, for he would not look at it. He had a deep sense of the unnatural solemnity that brooded upon it. He knew what lay within. He turned abruptly from the road to the flower-crowned redoubt. He crossed the ditch, climbed the parapet, and flung himself down in an empty embrasure, through which a great gun had once looked. There he watched the golden afternoon glow and ripen to redness, and drop at last out of the sky. The latest light of the day quivered on the wings of a throng of homeward-bound swallows till they were white, and scintillated like a flying constellation. The cows were coming home; he heard them low. The familiar voice of the river sounded with a new and dreary intonation. He listened to the fitful bleating of the baby, still rising and falling as it had risen and fallen through all the long hours that the child had crept about, neglected, and in forlorn surprise, on the rickety porch. Stars were in the sky, and suddenly a golden gleam sprang into the window of the little log-cabin. He lifted himself on his elbow to look at it, and as he looked he burst into tears. Why should a light ever shine there again!

It was strange to him that, filled as he was with an overwhelming realization of his misfortunes, he could still take note of external objects. He seemed endowed with keener sense. From far up the road he heard the regular hoof-beats of a pair of trotters and the smooth, light roll of wheels. He recognized Percy and Brennett as the buggy whirled by. He saw in the dim light of the closing dusk the face of the man who had testified against him, and whom he had learned to hate. And so, too, the man saw his face.

There was so hard, so fierce, so bitter an expression on its clumsy features that Brennett drove on in renewed perplexity. He had had some wild, reckless idea of taking advantage of Toole's straits by bribing him heavily to leave the place. But he began to realize that he was regarded as the direct and active cause of these calamities, and although it could not be divined that thus he had sought to subserve a personal interest, still Toole was an unreasoning brute, and this instinctive distrust and enmity could hardly be dissipated even by the most specious arguments. It was sheer madness to place himself in the power of a man who held a grudge like this against him. And so he cast the thought from him forever.

The swift shadows of the horses that had raced with them neck and neck along the sunset road were distanced and lost in the darkness. Only the red sparks of the cigars broke the monotony of the colorless night. The new ferry-man, who, silent and grim, pulled them over the river, was a suggestively lowering figure in the gloom, and the river was as black as Styx. Brennett felt in landing on the other side that he had left all hope and life, and was entering upon judgment. He arraigned himself fiercely. He might have foreseen; surely he might have been sharper!

He said to himself that this was definitive; the game was up. The man concerning whom General Vayne, with his fantastically potent rhetoric, blowing about the town, had raised a cloud of public interest, might now tell his story every day to a genteel audience. Other "companions in arms" would indulgently listen to Toole's reminiscences, when, in rehearsing his Iliad of woes, he would relate how the old commander held out the left hand spared him, although no one else would move; and so to General Vayne's qualities as man and soldier, to his feats on the field, to the wide subject of the great battle, to the details of personal experience, — and was it likely that the dramatic story of the burning bridge and the officer who fired it would be forgotten?

So it was all over. Brennett was so loath to realize it that he remained inactive for days in torturing suspense. When the Criminal Court was in session, and the case came on for trial, he watched the proceedings in a lethargy of despair. The fact of self-defence was so incontestably proved, that the jury found a verdict of acquittal without leaving the box, and the two men were free forever. They occupied so much public attention, that Brennett's mind was forcibly recalled to the dangers with which Toole's prominence menaced him. The veriest chance word that might come to Percy or Miss St. Pierre would ruin all, and Percy, in his utter idleness, made it a point to interest himself in such subjects as General Vayne took in hand, that he might find opportunities to present himself in an amiable light for that simple-hearted gentleman's approval.

He had not, it is true, done his sensibilities the violence of attending the trial, but he was much exercised about the cheerful verdict, and brought up the subject himself the evening after it was rendered as he sat in the library at General Vayne's house. The wide windows let in squares of moonlight that lay sharply defined upon the floor despite the yellow lustre of the shaded lamp. The white curtains fluttered in the perfumed breeze. From far away he could hear the melancholy note of the frogs monotonously chanting in the dank ditches of the works. It filled the pause that ensued when Captain Estwicke was ushered in upon the party, and the formal greetings were over.

Percy turned to him agreeably. It was an element of his self-love to include even every casual stranger in the demonstrations of what he mentally designated his "universal fascination system." Estwicke's hard metal, and the superficiality of his suavity were very patent when they were thus contrasted with these soft graces.

"You drove over, Captain? Then you haven't heard the news from our little burgh."

This was so obviously a note from General Vayne's bugle that Estwicke could have smitten Percy for it; why did he call the town a "burgh!"

Estwicke, silent, his elbow resting lightly on the table, looked at Percy with a challenging stare.

"You will be glad to know that Toole is acquitted."

"Toole?" Estwicke repeated, dubiously.

"The ferryman, or rather the ex-ferryman," Percy politely explained.

Estwicke's face was blankly unresponsive. He had not known that the ferryman was accused of anything; if he had noticed, he had forgotten that the office was filled by a stranger. He was a trifle confused to be boned on a point like this, as if he were expected, at such a distance, to keep up with the excitements of the village. His attention too was divided. He had never before seen Marcia wear a white dress. The material and make were of the simplest, but the snowy diaphanous draperies gave an added lustre to that fresh young loveliness. The sleeve fell away from her delicate wrist, displaying her rounded dimpled arm, and all the soft folds illustrated the grace of her lithe, slender figure. Her throat rose from a many-petalled ruche. Her hair sparkled with golden glimmers; with all this whiteness about her, she seemed trebly fair. Her cheeks were flushed, and she looked at him with a smile deep in her gracious young eyes. He felt that she was conscious of this sudden bloom into a beauty infinitely exquisite. He recognized her frank vanity.

And how came those other men here!

Thus his jealousy shut from him the suspicion that by the intuition of an awakened heart she had divined *his* coming. And so it was, he never knew that even after the lamps were lighted, she was still sewing, that the dress might be finished in time, and he should find her lovely.

He looked at Percy, not at her. And he said nothing of Toole, the humble fellow who had served his coming and going for a matter of six months, and who had lived a tragedy lately. General Vayne pulled hard at his mustache. But he had always thought that this man was peculiarly callous.

"Oh, poor fellow!" exclaimed Mrs. Kirby, shaking her curls compassionately, "so destitute — homeless — without employment — and so many children — so many."

She turned and bent the beaming blandishments of her smile upon Brennett. "Poverty in the country is more painful to contemplate than poverty in town, I think, Mr. Brennett. Deprivation in the midst of the abundance of nature; yes, very bad indeed, very bad. In towns, potatoes are measured by the bushel, and signify dimes. In the country they are meted out by the sunshine, and the rain, and the generous earth, and they signify the blessing of God on the rich season — yes. And these are the inalienable rights of the poor as well as the wealthy — the just and the unjust."

Brennett smiled vaguely, with a semblance of endorsing this romantic communistic proposition.

"It seems to me that potatoes belong to the man who plants them," said Marcia prosaically, from out the poetic shimmer of her white dress.

The slightest vibration of her voice thrilled through Estwicke, but he sat looking straight forward, and did not turn his head.

"Do you know, General Vayne, what Toole intends to do?" asked Brennett with some eagerness.

"What *can* he do?" said General Vayne with a deprecatory wave of the hand. "He is not a skilled workman; his only chance is to find an odd job, now and then."

"Ah, the poor man! So precarious!" exclaimed Mrs. Kirby. "He quits his little house next Thursday. But his aunt, old Mrs. Prindle, at the toll-gate, good old soul, will take one of the children, the youngest, yes, the baby. F-fat little thing!" she cried, with a cheery, grandmotherly smile illuminating the general desolation. "And no doubt he can find homes with some of the small farmers for the boys — boys, yes — so useful, you know — pick up chips."

"You have talked with him then," said Brennett, pursuing the subject.

"Yes; Marcia piloted me over there — long walk, dear me! and very warm to-day. Takes his wife's death hard, very hard. Seems really to feel it, you know. She was dead before he was released, before he reached there. The shock of his arrest killed her, and it was all for naught, since he was acquitted. And nothing consoles that poor baby. But it is all over dimples! It is a terrible reflection that that mother's life was sacrificed, and those children bereaved — all for nothing!"

"Oh, I beg of you!" exclaimed Percy, with a gesture of entreaty.

"Yes, very serious, I don't wonder it jars your nerves," said the old lady with solemnity.

"Why, that's a calamity — to jar *his* nerves!" exclaimed Marcia, with a light laugh. Light as it was, it had in it so tense a thrill of satire that the others looked at her in surprise.

She sat at her ease in the stiff old arm-chair, her hand toying with a full-blown white rose. She was very charming to look upon, and all the gentlemen were gazing at her. Nevertheless, Mrs. Kirby sighed. Surely it was not politic to show temper before so many unwived men. And temper for what — pray?

"A calamity!" Marcia reiterated, "but we must try to bear up against it!"

Certainly it is anomalous that a lover should grudge his rival the lady's displeasure. But the fact that she spoke thus freely to Percy reminded Estwicke unpleasantly of the friendship which had subsisted between them long, long before he ever saw her.

Percy was so accustomed to be regarded as an exemplar of all that is gallant, and generous, and high-spirited in youth, that now he was suddenly confused, self-depreciatory, and wounded.

"You mean my sympathy is so shallow that it is worthless?" he said, looking at her with a gentle deprecation, that the bewildered Mrs. Kirby thought must surely disarm her. Her aspect, however, was so impassive that the old lady, who believed herself the tactician of the world, and joyed in her little management, could not trust the conversation in other guidance, and seized upon the helm herself.

"Sympathy!" she cried. "Why Toole is held as a public martyr!"

"And that is very bad for him, and for the community," said the severe Marcia. "He *thought* he was breaking the law — that was his *intention*."

Oh, if a young lady only knew how unlovely she appears when she sets herself to discourse of affairs of public policy, she would forbear — she would refrain. Mrs. Kirby could have wrung her hands. So many gentlemen! And the moonlight was touching the girl's grave face with a spiritual glamour, and shifting over her beautiful dress, and the melodious nocturnal sounds pulsed along the perfumed air, and all the night was full of starlight, and poetry, and the bursting of buds, and the bloom of flowers — and she to be talking about the community!

Maurice Brennett's eyes were fixed upon Marcia with questioning intensity. What did she mean? What was she driving at?

"Help me to reconstruct my sympathy," said Percy, still grave and gentle.

"You give him money," said Marcia reprovingly, "because you have plenty of it and won't miss it."

Everybody winced at this frank mention of the young gentleman's wealth.

"You give him money, and it slips away immediately, and it is bad for him — he drinks it up — and when it is all gone — what then? You give him money because you are sorry for him — for a little while — and to give it makes *you* feel better. But you can't *think* for him — you won't give him so much as a thought."

General Vayne was nervously pulling his mustache, and staring at his daughter's soft young face, with its unwontedly severe expression, as if on the whole he did not recognize her. Mrs. Kirby could not even fan. Miss St. Pierre smiled from one to another, as if to make believe that this was a mere society conversation, and had no especial significance, no incongruities. Estwicke, with a heavy frown on his face, was watching Percy, who leaned eagerly forward, his elbow on his knee, and his hat in his hand, his temper unruffled, and his pride pocketed.

"I confess all that," he said hastily. "Tell me how I must think for him."

"You make him a beggar," Marcia continued, still indignantly accusing, "when you might give him a chance to work for his living, and support his children, and keep them together, instead of distributing them about the country to anybody who will take them."

"I shall make it my business to get him into something," declared Percy.

"Mind," said Marcia, lifting the white rose with a didactic gesture, "it must be something in which he honestly earns every dollar of his wages — it must be no pretence — charity in disguise. That, you know, can't last. What do you think of trying?"

"I had no definite idea," Percy admitted, a trifle confused. "I don't know of anything about here — in this town or neighborhood that would answer."

"*Here* — why it is not necessary, surely, that the man should remain *here!*" she rejoined impatiently.

Maurice Brennett scarcely dared to breathe. The anguish of his hope was hardly less poignant than the anguish of his fear. Great drops started on his forehead.

He could not, he would not speak. What incongruity of fate was this? That this girl, this saint on earth, should unconsciously lend her hand to his schemes — that she should help Toole out of the country!

"Can't you find work for him elsewhere?" she demanded imperiously. "You have interests away from this little treadmill of a town." (Young America is not always respectful to the good old "burgh" of its fathers.) "Don't you own an interest in some sort of factory — a furniture factory, or something or other, at Marston," she continued vaguely — "enough to make them employ a workman you choose to send them?"

"I reckon so," said Percy; he brightened at the suggestion, and rose with a triumphant laugh. In fact, he had no doubt, for he was a half owner in the flourishing concern; but he was modest in regard to his possessions, and affected a modicum of uncertainty. "If you will let me have pen and paper, I will write to them now, and give the letter to Toole as I go past his house on my way home."

"Yes — dear — yes. Get the inkstand for Horace," said Mrs. Kirby, having recovered the use of her palm-leaf fan. "Take your little key-basket off the table — yes — out of Horace's way," she added blandly. She was in truth anxious to make the girl wait upon him, and in trivial acts of consideration and deference afford a small compensation for the soul-trying experience to which she had subjected him.

But Percy, as he sat at the table, looked up with a bright protest in his dark eyes.

"No, it does n't disturb me, I assure you; don't trouble yourself." As he touched with an insistent gesture the stout little wicker basket, with its jingling contents of housekeeping keys, his hand met hers for a moment.

Estwicke saw this; he divined the wild, vague suggestion of close domestic association which made the ugly, housewifely little key-basket a precious thing in the young man's eyes, and its proximity a pleasure. He recognized the adroit tact by which she was kept hovering about the table, and knew that it seemed to Percy a foretaste, too, of the blissful unrestraint of a common home, that he should informally remain seated while she stood beside him and bent over to look at the paper and pen, when he called her attention to them.

Estwicke's heart waxed hot within him; was it for this that he had come so far to see her? With a sharpened sense he heard every word that passed between them, despite the animated chatter of the rest of the group. He saw and translated as full of meaning every gesture.

"Is this your pen?" asked Percy, examining it. "The General's? Well, there's a heavy stroke for you! Why does n't he write with a fence-rail at once!"

She laughed blithely as she bent down to look at the writing; her face was sweetly flushed; her eyes were so gentle now; her floating, diaphanous sleeve lightly brushed his shoulder; his eyes followed its sweep. He was so gay, so handsome, so alertly confident, and she was so pleased with him.

As she turned away, he glanced up once more. "Do you write the date on the top line or the next one? And how must I date it? — advise me. From Chattalla? Oh, how you shock me. Is this what you call candor? I'm not in Chattalla, thank heaven!"

As he began to write she went away and sat down, still flushed, and excited, and absorbed.

"Mr. Percy is very prompt in keeping his promises," said Brennett; his lips were dry; he enunciated with difficulty the commonplace.

"Oh, I'm a very promising young man," Percy declared without raising his head.

But it was only a moment before he again appealed to her.

"Can't you help me word this?" he said speciously. "I'm getting mixed up here in some fearfully awkward phraseology."

In the simplicity of her heart she rose instantly and went to help him. To Estwicke it hardly seemed simplicity. He could not understand how she should fail to know that a man like Percy was wont to write in whatever hasty and dishevelled style that pleased him to the stewards of his wealth, and had of necessity far more epistolary experience than she. The two together made a long, grave, and careful job of it. Percy was hypercritical; once or twice he objected to her suggestions on the score of tautology, and as she placed her dimpled, rounded elbows on the table, and rested her cheek on her clasped hands, and cast her eyes absently out on the moonlight in a cogitating search for a felicitous synonym, he, with his pen idly poised, looked with a satisfied proprietary admiration at the pretty picture she made. And Estwicke looked at him.

It was all over at last, and he had written his name half across the page.

She laughed as she glanced at this pompous signature.

"That is a very great man!" she said.

"*I* believe in him — for one," said Percy — which was the truest word he had spoken for a week.

"And so do I," protested Mrs. Kirby blandly.

And this, too, was true in a certain sense. Estwicke had felt more than once that they all liked Percy for himself — apart from his prominence and wealth, which to the eyes of a poor and jealous rival were formidable advantages. The handsome young fellow, with his subtle arts of propitiation, always contrived to appear here in an exceptionally genial and fascinating guise. With a disposition to make amends for all that he must have suffered in the crucial interview with Marcia, the kindly feeling of the elders was especially marked to-night. Estwicke was of course unaware of this motive. He was angry, sore, dismayed — he seemed to have dreamed that blissful termination of all his vacillations of hope and fear. But for the glitter of his own ring on the girl's hand he could not have realized that she had so lately given him a promise which he had fancied was dear to them both — which had made his future bloom like a rose.

Only when he spoke to her at last — he had risen to take leave — did his heart, grown so strangely heavy, beat with a quick, tumultuous throb once more. The group was breaking up, for it was late, and these two were standing quite apart from the others for a moment.

She lifted her eyes to his with so candid a disappointment expressed in them, that he was in a measure consoled.

"We have had a dull time, have n't we? But — but" — her eyelashes drooped a little, — "you know you 'll be coming back again soon."

"To-morrow," he said hastily. "In the morning," he added, frowning darkly over an intention of thus outmarching Percy. But she was so evidently unconscious of having given him reason for jealousy, that he began to be a trifle ashamed of it.

Percy glanced at them askance as he stood at a little distance, a victim of Mrs. Kirby's messages and remembrances to his mother. He had experienced upon first meeting Estwicke a vague uneasiness to find any personable man in her society, but it had been dissipated by the fact that the officer seemed a dull, heavy fellow, and there was no sign of a sentimental interest. Now, however, he detected something in Estwicke's manner that roused him from the soft delights of his self-satisfaction to the keenest anxiety. He had not time to make sure; he would have waited till Estwicke was gone, but Brennett seemed feverishly anxious to be off, and he must go with his guest. As they walked down the long pavement he strove to reassure himself with the recollection of the man's serious, intent, even frowning face. Surely this was not the self-gratulatory mien of a favored lover. And he had no reason to suppose that the officer frequented the house; General Vayne's political feeling would hardly warrant that supposition, and he had never before met Estwicke here.

Their host had accompanied them to the buggy; he was gesticulating with his left hand as he described to Brennett how the features of the country were utilized in a certain midnight assault on Fort Despair — an incident of the great battle. As Percy looked back at the door he saw, in the yellow flare of the swinging lamp in the hall, Mrs. Kirby and Miss St. Pierre standing there, exclaiming over the iniquity of Dick, who had robbed a nest among the roses on the pillars of the portico, and was bringing the young mocking-birds into the house. The conviction was forced upon Percy. Estwicke had lingered in the library that he might have a few moments alone with Marcia. And had she not lingered as well?

Percy drove away in moody silence, and very slowly. At every turn of the road he glanced back, expecting to see a shadow moving in the moonlight, and to hear the whir of wheels. Evidently Estwicke had not yet left the house, for he saw only the myriads of fire-flies, pulsing points of light, among the heavy foliage on the redoubts, and he heard nothing but the shrill, quavering wail of a screech-owl, jarring ever and anon the sombre stillness of the haunted thickets.

He experienced a thrill of dismay that he should suspect all this so late. Hitherto he had considered himself reasonably sure of her, although he had as yet given her no intimation of the state of his feelings. He had thought he might safely wait. They were both very young — there was plenty of time before them — and he felt, too, that his freedom was dear and that he would like to see a little more of the world before settling down to quiet home-life and conjugal felicity. He had been entirely at ease as to the completion of his romance, when it should suit him to recur to it. Now, however, his inertia, when the field had been clear, seemed to him inexplicable, and it required some agile mental processes to reason himself out of his despondency. But he remembered once more Estwicke's grave, intent, frowning face — he remembered, too, that she had scarcely spoken to any one but himself throughout the evening. He resolved that he would take heart of grace — if he had been too dilatory heretofore, he would compensate himself now.

His whip touched the off horse. They bowled along swiftly through the gloom. The wind seemed to freshen with the quickening motion. He felt its influence.

"It's a good thing I forgot that letter!" he exclaimed hopefully.

The sudden sharpness of Maurice Brennett's voice struck his attention even amidst his pre-occupation.

"Did you leave it there?"

"I left it lying on the table — and that's a good excuse to go back to-morrow," said Percy, laughing.

Brennett breathed hard — he remembered the broad open windows and the position of the table near them. He felt on his cheek the fresh wind — what more natural than that the letter on which so much depended should be blown upon the floor to lie there overlooked, until some careless housemaid should sweep it out in the morning. It was as likely that Percy would forget the "good excuse" when once there again, and the young lady, having carried her point, would probably recur to it no more. Thus Toole, narrowly missing the good fortune intended for him, would still remain here.

It was hard to say upon what pretext Brennett could interfere — how he could busy himself in matters apparently so alien to his interests without exciting surprise, anger, even suspicion of his motives. The fact that Miss Vayne had concerned herself in the incongruous affair added elements of difficulty — the jealous sensitiveness of her lover, and the delicacy requisite in speaking of a young lady. But he could not — he would not submit his recently rescued project to a contingency like this — so slight in itself, so portentously important in its effects. He had only a moment for thought, but he was wont to think quickly.

Percy saw his face in the flicker of a match which he had struck and applied to his cigar. He was laughing cynically, despite the weed held fast between his teeth.

The young fellow turned scarlet; he felt a fiery rush of indignation.

"I am glad to afford you so much amusement," he said, as stiffly as a punctilious host may allow himself to speak to his guest.

Brennett pulled silently at the cigar until it was fairly a-light, then he flung the match aside in the road, and leaned back luxuriously.

"My dear fellow," he said — and Percy knew from the sound of his voice that he was still laughing in the darkness — "I beg your pardon most humbly, I assure you. *You* do not amuse me — as Horace Percy. I only laugh at certain common human vagaries, which are very humorously expressed in you at this period of your career."

Percy's wounded pride was hardly assuaged. "I can't see the application," he said tartly.

Brennett laid a friendly hand upon his knee. "Don't ask me to translate your characteristics, and then quarrel with me for my version. It seems to me that a charming degree of youthful self-importance and self-love is suggested in leaving that letter as a good excuse to call on Miss Vayne to-morrow. Do you think she has no self-love? Will she be flattered that you forget a matter which she intrusted to you?"

"Oh — I thank you — she will guess why I forgot it," said Percy hardily. "If she can't, I will help her when I call to-morrow."

Brennett made no answer. That the success of such a scheme should be jeopardized by such puerilities!

Percy felt that this silence was almost impertinent. But their mutual position forbade any notice of it. Still he chafed under this sense of wordless ridicule.

"Oh, talk it out, Brennett, talk it out!" he exclaimed impatiently, at last.

"Why, it's no great matter, after all," said Brennett, laughing agreeably. "A disappointment will do you good. Life has been too easy for you. Lucky fellow!"

"A disappointment!" said Percy sharply.

"No grave disappointment, of course," said Brennett. "I was only alluding to the letter. In my opinion you will never see it again."

"Why?" Percy demanded shortly.

"Oh, confound it, boy," said Brennett, with a blunt, good-natured intonation, "why, she will give it to Captain Estwicke to hand to Toole as he drives by; and you may bet your immortal soul that *he* does n't forget it."

Percy drew the horses suddenly into a walk.

"What makes you say that?" he asked eagerly. "Did you notice anything?"

"Vaguely, very vaguely. But, however that may be, I can understand how she might think him a man whom she could intrust with a little matter like this; a man accustomed to responsibility, detail, duty. What do you mean? Where are you going?"

Percy was wheeling the vehicle round in the narrow road. "Going back for that letter, that's all."

"It's too late," Brennett remonstrated. He drew out his watch, and leaned forward, striving to see the time by the glow of his cigar. He heard the triumph in his own voice, he felt it in the relaxing muscles of his face.

Percy made no rejoinder. He lashed the horses savagely and they were dashing back at a great rate. The old house loomed close upon them, dim in the midnight, before he saw, slipping through the gloom, the moving shadow for which he had angrily watched.

It became suddenly stationary. A stentorian "Hello, there!" prevailed on him to check his horses, and the next moment Estwicke was standing in the road, with one foot on the hub of the wheel, as he leaned into the vehicle, and held out to Percy the envelope, with his own superscription.

"I am instructed," he said gayly, "to overtake you, and give you that, and charge you, very severely, not to forget again."

Both men in the buggy were looking keenly at him as

he stood in the full moonlight. He was elated; he had been laughing; his eyes were bright; there was a flush on his cheek; he spoke with an ease and a hearty comradeship that changed him out of recognition; he seemed utterly unlike the saturnine stranger they had left. He was disposed to hang upon the wheel and talk companionably.

"May I trouble you for a light, Mr. Brennett?" he said, reaching up for the other's cigar. "I might have gotten a match at the house, but" — glancing back at the lights which were disappearing, one by one, from the windows — "can't rouse it after 'taps.'"

Percy said nothing, and Brennett made amends for his silence.

"Do you drive far to-night, Captain?"

"Only a little matter of seven miles — first-rate road. It's a fine country, Mr. Percy, that you have about here," Estwicke added, as he turned away. "Good night."

They lost sight of him before they drew up at Toole's log-cabin, where they called lustily, to rouse its occupant.

Somehow, as they stood there motionless, and looked on the vast, dark stretch of country about them, and the lonely vastness of the sky above, with no sound but the quavering wail of the owl from out the recesses of Fort Despair, and the ceaseless monotone of the chanting frogs, and the vibratory clamor of the cricket and the katydid, and the weird echoes of their own outcry striking back from the parapets, it was so drear, so solitary, so infinitely forlorn, that some untried chord of Maurice Brennett's nature was smitten strongly for an instant and set jarring with an unwonted throb. He remembered the woman with yellow hair whom he had seen here walking up and down and striking her hands together in mute despair. She had walked thus all night. And thus she had been found in the morning. It was a mute despair, for she had spoken no more. She was brought to this pass by the shock of the arrest, the ignorant people said, — and they said it because they were ignorant. The shock had only evoked and given direction to some deep-seated disease of heart or brain, which would have come at last. But he had set it all in motion; and now he was sorry — he was very sorry. It was a great price to have paid; but, he argued, a very vague responsibility. Still, if he could have known, it should never have happened. And perhaps he did not deceive himself.

He was glad when Toole came slouching out at last; he was even glad to see the look of settled hate, as the man once more recognized the witness who had testified against him. It gave Brennett back to mundane associations, for this was a more familiar emotion than remorse.

He watched Toole's face change gradually from an expression of stunned astonishment to one of infinite relief, as he listened to Percy's explanation about the work, the wages, and the route.

"Oh, I'll light out right away!" cried Toole passionately. "God knows I don't want to stay hyar."

Brennett looked forward into the surly glooms hovering about the river, a smile relaxing his thin lips.

Percy was about to drive on. He hesitated, and glanced around doubtfully. He had enjoyed doing a real benefaction when once at it. The humble gratitude of its recipient agreeably titillated his self-esteem. But his mirror-like nature was reflecting the influences cast upon it this evening, and with a frankness, and justice, and modesty that were uncharacteristic, he had an impulse to disclaim the credit of the kindness. Still, Toole was a rough fellow, to whom he hardly liked to mention a lady's name.

As he gathered up the reins, however, he said, a trifle dubiously, —

"You don't owe me any thanks; all this was suggested to me. You are indebted to — to — the General's daughter."

The man raised his shaggy, tawny head and looked back over his shoulder with a light of comprehension on his face. "I might hev knowed that," he exclaimed naïvely; "'t ain't the fust time that us pore folks round hyar hev hed ter thank her."

Percy drove on, laughing a little; and Brennett was laughing, too, triumphantly. He was alert, revivified. He also had to thank her.

And in the days that came and went the hawk's bright eyes were cruelly vigilant, for the strong prescience of success was upon him.

CHAPTER XVII.

IN summer-time, always, Marcia and nature together did much to soften the traces of that terrible event in the history of the old house. Flowering vines curtained such of its windows as were still left glassless. In the black fissures in the stone wall of the terraces, and the curb of the pavements, where bombs had exploded, lilies grew tall and stately. The parterre was splendid with variegated color, and above it hovered always the fluctuating brilliancy of humming-birds and butterflies, that seemed themselves some impalpable undulatory blossoming of the fragrant air.

It was close upon noon when Estwicke checked his horse on the drive next day, and no one was visible except Edgar, who stood upon the front steps in an airy costume of bare feet and plump calves, brown linen knickerbockers and blouse. He intently examined something which he held in his warm, fat hands.

"Is your father at home?" asked Estwicke, in passing up the steps.

"Hy're, Cap'n — d'ye see my Juny-bug?" demanded Edgar affably, ignoring the question. "I've been on the terrus to ketch me a Juny-bug. An' I got him."

Upon opening his hand there flew into the sunshine a June-bug, its roving tendencies very effectually checked by a thread tied to one of its legs.

"Marcia says," continued Edgar, holding the end of

the thread, and watching with complacent eyes his victim's evolutions, "Marcia says that no boy who is mean·enough ter tie a string ter a Juny-bug's leg need n't never expec' ter go ter Heaven. He 'll make a mighty mistake if he does expec' ter go *there!* That 's what Marsh says!"

Estwicke was too pre-occupied to comment on this singular doctrine of election. He rang the bell without further questions, while Edgar, with that insensibility to appropriateness, eminently characteristic of the infant mind, sat down with a long breath of enjoyment upon the hottest step of the whole flight, in the broad glare of the sun, and watched his Juny-bug's airy gyrations and listened to the musical whir of its wings, totally indifferent to the prospective exclusion from eternal bliss.

From the library could be seen vistas of uninhabited rooms, with bare floors and curtainless windows, for all the doors stood open this June day. The wind swept through with a rush, bringing the warm fragrance of clover from the battle-field and the scent of the roses that climbed the pillars of the portico. There seemed in this fierce weather much method in the madly ostentatious proportions of the house. Within was a large breeze-filled, perfumed twilight, while without, the earth was scorching under a furious sun, and the drowsy drone of the cicada pervaded the heated air.

In the strongest draught General Vayne sat, alone, at leisure, reading his favorite Addison's Cato. The anxiety occasioned by observing his genuine liking for Percy had heavily re-enforced a wild fear, which had already beset Estwicke, that General Vayne might, from political prejudice, withhold his consent. These reflections had given the young man a sleepless night. But, with the revivifying matutinal influences, he grew more hopeful. He determined to put it to the test at once — to make the attack all along the line. He argued within himself that this friendship for his rival was not of necessity inimical to his interest, and, as to his principles and his position in the army, even when the war was at its fiercest, enamoured Yankee officers did not, as a rule, find the cruel papas of the South so very obdurate.

Perhaps it was well that he could not divine, as he made his demonstration, the amazement it excited in General Vayne, whose latest impressions of his guest were from the witness-stand in the Jartree case. His long absence from home had precluded all suspicion of the little romance recently dramatized here. He had never thought to ask if that forced invitation to the fishing-party had been accepted — for this had seemed out of the question — and he had supposed that until last evening Estwicke had not again been to the house. He was possessed by a towering incredulity when a modest allusion was made to his daughter's gracious acceptance of the devotion offered her, and with difficulty restrained himself from telling the young man, from the plenitude of paternal wisdom, that he must be mistaken. But when General Vayne once realized the situation, he quickly came to his conclusion. Marcia was too young, far too young, to know her own mind. He determined to put his foot down on this engagement at once. He believed Estwicke a coarse-natured, hard, cold, callous man, to whom no woman's happiness could be safely committed. He was always convinced of the justness of his decisions; but he recognized a certain awkwardness here, for he could not put this into words. In decency he could not tell a man who had just paid Marcia the highest compliment in his power that he was so contemptuously considered. The puzzled father cast about vainly for some plausible alternative. Even he appreciated the inconsistency that so unprejudiced and temperate a thinker as he deemed himself should base a grave objection on political differences. Estwicke's position in the army offered, however, a vague elusive prospect of extrication from this dilemma. General Vayne honestly did not think Marcia's happiness would be promoted by going some time to the frontier with a husband liable to be scalped any fine day. And he felt, with a sudden strong rush of emotion, that he would not intrust her to any man — *any* man — so far away. His humane intention was to keep his son-in-law as much as possible under his own eye — the average son-in-law would probably rather risk the Indians. But Captain Estwicke *might* offer to resign; for aught General Vayne knew he was a man of fortune, and his pay the merest superfluity. Thus the strategist determined he would not advance an objection that could be so summarily swept away.

To one whose tact and policy are, in his own opinion, boundless, no embarrassment need last long. General Vayne resolved, autocratically, that he would assign no reason for withholding his consent; he would merely intimate to Estwicke that his addresses were not acceptable, and no doubt the young man would at once withdraw.

In projecting plans of action, General Vayne took slight note of the volition of others. Experience taught him nothing, and he had occasion for great surprise when Estwicke urgently pressed for the reasons of the refusal, justifying his persistence by the altogether unexpected argument that his dearest interests were at stake. And now was presented the striking and unique spectacle of one man eagerly insisting that another should insult him, which the other politely but firmly declined to do.

They were restrained in manner, voice, and word by the rigid decrees of the conventionalities, but, nevertheless, in their opposing determination they fretted each other like a pair of fiery horses.

In the subsequent interview with Marcia it was still more difficult for Estwicke to cloak his indignation.

"Your father will not give his consent," he said briefly.

A startled expression sprang into her eyes. "Why?"

"He vouchsafed no reason!" cried Estwicke with angry sarcasm. "When I had the audacity to ask for his reason, he said that it was not necessary to discuss the matter further, and that he hoped I would consider it definitively settled."

Marcia walked in silence to a chair and sat down, revolving in her mind the unexpected complication, and hardly sure of what she felt and thought in the shock of the surprise.

The library was dim and shadowy, for the blinds excluded the sunbeams, except one glittering marauder that forced an entrance through a crevice and raided fantastically about the room when the wind stirred the vines outside. Now the bright gleam touched the girl's hair, now it shimmered over the fluted petal-like ruffles of her dress, and now it flitted across her face as she looked up at Estwicke, who stood opposite her, leaning with one elbow on the mantel-piece and his hat in his hand.

"Perhaps," said Marcia, with a sinking heart and a keen despair, "it's because your politics are all wrong."

His feelings were so deeply involved that he did not resent even this sweeping imputation of wholesale error.

"I'll vote for Genghis Khan if he wishes!" he declared impetuously. "I'll swear allegiance to the king of Dahomey! I'll renounce every political and religious conviction. But I can't believe that's the reason," he added more calmly. "We might as well imagine it's because I don't belong to the church."

"What do you think is the reason, then?"

In all Estwicke's efforts and schemes the cohesive element of policy was lacking. And thus his life was full of rugged incongruities; there were great rifts in his friendships; and now, all unconsciously, he was driving that wedge of tactless speech in among his own heart-strings.

"It is very plain," he said bluntly, "he wants you to marry Percy."

"I should be glad, Captain Estwicke," cried Marcia angrily, "if I could never hear you call that man's name again."

"Well, forgive me this time. I'm not jealous about your feeling for Percy, *now*," stipulated Estwicke. "I have given that up."

Which was indeed true, as his every faculty was absorbed in apprehensive jealousy on account of her father's feeling for Percy.

He turned his hat in his hand, and eyed it for a moment with exceeding bitterness. When he again looked down at her, he detected something in the expression of her face which gave him a sudden comprehension of the manner in which she regarded her father's opposition. For once in his life he was not precipitate. The knowledge of all he had at stake steadied him. He sat down near her. "Tell me, Marcia," he said, with a calmness that sub-acutely astonished him, "Tell me that all this shall not make any difference between us. Shall it, dearest?"

"No," she replied softly.

He felt a thrill of infinite relief. He leaned forward and caught both her hands in his. "And if you marry me now, at once," he began, more confidently.

There was a flash of astonishment in her eyes. She drew back suddenly.

"I only meant — that — that I can never care for anyone else; but I couldn't be married without papa's consent; how can you think it?"

Estwicke did not intend to be tragic or theatrical, but his manner as he dropped her hand and walked away to the window would have done him credit on any stage. Presently, however, he came and stood opposite to her, leaning against the mantel-piece once more.

"If your father would advance any objection in which sensible people could acquiesce," he argued, "I might understand the position you take. But he has no objection. It is because he prefers Percy. Don't break my heart, Marcia."

"Papa would never forgive me — never. But don't say I break your heart. You must wait, and be cheerful while you wait. And if he does not change at last, you must forget it all. I don't mind being miserable, much." Her lips quivered. "But you — *you* must be happy!"

In discussing the subject with her father that afternoon, Marcia was not so dutiful as she had been in his absence.

"I think you were needlessly rude to Captain Estwicke," she said.

General Vayne had tried to shirk the interview, fearing an unpleasant scene. Even now he had his papers before him on the table, and had dipped his pen in the ink. He made no reply, and did not raise his eyes.

"I don't intend to marry Horace Percy," continued Marcia. "It is useless, papa, for you to insist."

Now indeed her father looked up. "And pray," he said, with cold constraint, "who told you that I wanted you to marry Horace Percy?"

"Captain Estwicke," promptly replied the guileless Marcia.

She was not prepared for the effect of her words. In the instantaneous change on her father's face she saw in astonishment that he was deeply offended. She had so little knowledge of the sordid ways of the world that it did not occur to her that there could be any preference between Percy and Estwicke, save that which her heart might dictate. In a normal state of affairs General Vayne would have been equally free from imagining that any one would attribute to him mercenary motives. Lately, however, he had been greatly harried and pressed to the wall by his debts; he knew that even a stranger in the town could not remain unaware of his financial straits; his anxieties had made his sensibilities tender, and in a flash he ascribed to Estwicke that unworthy suspicion. He resented it as he would have resented a blow. He could have forgiven it as readily.

"I have nothing whatever to say to you about Horace Percy," he replied. "And only this about Captain Estwicke — that if you do not break this engagement you will disobey the first positive command I have ever seen fit to give you."

"I hope you are not angry with me, papa," she said. Her fair young face was full of trouble; there was a suggestion of unshed tears in her heavy eyelids. He was a trifle softened as he glanced toward her. "And I don't see why you are so prejudiced against Captain Estwicke," she continued.

He hardened instantly. "I don't care to discuss the matter further," he said. "And I am busy now."

But when she had left the room he pushed the papers from him, and leaned back idly in his chair — not even his tangled financial tribulations could operate as a counter-irritant. He had never been so deeply stung, this *ci-devant* magnate and millionaire, as by the fancied imputation that he would scheme to prop his fallen fortunes by marrying off his daughter to a rich man. It was intolerable that this gross slur should be cast upon him. And he had never known so strong an emotion as the repugnance it induced for Captain Estwicke.

CHAPTER XVIII.

GRAFFY BEALE had skulked back from the jail to his old burrow in the huge traverse. His sense of liberty expressed itself only in the fact that he was free to lie here in the deep glooms under the earth as if he were dead. Through the jagged fissure, where once was the door of the powder-magazine, he had no glimpse of the midsummer world save a narrow section of the parapet on which the lavished blood had bloomed so splendidly in trumpet-flowers. To his upward glance they defined themselves gorgeously against the blue sky, where sometimes a pale poetic moon swung among them in the full glare of the yellow sunshine. A bird might flit by; the grasshoppers drowsily droned; lizards basked. When the sky grew gold, and purple, and faintly green, behind those swaying red blossoms, he looked up to see the evening star in the amber haze, and it looked down to see the haggard misery in his mowing face. Sometimes a moonbeam stole to the fissure, and the mists entered into fellowship with him, and they inhabited the powder-magazine together. When they fell to shifting and shimmering, and asserting weird forms in the dusky dreariness; when a strange tumult sprang up all along the parapets; when the tramp of marching hosts and the clash of arms shook the earth; when the whirling wheels of the light artillery went by on the wind; when all the night broke forth with those strange lipless shrieks of the dead, with the blare of their bugles, with the roll of their drums, he shivered and trembled, and turned his grimacing face to the wall. But the ghosts had done him no harm — and in these days they seemed nearer akin than the living.

Now that his terrors of the law were over, he had developed in the reaction a morbid shrinking from the world, and his griefs — they were many — renewed their power. He said there was no place for him — he wanted no food, no drink, no home. He would waste out his life, wear it out, offer it in expiation, here.

Days had passed since he had heard a stir close at hand other than the flutter of a bird or a rabbit's leaping rush. Suddenly there sounded, on the parapet without, hesitating footsteps, heavy panting, the sharp cracking of brush and weeds, which indicated a struggle with the brambles. He rose from the ground, tremulous and weak, and, holding in his hand his wool hat, which had the best of reasons for being fresh and unfaded by the sun, he stepped out through the fissure. The light struck full upon his yellow hair, that was as fine and soft as a woman's, and gave out a glimmer like burnished gold. As he turned his head upward there was something ineffably repugnant in his pitiful, jail-bleached, mowing face. But delighted recognition resounded in the shrill cry set up suddenly on the parapet — there was a great scuffling under the blackberry bushes, and a dirty, tattered, tow-headed urchin came sliding, with an avalanche of dislodged stones, down the steep interior slope.

"They tole me ter fotch ye!" he piped out tumultuously on a high key. Then he sat down on the tread of the banquette, placed his hands on either knee, and drew a long breath. His attention was abruptly arrested by the sight of the sun-blanched skull of a noble charger, flung here, perhaps, when upturned by the plough in the fields without. The boy's curious eye detected the minie ball still half embedded in the splintered bone. He glanced over his shoulder, furtively, fearfully, for the unseen terrors that lurked about the place. "Why n't ye go 'way from hyar, now that ye air out 'n jail?" he demanded impatiently.

Graffy said nothing. He was only wondering vaguely why Pickie Tait should have sought him here. The boy was called "Pickie" by reason of a certain deft accomplishment of picking and stealing, sometimes — "Quick Pickie;" he was the hardiest urchin in the county, and all the juvenile iniquity perpetrated within five miles was easily traced to his door. "Waal," he observed, wiping his hot, dirty face with his tattered shirt-sleeve, "I ain't a-goin' through these hyar harnted forts agin by myself, ye hear me! Like ter hev been skeered ter death fower or five times whilst I war a-gittin' hyar. The folks hev sent fur ye ter kem an' play the fiddle at the infair. Las' night they scoured the country, mighty nigh, ter git a-holt o' ye in time ter play the fiddle fur Jeemes Blake's weddin'. They rid hyar, an' they rid thar! Nobody knowed whar ye be."

He cocked up his sharp eye reprehensively. Then he rose, went nimbly to the old powder magazine, and peered in with amicable curiosity. "Got yer fiddle in thar?" he asked, looking back over his shoulder and nodding gayly, his broad mouth a-grin.

"Ye-es." The man flung out the word between his chattering teeth and his unruly muscles. "The fiddle is thar."

"I'll tote it," said the boy officiously. He treated his red, round face to another smear from his ragged sleeve. Then he cut a wiry caper, kicking up a festive heel. "Kem on!" he cried imperiously. "They say that now ez ye air out 'n jail ye hev got ter play the fiddle at the infair."

And Graffy followed.

Perhaps it was by way of making her flout at humanity more complete, of pointing her grim jest, that Nature encased a great gift here — a gift that should be as useless, as unavailing as a wayside weed. But like the wayside weed, it throve mightily in sterile conditions where naught else might grow.

His wild, barbaric melodies came to him as the wind comes; no one knows how, nor whence. They were a defiance of science, but in their spontaneous ecstasy they swayed, they thrilled, they held. In the midst of the infair that night, when their passionate, tumultuous, shivering chords set all the midnight a-quiver, the strong rapture of his rude art once more laid hold upon his heart, and it grew warm again. As he sat on the cabin porch, his unnaturally white cheek pressed to the instrument, his eyes were fixed sometimes on the stars which seemed to throb in sympathy with the rhythmic vibrations of the strings, sometimes on the red interior, where the dancing figures of young men and girls whirled in a cloud of dust that was idealized into a golden haze by the soft light of the kerosene lamp. Merry guffaws proceeded from the elders, ranged against the wall or thronging the cooler porch, where they smoked and spat profusely through the white and lilac blossoms of the luxuriant jack-bean, and among the yellow globes of the gourd vines which climbed to the roof. Once there burst forth from the violin a strain so rapturous, so poignantly beautiful that its effect was like that of some impassioned eloquence. A slow, white-haired codger, the bridegroom's father, paused in lighting his pipe, and let the match burn to his fingers, while he stared at the instrument and the uncouth musician. "Graffy do fairly make that fiddle talk!" he exclaimed.

When the bow paused, and the reel was finished, and the elders made way for the over-heated young people to get out into the air and walk in couples, arm in arm, up and down the dusty turnpike, or flirt and make love under the apple-trees, or sit — a noisy, hilarious crew — on the rickety steps, this man, the host, sauntered up to the musician.

"S'prisin' how ye play, Graffy," he remarked affably.

Graffy looked down at the violin and twanged the strings. "Toler'ble well," he admitted, in his shrill, gasping voice, "cornsiderin' I never hed no showin'."

"Shucks! showin''s nothin'!" said the old man, with that supreme contempt for science so characteristic of ignorance.

"I hearn tell in town," said a black-bearded, jeans-clad fellow lounging against a post close by, "ez Patton — I don't mean Bob; I speaks of his brother Jim, the jailer — waal, Jim say ez he air a-tryin' mighty hard ter put up some sort'n job on ye ter git ye an' yer fiddle back thar agin. He say they air all mighty lonesome round them diggin's now, sure. He say they all 'low ez ye wouldn't know it fur the same place. He say ye kin play all sorts o' chunes out o' yer own head. He say ye kin even play hyme chunes wonderful."

The musician glanced from one to the other, his pallid, grimacing face indistinctly seen in the light from within the door. They might not know if he smiled, but he twanged at the string with the air of a man who receives a compliment.

"I'd a-reckoned ye'd hev furgot how ter play all them months ez ye war a-hidin' out," said the black-bearded man. "Ye never tetched yer bow then, I'll bet, fur enny fool would know yer whank from enny other man's sawing, ez fur ez they could hear it."

Even Graffy's face, debarred though it seemed of expression, changed subtly. He took the fiddle and began to turn it about mechanically.

"That was a mighty queer dodge ennyhow, yer hidin' out," said the rough, black-bearded man, whose coarse disregard of the other's sensibilities was perhaps unintentional. "Ye ought ter hev lef' the thing ter men at fust," he pursued didactically. "That's jestice. Ye *hev* ter leave sech questions ter men. I can't understan' how ye hed grit enough ter face shot an' shell in the old war times, an' now ye air afeard ter leave things ter men."

"Whar hev ye been stayin' sence ye been out — at Tom's?" asked the host.

"No," gasped Graffy; "Tom an' me hev bruk."

"I hearn," said the black-bearded man, animatedly retailing the gossip, "ez how Tom hev never said nare word ter ye sence he was took; they say he warned Patton 't warn't safe ter leave ye an' him tergether, kase he 'd do ye a damage, sure; they say he hev jes' gin ye up an' cast ye off."

"Laws-a-massy!" exclaimed the master of the house, upon this dramatic recital, "I dunno what ails Tom Toole, to sot hisself up ez better 'n Graffy Beale."

"I s'pose he thinks Graffy fotched all his troubles on him," said the black-bearded man dispassionately.

"Ef he hed a mind ter renounce ye he oughter hev done it a-fust," declared the old codger. "Then he 'd 'a' been cl'ar o' blame an' trouble too. That's like Tom Toole — do all he kin fur a-body, an' grudge it arterward. But law! we hain't got time to be a-talkin' 'bout sech ez that. The folks air on the floor agin, standin' up ter dance. They all look powerful peart, an' spry, an' straight, don't they?" He admiringly surveyed the two rows of rosy-faced young rustics through the gleaming haze of dust. "I'm mightily afeard, though, that hell is a-gapin' fur 'em."

"Shucks! They're young yit," said the black-bearded man, too leniently for the "perfessin' member" and anti-dancing theorist that he was.

"Jes' fryin' size, I'm thinkin'," chuckled the old fellow. "Play up, Graffy; gin 'em a good chune ter dance ter the devil by. That's edzactly whar ye air all bound fur," he added, raising his voice, as he leaned through the open door and admonished the young people with a gesticulatory, skinny forefinger. "Play up, Graffy, an' let 'em dance ter the devil."

So Graffy played up.

The freshness of dawn and dew was in the air when he was tramping along the turnpike. Only by degrees the fences on either hand detached themselves from the dense gloom. The sad, gray light made day seem hardly less drear than darkness. But in the distance a purple mass, which he knew was Fort Despair, slowly outlined itself against a faintly roseate suffusion in the east, that was deepening and reddening all along the horizon. Suddenly it expanded into a myriad of divergent lines, that shot up into the sky, quivering from red into the purest gold, then into a dazzling white effulgence that the eye might not gaze upon. The birds burst into song, the wind rose, and for a mile throughout the level country he could see the jagged line of the works take the first benedictory touch of the sun.

Perhaps it was the matutinal purity and peace that rested upon the land, less like holiness than forgiveness, which revived in him a yearning to which he thought he had grown callous. He watched for a long time, from the opposite bank of the river, the smoke stealing timorously up from Tom Toole's log-cabin, and when the first wagoner of the day came down the turnpike and hallooed lustily for the ferryman, he, too, went to the water's edge and waited for the boat.

"I'll be fixed nigher arter this, an' kin hear folks call," said the new ferryman apologetically to the teamster. "Tom Toole gits out 'n his house terday, an' I gits in termorrow. Mighty ill-convenient it's been fur me at my brother's place, way down yander round the bend."

When Graffy had trudged up the steep bank, he paused and laid his hand on Toole's door; then he looked back over his shoulder at the cruel old redoubt, with its flaunting flowers, its darting birds, and the grace of the sunshine upon it. The memory of all that had come and gone swept over him tumultuously, and he turned away without a sign.

He vacillated when he was again in the road; he glanced at the house; he turned toward it; once more he turned away, shaking his head tremulously and smiting his hands together.

He was sitting, when at last Toole opened the door, on a rock beside the milestone, mowing and grimacing at the house like an ugly dream. The burly master of the cabin stood staring, his tawny head unkempt, his great beard streaming tangled upon his breast, a lowering, dogged, dangerous look usurping the surprise in his eyes.

But the sight of Toole intensified the longing that had seemed to wear itself out in the hardships of prison and the loneliness and despair of the old powder-magazine. Now it asserted its redoubled force.

"Oh, Tom," quavered Graffy, extending his long, deft fingers that were unnaturally white, too, "I hev kem hyar ter shake hands with ye afore ye goes away. Ye hev done too much fur me ter grudge me that. I never knowed how 't would end — fur *her* — no more 'n ye did. What ye hev done, an' tried ter do fur me, air wuth all my life's work, an' more, too, — more, too."

"Yer life's work!" cried Toole bitterly. "Yer life's work air them two graves what ye hev holped ter fill. When ye gits ter studyin' 'bout me, go look at them."

And he shut the door.

CHAPTER XIX.

THE great sun that went down over the vast sweeps of the battle-field, and slipped into the dawning day lying in wait beyond the wide horizon, had a potent solemnity and majestic breadth of effect, which were lacking in the sunsets of the mountains, despite their melancholy. Here all nature besides was subordinate to the everlasting hills. The dark, mysterious, heavily-wooded Cumberland spurs cancelled the rest of the universe. They piled, one above another, their long, craggy, horizontal barriers against the clouds, and limited the infinite sky. The sun was dragged down beyond them before the day was done, leaving the afternoon valley dominated by their moody shadows. Diana and her hounds had an up-hill jog of it, till they could slip her silver leash on the purple heights, and course after the fleeing darkness through the wild world of ravine and cliff, roaring cataract and placid lick, tangled woods and scanty clearing.

For it was a wild world, so rugged and primeval of aspect that it might seem it was not made for man. The impression humanity left here was slight, discordant, — only an alien incongruity foisted upon the scene. The savage fastnesses were a wilderness still, although the gay, flimsy, many-galleried buildings of a summer hotel tectered on the verge of a frowning precipice. A cataract, that dashed headlong down the gorge, charged with some thunderous message to the forests, gave it voice, overwhelming with its sonorous periods the flippant chatter of bevies of young girls, who, attended by few and highly-prized cavaliers, drank of the chalybeate water bubbling out from the neighboring cliffs. The cicada sang deep into the night. Myriads of fire-flies quivered over the inaccessible heights of the looming black mountain opposite, whence one might hear the wildcat shriek, while the band in the ball-room was playing a waltz, and the throb of dancing feet kept time to the rhythmic strain. Nowhere had nature and art demonstrated an affinity save in the fresh, delicious fragrance of mint which lurked alike among the abysses and on the piazzas, and rooted in the mind a deep, immovable faith that somewhere there was a julep in the air.

It was an infinitely tame world to John Fortescue.

"This is the length of my tether," he was in the habit of saying, with an air of resignation. He felt that there was a certain inappropriateness in the presence of a man of his stamp and pretension at an obscure little watering-place like Bandusia Springs, for its halcyon days preceded by ten years the present summer, when it was timorously entering upon its first season since the war. Only the fact of important litigation in Graftenburg, which might be favorably compromised at any time, and necessitate his return thither within twelve hours at a call from his counsel, might explain how he could reconcile himself to the flat and spiritless conditions of existence here.

The place seemed the paradise of connubiality. It was overrun with children, whose health was understood to be fostered by mountain air and mineral water. The rocks everywhere echoed their shrill clamor. Perambulators occupied the plank walks, to the confusion and exclusion of pedestrians. The society was largely composed of sober, unimaginative Benedicts, who could evolve no more original idea of life than the routine of talking politics in the morning, driving out in the afternoon, each with his own wife, and gracing the whitewashed walls of the ball-room in the evening, solemnly watching the young people dance. Of these young people, the ladies were in their teens; their partners, callow collegians, — callow enough to be conscious of their fledgling state, and to entertain a self-immolating admiration of Mr. Fortescue, a man who had progressed so far up the scale of being, and who was so handsomely schooled by experience, as to care nothing for the eventful balls at Bandusia. He might hear only the vague swing of the waltz music in the distance, while he consoled his loneliness in the billiard-room by fancy shots that made even the thoroughly-seasoned attendant stare. For they were wonderful. Sometimes the youth of Bandusia stood around the table and looked on, feeling effaced the while, since Fortescue, although the centre of a crowd, skilfully preserved the manner of being alone, cognizant only of his own presence. He would have no opponent to quake before those marvellous runs and stand aghast at his "nursing," so delicate and dextrous that it rivalled the zealous coddling of the infants at connubial Bandusia; for, somewhat contemptuously, it is true, he recognized the adolescence of his spectators.

"I should like to take a game with you, Mr. Fortescue," said a young sprig, one day, rendered reckless by that potent elixir, chalybeate.

Fortescue glanced up quickly, his cue poised above the table, and the attitude displaying his fine, lithe figure to great advantage. "My good young friend," he exclaimed presently, "you discredit my humanity."

But there came a day when Fortescue's humanity was lightly esteemed at Bandusia. That exuberance of notoriety in which he had flourished in New Orleans, and which had so vexed the sensitive soul of Maurice Brennett, had been checked by the narrow restrictions of life here. He seemed to the casual observer only a quiet gentleman, who, by reason of a long absence abroad, had become unacclimated to his native New Orleans, and, pending the adjustment of business affairs, sojourned in these salubrious mountains. Now and then accident threw him into the heavy company of the other quiet gentlemen of the place. Under the stress of his exile from his own accustomed sphere he was for a time as lethargic as he deemed them. But the singular fascination which he was wont to exert upon other men began, even in this trance-like existence, to unconsciously assert its power. His interest was half dormant, and he did not notice, until it grew very marked, the preference for his conversation which had been developed by one of the party, a man of considerable prominence in business and social circles, of some mental and colloquial activity, but a heavy weight physically. They became familiar associates after Fortescue's discovery of this predilection. They talked away long, idle hours, as they lay at length on some fern-covered slope, and watched the distant mountains changing in the sunset from purest azure to an illusory, amethystine tint that was itself a poem. They smoked many a meditative cigar in the observatory, a mere skeleton of a building, perched on the verge of a sheer precipice. In company they visited the stables, where, however, Mr. Fortescue exhibited more zeal and knowledge concerning horse-flesh in general than interest in his new acquaintance's sober, fat, sleek family trotters; they cemented their friendship in the domestic circle, and he decorously accepted the position of a friend of the family. Often the two were together until late at night in Fortescue's room. It was at some little distance from the fair and flaunting hotel, and situated in a dark, unlovely, unpainted building, which was consigned to the use of the bachelor fraternity, and grimly called "St. Paul's." But, although still vulnerable to malice, the bachelors were out of earshot of the babies.

Strange rumors concerning these vigils got afloat somehow. Certain cabalistic words drifted through the open windows to belated strollers in the woods below. But the suspicions which seemed too grotesque for fact were merged in certainty when a couple of the callow youngsters, going out betimes on some mountain excursion, chanced to encounter this elderly wight as he emerged from Mr. Fortescue's room. The first sad, pale glimmer of dawn was straggling through the high, unwashed window of the narrow hall and fell upon his puffy, red face, that, despite its superabundant flesh, had a rigidity of aspect. His eyes were bloodshot; his gait a trifle unsteady; he recoiled from the stare of the bewildered boys as if he had received a blow in the face. Through the open door streamed the soft lamplight, and in its midst was Fortescue, fresh, flushed, triumphant, a pack of cards in his hands, a decanter and a couple of glasses on the table by which he stood, a bottle or two rolling empty on the floor beneath it, and a tense vibration of elation in his voice.

"Your revenge, Colonel, whenever you like," he was saying. "I can't sympathize, you know. Good morning, gentlemen;" and *his* eye fell unabashed on the passers-by. "But I offer you all the comfort in revenge — that you can get."

And so it came about that the "Colonel," instead of

paying his board-bills, was obliged to borrow the money of another Colonel who kept the hotel, to take his family and himself home in the dog-days.

And all Bandusia was agog.

Although Fortescue thus contributed much to the entertainment and excitement of the place, his own idiosyncrasies had not with himself the force of novelty, and proved less edifying. Bereft of the diversion of this new friendship, his days grew dull. One afternoon he was so far reduced as to share a petty interest that swayed all Bandusia at this hour: when the cliffs began to echo the mellow resonance of the stage-horn from the foot of the mountain, and the arrival of the coach, the great event of the day, was expected. With his cue in his hand, he leaned out of the window of the billiard-room and gazed far down the bosky recesses of the precipitous slopes where, now and then, a gap in the foliage gave glimpses of the winding road. The purple splendor of the sunset glorified the distant mountain-summits; they glowed transfigured, like the heights of heaven. Below, all along the coves and ravines, and in the heavily-timbered valley, skulked the dusky shadows of the coming night, like troglodytes emerging from the cavernous earth. A mist sifted through the chasms. Among the wild tangles of "the laurel," a cow-bell jangled faintly. The cicada's song grew loud. The pungent fragrance of the humble herbs, nestling by the waterside, drifted by on the air that throbbed responsive to every eloquent apostrophe of the declamatory cataract. Human voices rose thence after a time, for the rocks below the fall had been made by immemorial custom a resting-place for those able-bodied passengers who were constrained, either by the tyranny of the stage-driver or motives of compassion for his horses, to walk up the mountain. Something in one of these voices struck John Fortescue as singularly familiar — something *ore rotundo*, something indicative of a benignity of patronage, as it descanted on the sublimity of the scenery; it convinced him that Colonel Walter Percy had, for the present, forsworn condescending to his fellow-men, and had come to pat Nature on the back for a while. Thus the sight of the old man, pompously trudging along in advance of the vehicle, the dust of his journey thick on his hot red face, his linen duster, his big Panama hat, and dimming the lustre of his silver hair and beard, was no surprise to the sybarite who, cool and clean, looked down from the giddy heights of the billiard-room on the summit of the crags, waved his hand, and shouted out a welcome.

Colonel Percy glanced up and bowed in response with as much dignity as it is in human anatomy to bow upward vertically. Then the clustering leaves enveloped him and hid him from sight. Presently a heavy tread on the steps of the billiard-room announced that he had taken the short cut thither. "I knew you were at Bandusia," he said, as he held out his hand. "I heard something to that effect; yes, I heard so when I was in Graftenburg — the city."

Fortescue supplemented the fact of his presence with the story of his involved interests, and the tyranny of his counsel in reeling out so little line. "I find it dull as the grave here. But for the fear of yellow fever I should as soon be in New Orleans, deserted though it is."

"Why, — my — dear — sir!" exclaimed the old man, with a supreme ridicule that might well become a medical authority, striving to dispel the vaporings of an ignorant superstition, "believe me, you can have the yellow fever but once. It is not in human nature to do that thing *twice*. Not in human nature. No, sir!"

Fortescue's face changed suddenly. He stared blankly at his interlocutor, as if some strong surprise or doubt lurked within him. It was only thus suggested. In a moment he turned lightly to the table, bent down, and with an airy stroke of the cue sent a red ball glowing across the green cloth.

"And you think once isn't enough, eh?" said the elderly joker, continuing to twinkle upon him with the affable superiority of rallying laughter. "Let me see — that was in '39 — terrible epidemic! I was going down, by invitation, to your father's place for safety — Paturin — yes, the plantation — met a runner to stop me — the fever had appeared in the family — yes — you, and your sister Estelle, and your mother, and — let me see — no — no — your father had it before — years before. They had my sympathy — my dearest sympathy. I wrote to them. I did write. But I pledge you my honor I accepted no more invitations to Paturin for a season. Cure means future exemption. *You* need never shun New Orleans."

But Fortescue, still knocking the balls about on the table, said that nevertheless he *was* afraid. And when he lifted his face he looked afraid.

The old gentleman, however, was now absorbed in a budget of envelopes, which he drew slowly and magisterially from his pocket, closely scanning the superscription of each. "I had the pleasure, sir," he said, detaching his attention with difficulty from the papers, "of meeting — before I quitted Graftenburg — a gentleman — ah, is this it? — no — a gentleman who has some connection with you in business matters. He sought an introduction to me through the kind offices of — of — what have I here? — of Mr. Maurice Brennett."

Once more Fortescue's manner and attitude changed.

That strong, fully vitalized look was in his eyes again. Its spirit was expressed in every gesture. "Is Mr. Brennett in Graftenburg?" he asked eagerly, disregardful of the vague gentleman who had business with him, and who had apparently sent him some token which Colonel Percy was striving to separate from the chaos of his own correspondence.

"He was there only for a day," Colonel Percy answered, still dexterously shuffling his letters as if he were stocking cards; "let me see,— the day of his encounter with Mr. Travis."

"An encounter with Travis!" Fortescue exclaimed sharply.

The old man's hands were still, and he looked up, laughing with a sort of cumbrous slyness.

"Aha! you see, when you tell the world good-by, and say, 'I have done with you,— you baking, broiling planet, — I go for my good pleasure to the cool retreat of sylvan shades,'— the first whiff of a mundane sensation makes you quite ready to get back into the frying-pan and stand the temperature for the sake of the company,— take a hand, as it were, in this little sublunary game, which we call life. Chip along,— yes, chip along."

Somehow the propinquity of Mr. Fortescue suggested this wicked phrasing, and the old man repeated it with the relish of feeling in a degree up to snuff. "Chip along — yes. Well, sir; well, they contrived to keep this altercation out of the papers,— the public prints. Still it was notorious. Deeply regretted by the friends of both gentlemen — although Mr. Brennett was popularly held blameless in the matter. Blameless. But, in fact, he is a blameless man."

"Emphatically," assented Fortescue; there was, however, so strong an expression of irony in his curving upper lip that perhaps he himself became conscious of this lapse of facial control, for he drew down the long ends of his auburn mustache as he continued with his gracious air. "Let me remind you that you have not yet told me the story."

"Aha! the frying-pan is pretty interesting, eh? — you would like to hear a little more of the sizzle and sputter? Well, sir, — well, — let me see." Colonel Percy hesitated, looking meditatively upward, his sheaves of papers in either hand, and slightly balancing himself alternately on the heels and toes of his boots, which creaked pleasantly with the motion. "They met in the office of some hotel in Graftenburg, — the city, you know. Travis made an effort to strike Brennett in the face, without a moment's warning. In the face, sir, in the face. Brennett caught his arm, tried to quiet him, demanded an explanation. Travis stated that he wished to strike him for the purpose of forcing a challenge, when he would take the utmost pleasure in shooting Mr. Brennett."

This suggestion seemed to please Fortescue. He laughed out buoyantly, gayly, irrepressibly, boyishly. Then he leaned forward, half supporting himself on his cue, so eager a listener that Colonel Percy felt all the stimulus of oratory and an audience.

"Well, sir, — well, the altercation came about from this cause: — Travis accused Brennett of having, with interested motives, set his creditors on him, — the usurers, you know. Usurious money-lenders. It seems that Travis's affairs here in Tennessee were much involved, aside from his mining interests in the West, which I understand were hopelessly embarrassed. Nevertheless, Mr. Brennett bought out these interests, assuming of course their liabilities, and with the money thus furnished Travis was enabled to make a satisfactory compromise with his creditors here, and retain a handsome surplus. Generous of Brennett, eh? Generous?"

"Characteristically generous," Fortescue agreed.

"But Travis, although he was reconciled personally, and apologized for his violence, was not satisfied. He declared openly that Brennett had 'skinned' him. That was the expression he used. Skinned. Still he sailed for Liverpool, — without his cuticle, I presume, — last Monday."

He glanced at his companion, expectant of a bravo for this jest, but Fortescue's attention had failed mid-way. He had fallen suddenly into deep, absorbed thought. He understood all this in a sense of which Colonel Percy, wise as he was, did not dream. So Brennett, at some comparatively trifling outlay, had contrived to double his stake. The future profits and prospects of the mine were secured for himself alone, in case the compromise with Miss St. Pierre should be effected and the debt cleared away with the funds thus secured, for Fortescue could easily divine that Travis had sold, too, all the interest in the Graftenburg property which he had bought of the claimant. No doubt, deceived as to the probability of a compromise, and heavily harassed by Brennett's clever maneuvres with his creditors, Travis was easily pacified with a little ready money, and content to make off with his meagre pickings in lieu of the full feast he had expected. Brennett was a wonderful fellow! No hint of all this to his coadjutor, no word, no letter. The compromise was imminent, and doubtless Brennett feared that because of this he would be bled as he was wont to bleed others.

The darkness had come at last. The mountain in the distance, sad and sombre of aspect, doubly bereaved as one dropped again to earth from the ecstasies of a vision, touched with its jagged purple summit the last faint greenish line of light in the sky. The lamps were glimmering in their places against the unplastered, unpainted walls, and the soft yellow radiance brought out the rich tints of the maple and the cedar and the walnut and the oak, which in their rude, undressed state made this building so primitive, so sylvan, that it seemed still nearly allied to the trees of its kindred standing in the forest without. The pallid mist pressed close to the broad windows; sometimes it shifted through in a ghostly, elusive fashion.

As Fortescue leaned against the window-frame, he was laughing a little; it was a low laugh of elation.

Colonel Percy suddenly faced round upon him.

"John Fortescue," he said impressively, "you lost something on the battlefield of Chattalla."

The man received the words with a palpable shock. It quivered through every fibre, and blanched his face, and shook his laugh to a husky mutter. He turned with a stony stare.

"My life!" he cried out shrilly. "I lost my life!"

A tiny package that Colonel Percy had drawn from his vest-pocket fell from his nerveless clasp and rolled away on the floor, while he stood as one petrified.

The moon was dim and the wind came up the gorge. The sudden gust tore away the fantastic white mists from the window, and the uncertain light fell through the shivering rifts and traced upon the floor a dusky outline of the serrated leaves and acorns of the chestnut-oaks without. Perhaps it was well for John Fortescue at that moment that the convulsive motion of the boughs dashed into his face their wealth of dew, cold and fragrant, and with all the freshness and strength of the woods distilled into it. When he drew out his handkerchief and brushed it away, he brushed away other drops, colder and clammy, which had started from within, and his long sigh of physical relief was blended with a groan as of mental anguish.

The commonplace gesture restored Colonel Percy's normal self-possession. He stooped with difficulty, regained the package, and, as his fingers curled around it, he felt that he had mastered the situation.

"The lady's letter to the lawyer suggested as much," he said, with the stiff pomposity of a conscious appreciation of delicate matters.

"The lady's letter to the lawyer?" Fortescue echoed tremulously.

The old man nodded gravely. "She spoke properly — the lady did — quite properly, in fact. She said that in finding this trinket on the battle-field she was aware that it must be of great worth to its owner from association — its character being that of some loved one's gift. A gift, — yes. Therefore she was willing to retain it no longer, although she was as yet unable to decide as to the matters of business touching which your counsel had approached her. She states," he continued, drawing from an envelope some flimsy sheets, which fluttered in the breeze, "that she intends to write again soon to her legal adviser who, for some reason, did not reply to her former communication, and she hopes then to — to — ah yes, — this is the lady's letter to the lawyer."

He adjusted his spectacles and strove to read. "Ah well, sir — well — your eyes are younger than mine — you see she fails to say anything whatever touching the intrinsic value of this gift — this trinket — which she sends by express to you, in care of your lawyers, as she is ignorant of your address. It is in a sealed packet. Sealed — hermetically sealed. And your lawyers are cautious fellows. Very prudent. They say a 'trinket' may be diamonds and may be oroide. They decline the responsibility of forwarding it by mail. There is no express to Bandusia. No express. None. So they beg of Brennett to introduce them to me. 'As you are going, my dear Colonel, will you be so very good'—And I am always very good— So, you see, I have the pleasure—pleasure, I am sure—"

He paused expectant. But Fortescue had forgotten the elaborate courtesy that so well graced his splendid presence. He did not even thank Colonel Percy, who felt that for his friend's behoof he had done much in waiving his dignity and fetching parcels like a common carrier. As Fortescue hastily tore the papers enveloping the package, his breath was quick, his hand unsteady, and when the locket, that the girl had found in the empty grave on the battle-field, lay exposed to view, encrusted with clay, tarnished, stained too by some dark current, and jangling from the bit of watch-chain cut smoothly off by the bullet, which had gone close to the heart of the man who had worn it there, he winced with a shocked recognition so unmistakable, so simple in its expression that it touched Colonel Percy into momentary forgetfulness of his own importance.

This was what he had lost, and, so strangely, he called it his life! Once more in dwelling upon it the old man was bewildered, mystified. But after all, he thought, with a not unkindly accession of sentiment, are not the feelings we cherish for others, for even the inanimate things they have hallowed, the most vital principle of life, the essence of existence — worthier of the name than the involuntary functions of the lungs or the merely animal mechanism of the heart?

He was satisfied with his own explanation. He could not understand, and he did not stay to ponder on, the change that usurped this look when the spring of the lid gave way suddenly in Fortescue's hand — as it had given way in Antoinette's hand when she stood by that yawning empty grave in the haunted thicket.

Fortescue glanced hastily at the hair beneath the shattered crystal; then he held up the burnished lid to the light, and read the words engraved within, —

John Doane Fortescue
from
"Adelaide."

The intent curiosity in his gesture and eyes immolated every other suggestion of his face and figure. After a moment it was supplemented by surprise, by a vague doubt, even by a grave and gathering fear.

But the old man was turning away. Fortescue, observing the motion, silently offered his hand, which was silently accepted. Then, thrusting his hat upon his head, he went out from the flickering flare of the lamps into the dark encompassing wilderness.

The wind was laid. The silvery impalpable mists contended with the silvery impalpable moonbeams. Together in a splendid sheen they hung about the little observatory that quivered over the dark chasms below. It quaked even more beneath Fortescue's weight as he strode within it and threw himself, panting and exhausted, on one of the benches.

"And who the devil was 'Adelaide'?" he muttered.

Then he fell silent again, and for a long time he did not move.

He might have heard, yet he did not hear, the music in the ball-room that told of the tide of enjoyment, rising gradually from sober lancers to waltz, to the culminating gayety of the wild Virginia reel, then ebbing away at last in the sentimental measures of "Home, Sweet Home."

He might have seen, yet he did not see, the orange-tinted points of light as they disappeared one by one from the rows of windows till the wilderness knew no gleam but that of the pallid moon which had waxed and waned here when the savage fastnesses first rose from the sea.

More than once he turned his eyes toward the west, where the sombre summit of the distant mountain, rising above the illusory vapors, was sharply outlined against the midnight sky. Beyond that mountain lay the nearest railroad.

The moon went down behind it. The mists closed more densely about him. The night grew chill, and because of this, perhaps, when he chanced to slip his hand in his pocket and it suddenly touched the locket, which he had thrust away there, he shivered.

CHAPTER XX.

A FERVID Fourth-of-July sun was blazing in the sky, and Chattalla responded, for the first time since the war, with a celebration of the day. That favorite rural diversion, a barbecue, had been projected, and certain optimistic souls, spending the day thus in the forest beside a flowing rivulet, drinking of its crystal clear water, flavored with mint and dashed with "Robertson County," grew patriotic enough by degrees to declare that it was altogether like the good old times, and "damn the bloody chasm." The disaffected absentees who remained in the town were of opinion that it was a "mighty pore little Fourth," for Independence Day was here represented only by a banner on the court-house, hanging motionless in the sultry air, and all the "underfoot trash" of the village, white and black, rioting in fire-crackers and small explosions of gunpowder.

The ringleader of this motley juvenile assemblage was Pickie Tait. How he came by so large a quantity of powder was then, and afterward remained, a mystery. When, through its agency, disaster was developed, there was some speculation on the subject. Very possibly he stole the money to buy it from the drawer in which his father kept the change taken in at the toll-gate; or he might have stolen the powder itself from the store where he had "done yerrands" for a week, and in that time had contrived to perpetrate more mischief than could be rectified in six. He never divulged the source of his secret supplies, and his silence baffled conjecture. As the morning waned he went home to dinner, and the town heard no more from him till late in the day.

At the barracks the patriotism was of a somewhat more glittering and imposing quality, and there was martial music and a dress parade. It was a great relief to Estwicke when it was all over, for every distraction grated on his preoccupied thoughts. He mounted his horse and galloped aimlessly away in the lingering sunset, glad of the solitude and the woodland quiet, and finding in the swift motion some expression for his impatient spirit.

He had determined to make General Vayne's position as difficult as possible, and continued to visit the family as heretofore, divining that a man who held hospitality as a sacred obligation would flinch at the idea of forbidding him the house, and resolved that, unless this extreme measure were resorted to, he would see Marcia as often as he might. Now and then he had a twinge of self-reproach for thus making use of this fantastic view of the duties of a house-owner to persuade his host's daughter to marry him without her father's consent. But what could he do? Must he tamely give up the woman he loved, and who loved him, because, forsooth, her father was vaguely supposed to prefer another man? He swore that he would not, and he put his sensitive conscience down.

He carried his fierce moods there. Sometimes he bitterly upbraided Marcia with her broken promise. Sometimes it was almost a pleasure to him to know that, if he suffered, she too suffered. And then would come a great revulsion of feeling, and he would beg her with passionate tenderness to care for him no more, and protest that he was not worth one of her tears, and declare that, if she said the word, he would go away—he would go away and blow his brains out, and trouble her never again.

He had been more peremptory when he had last seen her. He had insisted that he must come to terms with this suspense; he could better endure despair. She must make her decision at once and forever. If she definitely gave him up, he would know how he stood; he would try to reconcile himself as best he might to the worthless conditions of his life. He might at least seek to make it of some value to others. He could go and fight the battles of his country with the Indians; he was still first-rate food for powder.

He had placed great hopes on this effort to coerce her from that neutral ground which she had striven to hold. But she had only cried and besought him not to be unhappy. And he had parted from her in anger.

To-day the horse had taken of his own accord the familiar, oft-travelled road, and checked the sweeping gallop only at her father's gate. Estwicke, roused from his absorption, realized where he was with momentary surprise. He had not intended to come, but now that he was here, he hesitated. Then he suddenly turned the horse aside, and went on slowly down the road along the river bank.

The green expanse of the battle-field lay before him, stretching to the horizon, and set, a gigantic, enamelled circle, in a circumference of gold and crimson clouds,— for the east was flushed with western reflections. The cows were coming home through the haunted thickets; the faint clangor of their bells reached him on the perfumed stillness. And in the midst of the shining river rose the massive piers of the old bridge, burned so long ago, leaving these great, useless, detached columns as still another reminder of the days of conflict.

As he glanced toward them Estwicke abruptly checked his pace. On the summit of the central pier was a small figure pottering about with an uncanny show of industry. A dug-out was tied to a bush that grew in a niche near the base; this showed how the boy had gone, and how he proposed to return. But what could he be doing?

"Now, that's odd," murmured Estwicke speculatively. "I have seen that boy there every day for a week."

A man was lying on the river bank with a crazy violin beside him, across which he now and then aimlessly drew a shuddering bow. Estwicke thought him a mowing idiot until he spoke. He was beginning to hold a long-range colloquy with the pigmy on the pier.

"Hello, Pickie!" he shouted in a convulsively chattering fashion. "What air ye up to?"

Pickie Tait turned his preternaturally solemn face toward his interlocutor.

"I'm up ter — *here!*" he replied.

Graffy changed the form of address.

"What be ye a-doin' of?"

"It's *me* that's killin' this here cat, — ye onderstand?" said Quick Pickie significantly.

"Ef ye war ter fall off'n that pier ye'd git yer head bruk," Graffy admonished him.

"'Tend ter yer own head — ye may find a use fur it some day," retorted Pickie.

The sound of the horse's hoofs as Estwicke approached diverted the man's attention. He turned, leaning upon his elbow, to see who might be passing, and the casual curiosity expressed in his glance intensified to a deep concentrated interest.

It was a somewhat brilliant apparition thus springing

up in the lonely country road. The young officer was gallantly mounted, and his blue uniform took the light like velvet. His bearing, surcharged with spirit and pride, and a certain challenging boldness in his eyes, suggested the phrase, "every inch a soldier."

There was a melancholy envy in the gaze that intently followed him till the jagged bluffs of the river bank interposed, and he disappeared. Then Graffy sighed — not because of the contrast with the mettlesome full-pulsed soldier, but the band at the barracks was the best in the service, and there rode a man who heard it every day. He took up his old violin and began to draw gently forth the vaguest echoes of crashing melodies, — souvenirs of his pilgrimages thither, where he had earned notoriety among the troops as the "damn fool who would tramp fourteen miles just to hear the band play a march." He was instantly aware when the regular dash of a paddle, growing momently more distinct, began to beat an accompaniment to his rhythmic recollections as they quivered along the string. But he was entranced with his own music, and gave no heed till his name was twice called in a nasal snuffling whine that was intended to be propitiatory.

The ragamuffin had come down from his airy perch, crossed the river in his dug-out, and run it upon the gravelly bank. Then he stood up in it, the paddle in his hand, and looked at the man from beneath his shapeless hat-brim with a blandishing expression in singular contrast with the cool impudence his dirty face had worn ten minutes ago. His tatters hung picturesquely about his skinny little limbs, and as he talked he placed one grimy, cut, and scarred bare foot upon the other, and thus clubbed he teetered forward and backward, as if this gesture were one of the accepted graces of cajolery.

"I kem over hyar," he remarked affably, although somewhat indistinctly, for he investigated, even as he spoke, the corners of his wide mouth and a row of jagged, squirrel teeth, with his large, deprecatory, red tongue, "I kem over hyar ter — ax ye — ef ye plissir — do me a — a favior!"

"I dunno ez I hev enny call ter do ye no faviors — sech a sassy critter ez ye be," said the musician, bending his head low to a series of deft touches.

Pickie looked up the river, then down the river, then high into the air, where he followed, as it were, a jay's flight with the widening motions of his mouth. Then he teetered forward, and with his former beguiling demonstrations he glanced up once more at the man.

"I hev got some fi'-crackers thar on the pier what I'm a-aimin' ter set off fur the Forf o' July, an' — an' — an' some gunpowder." Graffy lifted his head to look at the boy, who suddenly became embarrassed. He succeeded in clubbing his feet together more tightly, and thus inspired, he speciously explained. "A *leetle* gun-powder wropped up in a piece o' newspaper. An' I'm a-feard ter leave 'em thar whilst I skedadles home fur some candle wick fur a fuse, 'kase them Peters boys will raid on 'em, an' set 'em off tharselfs fur the Forf o' July. An' I hev got the fi'-crackers all stuck round in the rocks, an' I don't want ter — ter — unfix 'em, an' tote 'em off with me. So I 'lowed ez mebbe ye 'd git inter the dug-out, an' scoot over thar, an' sot on the pier whilst I'm gone. Them sly, sneaky Peters boys mought kem up on t' other side, an' ye could n't see 'em from hyar."

He stepped nimbly out of the dug-out, and waited for the man to signify his assent, but Graffy still delicately and deftly touched the instrument, and Pickie at last was fain to start off at a shambling gait, looking over his shoulder now and then to make sure that Graffy would relent toward him as of old. Presently the rocks intervened, but when the river next came into view he saw the dug-out in mid-stream and nearing the pier.

When Graffy had climbed it, which was no difficult matter, for some of the stones had fallen away, leaving crevices and jagged edges, he was surprised to see on the summit deep rifts into the interior.

"This hyar old pier ain't haffen ez solid ez ye might think ter look at it. More'n likely cannon-balls or su'thin' must hev hit it an' jarred it powerful in the old war times."

He looked down at the puerile preparations for noise — the fire-crackers set around in chinks in the mortar, a tin canister, flaring and empty, and a little roll of newspaper which he supposed contained the powder.

Then he seated himself and gazed silently upon the landscape.

It was all very still. Far away for a moment he heard the metallic jangle of trace-chains as some laborer jogged homeward on his plough-horse through the peaceful battle-field. A pair of mocking-birds fluttered back to their nest in a niche in the old pier, the male circling about the head of the motionless figure on the summit, and striking boldly at it. Then arose the shrill, vibrating clamor of the nestlings, and presently a line of light down the river marked the swift flight of the white wing-feathers of the little freeholder, still on provident thoughts intent. Graffy peered over to see the mother-bird hovering about her brood. "Ye air mighty nigh neighbors ter Pickie, I'm afeard," he said, with melancholy forecast. Then once more there was no sound — and no motion save the silent shifting of he crimson and purple clouds and of their gorgeous reflections in the deep water below.

The subject never far from his thoughts had returned now. In these days, with his untutored intellect, his narrow experience, his poignant conscience, the man who had been accused and acquitted, sought to sift the evidence and weigh the argument. He was wont to lie in wait for the witnesses who had testified in his trial, forcing from them the story they had already told under oath, and waiving their half-angry, half-startled remonstrance with the breathless protest, "I hev furgot — I hev furgot — 'T war all so suddint — an' so much come arterward." In like manner he once stopped the judge, presenting a clumsy disguise of the circumstances, and begging an opinion on a "p'int o' law." When the judge instantly stripped them of their fictitious integuments, detecting his purpose, and admonishing him to rest satisfied of the justice of his acquittal, he burst forth suddenly, "Your little court and the jury's say-so don't seem ter hender me none now." He smote his breast. "I hev jes' come ter jedgmint!"

Perhaps it was well that his ragged following of street urchins and shiftless loafers would not let him and his crazy old fiddle be, and that it was exacted of him as an imperative public duty to play at all the rustic merry-makings. Thus intervals, such as this when he sat alone and idle on the old pier, were rare. Now, in his ignorant fashion, he was reviewing the prosecuting officer's speech, weighing the fierce phrases as he muttered them. The cogent arguments of a man trained to debate had given voice to his dumb conscience. The trite truculence had for him all the actuality of doom. Once he rose to his feet, and with a violent gesture unconsciously imitated the muscular oratory of the Criminal Court as he mouthed the extravagant denunciations which had been forgotten long ago by the mild man who had first uttered them.

The muffled sound of hoofs pacing slowly on the grassy margin of the road restored Graffy to a sudden realization of the present. Captain Estwicke had wheeled his horse, and was riding back along the river bank. Under his intent, astonished scrutiny Graffy was painfully deprecatory; he mechanically laid hold on his violin. As he began to draw forth the strains of a melodious country-side song, he heard the plash of oars keeping time to the music. Presently the shrill voices of children broke on the air, singing,—

> "When I lived down in Tennessee,
> U-li-*ah!* U-li-*ee!*
> Beneath the wild banana tree,
> U-li-*ah!* U-li-*ee!*"

There were five or six urchins, black, white, and yellow, in the approaching skiff, all in imminent danger of a watery grave under Pickie Tait's guidance. But the tipsy craft reeled safely to the bank, and landed all but Quick Pickie, who then rowed across to the pier. He climbed it like a squirrel, and as he scuffled up on the summit he looked at Graffy with a triumphant grin on his broad, dirty face. It suddenly turned white beneath its grime. Graffy had filled his pipe, and was kindling it with a match which he flung aside still blazing. Its pale flicker disappeared as it dropped into a deep rift in the masonry, and a wild, incoherent protest from the boy rang out across the water.

Estwicke heard it. His eyes, following the sound, turned absently upon the great obeliscal pier, outlined in sombre tints against the gold and purple splendors still flaunting through the western sky. All at once there sprang into their midst an ethereal, corollated, crimson presence like some great evanescent flower of flame. Shooting through it, high into the air, were strange black projectiles. A sulphurous cloud of smoke surged over the placid waters, and far along the peaceful battle-field rang a mighty sound as if the very foundations of the earth were rent asunder.

And in an instant the flower of flame was gone as suddenly as it had bloomed. The smoke and the wind, in an airy embrace, swept together down the river. Here and there on the face of the current an ever-widening circle of golden light described its elastic periphery above the heavy masses of masonry that had fallen into the shining depths.

And with its jagged edges and maimed proportions, grotesquely defined against the calm sky, was the great pier, the right side torn away, leaving the other of a taller aspect. On its summit lay a writhing little figure.

The momentary silence that followed the report was broken with a shrill, quavering, wail of pain, terrible to hear.

The half dozen urchins on the bank were looking with frightened, deprecatory eyes at Estwicke as he flung himself from his horse.

"'T war n't us that done it," they cried in chorus. "'T war Pickie Tait. That's him a-hollerin' up there now. He had a fuse what he war goin' ter fix ter light, an' he laid off ter git away quicker 'n he done. But Graffy Beale drapped a match thar. *'T war n't us!*"

Two or three ploughmen returning from work came clattering down on their horses to join the little group at the water's edge.

"Graffy an' Quick Pickie?" said one.

"Well; they've blown themselves into Kingdom-Come this time, I reckon."

"We must get them away at once," exclaimed Estwicke, hastily tearing off his coat. "That pier is badly shaken. It may come down and crush them."

"Hold on a minit, Cap'n," said one of the men. "Then I'll go along o' ye — though it's skeery under them shattered rocks, I tell ye. Still, if they hain't got no more powder 'mongst 'em, I'm willin' ter resk thar fallin' down on me."

"Don't try it jes' *now*, Cap'n," said another burly fellow. "I'll bet that leetle scamp hev got that thar pier ez full o' powder ez an aig o' meat. Hold on a minit an' I'll go too when I'm sati'fied thar's nothin' thar likely ter explode. Any way ter die but that."

The horror of being blown into the air, dismembered and torn, was upon Estwicke with a terrible realization. He hesitated; but once more the child's woeful shriek, with all its cadenced anguish, rang out. And he flung himself into the water. He swam rapidly to the base of the pier, although the time seemed long to those who stood in suspense, watching him through the blue twilight which was softly slipping down upon the earth from the blue sky. He deftly climbed the jagged column and, as he neared the still figure of the man, he put out his hand and touched it. Then he spoke to the boy. From the bank they could not hear the words, but the sound of his voice came over the water. There were gentle suggestions in the tones, and after that the woeful shrieks were stilled. Even the distance did not disguise the careful tenderness with which he took the writhing, quivering creature in his arms. And suddenly, once more a-bloom in the blue twilight was that evanescent flower of flame. From among its fiery petals the black projectiles were flying upward — fallen instantly. And the red flower was withered. When the smoke cleared away the pier was a shapeless pile of stone hardly rising above the surface of the river, and the two men and the boy were gone.

It seemed a miracle to those who dragged them out of the water that there should be a spark of life retained in Pickie Tait's mangled little body. And even that pulpy mass of agonies which they knew as Graffy Beale was yet all a-quiver. They could not judge whether Estwicke's injuries were less serious. There were evidences of broken bones, he was insensible, and he bore some deep gashes and ghastly bruises that were unpleasant to look at. They carried him to the nearest house, which was the little log cabin by Fort Despair, and, when the physicians arrived, popular awe was increased by the professional utterance. After an examination they said, in consultation, that his left clavicle was fractured, and the joint of the scapula dislocated, and to the staring simple folks it seemed that no gentleman who had such things inside of him could be expected to survive. One of his ribs was broken and his left arm shattered in two places.

"Pretty bad fracture,— that arm,— I reckon," suggested the local physician.

"Ah—I guess so—I guess so," assented the post-surgeon, who had been summoned by telegram. "It's— ah—um—humerus"— with a meditative smile —"humerus—don't you know."

A great country lout who was assisting in the quality of curious spectator, stepped suddenly out of the room with a surly, lowering brow.

"I'd like ter beat that derned Yank inter a jelly," he declared to a crony outside. "Mighty funny ter *him*, I reckon. '*Humorous*'—hey!" with a sardonic sneer. "He wouldn't think it was 'humorous' long if *I* hed a crack at him."

For this episode had roused an intense local sympathy

for Captain Estwicke, and the feeling widened and deepened when all the circumstances were duly set forth in the Marston "Daily Chronicle." Not every day does a man of "quality" risk his life to succor humble folks, and the reporter, who felt himself destined for better things than writing up dog-fights and ward politicians, made the most of the opportunity. It afforded as broad a scope as an obituary. In fact, it was quite as satisfactory to the reporter as if Captain Estwicke had really died. It enabled him to dwell upon the generosities of character intimated as well as that passion of courage illustrated. It admitted of biographical detail which the enterprising representative of the paper gleaned in abundance at the barracks from Estwicke's brother officers, who were peculiarly eager, anxious, and enthusiastic. If their comrade had bravely encountered death and danger and paid the forfeit of serious wounds upon some stricken field, they would have held it an obvious duty and accorded varying degrees of soldierly commendation. But to have disastrous dealings with gunpowder out of the regular line of business seemed to these men of the sword abnormally daring and intrinsically heroic.

The reporter found much geniality housed in the unsubstantial white buildings with their flimsy galleries that shook beneath his tread. A potent nicotian fragrance permeated the air, as if it were geographically appurtenant to the spot — like the resinous odor of piney woods or the briny flavor of a sea-breeze. A veteran of the late war told some stirring stories with effect, annotated by the measured tread of the sentry without. A young lieutenant gave items of Estwicke's experience as an "Indian Fighter;" and while the reporter took notes, he was ever and anon exhorted to take also what was modestly designated as "something." And somehow the mellow generosities of this same "something," and the manly good-fellowship of his entertainers, and that fine thrill which the contemplation of a deed of daring, blended with kindness, excites about the heart, were subtly infused into his simple narrative, and surprised him when he saw it printed on the smoking sheets in the morning.

It surprised others. It suggested to more than one subscriber of the "Daily Chronicle" that there might be some fine fellows among those Yankees at the barracks; and a wonder if it were not a trifle too unfriendly and inhospitable to leave them shut off there like aliens; and a resolve to go and see Captain Estwicke, who had been already removed to his quarters, and tell him what was thought of him, and virtually, though unavowedly, shake hands across the bloody chasm.

Now, this feat of moral gymnastics is remarkably simple when one fairly tries it, and was successfully exploited by his brother officers and *ses amis les ennemis* so long as Estwicke lay too ill to take a hand in it. But in a short time, when he began to pull together and this amicable ceremony was celebrated in his quarters, a chill suddenly fell upon it. He hardly knew how to receive the unwise, ill-chosen superlatives of these fraternal strangers and his hearty, chorusing friends. Among them he was heavily badgered. He had all the shyness of intense self-consciousness. He was wont to approach his own identity with misgivings, and an undue respect. Had any man come to the barracks to pick a quarrel with him he would have been bold enough. Since they had only come to sing his praises he was all at once timid, gruff, uneasy, ashamed of himself, and very much ashamed of them.

The behests of hospitality held this grum mood painfully mute so long as the visitors were present. But the sudden change from whole-souled cordiality, which had earlier characterized their welcome, to this congealed stiffness was very marked, and the quality of his demeanor was variously reprehended as affectation, or "barrack manners," by these ex-soldiers who had seen only service in the field, and knew little of the life and manners of barracks.

But plain-speaking is one of the prerogatives of friendship. "You mortify me with your confounded twaddle," Estwicke was wont to say fiercely to his Damons when the wheels of the last departing guest were heard rolling away on the broad, gravelled drive. "Yes,—I do feel worse,—very much worse. They all make me worse. And *you* make me sick! I'm sick with shame!"

Whereupon the Damons would roar with good-natured laughter, and demonstrate jovially the feasibility of once more taking "something."

It was eminently characteristic that by his exacting reserve Estwicke should repel much kindly feeling, and that with this opportunity he should make not one friend in Marston for himself, but many for other men.

Beyond the reach of his personal influence, however, his action continued to levy a heavy tribute of good-will and admiration. It seemed in Chattalla an incredibly brave and generous thing to do,—so vast was the incongruity in the imperilling of a valuable life for poor Graffy Beale, that ill-starred fleer of fate, and "Quick Pickie,"— who, when he was pronounced out of danger, was universally conceded to be "a grand rascal, though I'm sorry for the little chap."

And just here was where it appealed to General Vayne. The whole episode was instinct with a fine humanity. It gave evidence of high impulses and a latent nobility hitherto undivined in Estwicke's character, — hitherto doubted.

And why doubted? In these days it seemed to General Vayne that his own conduct had been actuated by some strange, unreasoning malice. He could not recollect how his deep prejudice had taken root. He could not remember his grievance; the blow that Estwicke had seemed to sordidly deal him when he was already sore smitten and pressed to the wall. Mentally he fumbled for it. It was gone.

His own fine deeds of valiance stretched out in the darkness of the Lost Cause like the brilliant track of a falling star. He had thought them then only prosaic duty; now they had loosed all hold on his memory. But every enthusiastic pulse throbbed in accord with this fine deed that another man had done.

So it came about that he listened with an unclouded brow to something his daughter said one day, — something she said with her eyes full of tears, her face suffused with flushes, a quiver in her voice.

"Papa," she cried, "I don't need this to teach me how good — how good — Captain Estwicke is. It only teaches me how dearly I love him. And now — *now* — I shall never care again because *you* choose to undervalue him. And I don't want your forgiveness! He is more to me than you are. And some day when he comes again I shall tell him that now I — I will marry him, — whenever he likes."

There was something hard in this too frank avowal of a transfer of allegiance. But father and daughter alike were inexpert at half-measures, and the thoroughness of the new departure surprised neither of them.

"Why, my dear child," exclaimed the consistent man, with a fine gesture of expostulation, "I have not the slightest objection, — not the slightest."

There was an unfilial flash in his daughter's eyes as she looked at him. She remembered Estwicke's passionate unhappiness, and her own conduct to him seemed very harsh. She had thought obedience to her father her first and highest duty. So it was valueless, intrinsically, and wasted besides. But obviously policy forbade her to urge upon him the grace of consistency, and she said nothing more.

She had wanted to go to see Estwicke. But Mrs. Kirby, with a heavy support of proprieties, took the field in force. "My dear," remonstrated the old lady gravely, "you are not really, formally, engaged to him now."

"Oh, he knows how it all was," declared the girl impatiently.

"But other people know nothing about it, — nothing whatever. It would be very queer for you, and your papa, and me to go to him together as you suggest; very queer indeed, unless we could give out that you are engaged. You ought to have foreseen this, my dear. You broke it off; yes, you gave him back his ring. Very pretty ring, that. Oh, yes; I know what your papa said; he made you do it. But,"— with a funereal shake of the head, — "*never* give back a ring. So significant; so-o conclusive. Remember that, my dear. *Never* give back a ring, — no!" Mrs. Kirby laid down these valuable rules of guidance with as much solemnity as if her niece expected to be engaged a score of times yet, and be tempted as often to thrust back rings upon their donors.

So Marcia wrote a little note to Captain Estwicke, and Mrs. Kirby wrote a longer one, and only General Vayne drove over to the barracks. There were several other gentlemen present at this interview, and the conversation was chiefly general and impersonal; hence Estwicke had scant opportunity to exhibit that morose disinclination for laudatory sympathy which had so unfavorably impressed former visitors, and General Vayne went away with his rose-colored views of the incident unimpaired.

As it had occurred so near his plantation, he was popularly supposed to be peculiarly well posted, and more than once his account of it was sought by guests at his house. It gained much impressiveness from the noble graces of his rhetoric and the largess of his generous admiration. It was pretty to see Marcia listen on these occasions, her cheeks crimson and her crimson lips parted, an enthusiastic gravity on her face, and her eyes alight with that wonderful radiance which can shine in a mortal's eyes but once in a lifetime. Most of these visitors were stolid, unspeculative people, long past their romantic hey-day. With them this voiceless language of love was already a dead language, and they translated none of its glowing characters. Horace Percy was younger, and he had his own reasons for being observant. When he saw that look on her face — although it was but a look — his heart sank like lead.

Any grief with him was nearly allied to a puerile irritation, and he was rather cruel to his horses as he drove homeward. He said little to Brennett, he was absorbed in canvassing the matter silently, and seeking to reconcile himself to giving up his love with the doubt still upon it. He did love her, but he loved himself more. He tenderly deprecated for himself the jeopardy of rejection. Hitherto he had felt so sure of her; he would have felt equally sure of any woman whom he might seek in marriage. He had brought himself to regard the avowal of his preference, not as something that might give her to him, but as of great value because it would bind him to her. His was the important promise, and he was chary of bestowing it. That exaltation which dwarfs the opinion of others to but a mote in the wind was an exaltation to which Percy could never attain. The calamity of losing her, he dreaded less than that the world should know of his loss. It did occur to him for a moment that she might feel tenderly, in a manner, toward the love she could not requite; that she might respect it as a confidence. But no! his was a famous scalp. She would joy to wear it at her belt. At the least she would tell all to her aunt — that would be only natural. That Mrs. Kirby should not tell it to Mrs. Ridgeway would be supernatural. Mrs. Ridgeway would tell it to the county. And then it would go! A young man of great social prominence finds sometimes in his notoriety a painful difficulty.

But even should he draw off at once, he was not safe from the gossip. Percy ground his teeth when he reflected that if all he suspected were true, and it should become known that she had accepted Estwicke, the sharp-witted Maurice Brennett would understand his position, having witnessed throughout the summer his persistent efforts to propitiate General Vayne. Brennett was a man who gave no quarter, and Percy had a vivid realization of the infinite zest with which the *jeunesse dorée* of New Orleans would laugh at the story of his fatuity in making love to the old gentleman while another fellow made love to the young lady.

And these cheap things vexed him. He continued moody and silent until they reached home, but at dinner he was vivacious in a desultory fashion, had much to say, and seemed to find nothing amiss with his appetite. When he and his guest were lighting their cigars in the library, he observed with a laugh: "Did you notice, Brennett, how much interest Miss Marcia takes in Captain Estwicke's — a — a — blow-out — as you might call it?"

Brennett looked up with genuine surprise expressed in

his face. "Why, yes," he admitted, in a tone that was evidently meant to seem casual.

"Do you know," said Percy, his eyes fixed on the dark shrubbery close by the open window as he lounged easily in his chair. "I'd be willing to bet you something very considerable that they are engaged."

The crafty Brennett was embarrassed. "Why, I don't know about that," he said, hesitating.

After a moment he put a bold face on his uncertainty.

"To tell you the truth, I thought you were in love with her."

Percy glanced up laughing. "With Miss Marcia?" he asked, a note of incredulity in his voice. "I never should have credited *you* with a sentimental imagination, Brennett. What made you think that?"

Brennett vindicated his logic. "Because you seemed specially anxious to stand well with her father and please her," he said sturdily.

Percy made no rejoinder for a moment, while the servant came in and placed the lamps on the table. Then he laughed again — a trifle mysteriously this time.

"Well,"— he glanced over his shoulder about the room — "is that old darkey out of hearing? Well, as I was about to say, General Vayne is a man of influence, and in fact I am a man of some influence myself. Moreover, I am twenty-four — nearly twenty-five years of age."

Brennett stared. Percy turned his cigar between his fingers and gazed gravely at it.

"You're not a man that blabs, Brennett," he continued, presently. "I may as well say plainly that within a year I shall be eligible for Congress, and my friends want me to knock the old fossil, who has been going from this district, back into the Jurassic period where he belongs. I don't know certainly whether I shall consent to make the race, but in view of that possibility, I must, in the meantime, propitiate men of influence, and smile at their daughters, and humbug their Mrs. Kirbys as well as I can."

He filliped off the ash, grown long and white upon his cigar as he talked, looked brightly up at Brennett, and laughed again. He had told his little story very well, and the wily Brennett believed it—perhaps because he esteemed any scheme of advancement a stronger motive than love. Percy detected credulity in his face, and, having succeeded so well, concluded to delay. If she were in love with Estwicke she would demonstrate that fact by marrying him. If not, she would still be here next autumn on Percy's return from a little tour of the northern seaside resorts which he had in contemplation. When he had determined upon this course he waited only for his friend's departure to carry it into effect, and he waited in secret impatience, as Brennett showed no sign of bringing his visit to a close. Percy had lost all interest in the quiet rural existence that, but so short a time ago, was instinct with the keenest zest. It was painful to him to go to General Vayne's house and meet Marcia. But Brennett often proposed a drive or ride tending thither, and he must accompany his guest as behooves a host. He bitterly upbraided his folly in having hampered himself at this crisis with the restrictions of hospitality, for who knew so well as he that a guest in the country is like a soul or a conscience, impossible to be decently rid of for a moment.

In these visits Mrs. Kirby observed with some surprise that Antoinette sedulously avoided Mr. Brennett, and, although he did not talk to her with an eager interest, as when he had first come among them, he adroitly contrived, continually but unobtrusively, to throw himself in her way as if to keep her attention directed to him — to remind her of him.

And Mrs. Kirby pitied the hopeless love of which she imagined he was the victim, and wondered helplessly that dear Antoinette should be so cold.

Marcia noticed nothing of all this, for she was absorbed in a fact which she had at first vaguely perceived in doubting, chilly apprehension, and realized at last with an amazed despair. Captain Estwicke intended to come no more. She had experienced a sharp surprise to hear from others that he was already out again with his arm in a sling. Naturally she had expected to be the first to see him. But she had accounted for this as an accident, and for a week thereafter she herself gathered the flowers for the vases in the library; and in the evenings the lamps and the fire-flies and the moon were early alight in the big, square windows, with their sheer snowy curtains and their clinging vines, where the dew glittered on the climbing roses, and the mocking-bird sang for his welcome. But only the lagging hours came in his stead. She began to take account of that last interview when he had said his suspense should end. Did he, indeed, hold it definitive? Had his love worn out — and now when she was ready to renounce for it all the world besides? She could not have so doubted him, but for the little letter she had written. If he had felt thus, she argued, it must have seemed an appeal, a recall. And he gave it no heed. To be sure, he had not been able for weeks past to hold a pen — but he might have come, if he liked. That letter grew to be a poignant humiliation. She brooded upon it until the words, simple and few, were burned into her brain. Yet she told herself scornfully that it was no great matter — the letter was doubtless gone long ago — it had served, perhaps, to light his cigar. And then she remembered the fervor of faith and the glow of delight with which she had written it, and she felt that the best of her, the essence of hope and youth and love was exhaled with the smoke, and that all her life had flickered with the paper and had faded and fallen to ashes.

Estwicke did not light his cigar with it, but he smoked many cigars over it, and it furnished him, too, midnight vigils and bitterness of spirit. This was the first time she had ever written to him. Heretofore he had come and gone so often that there had been no need of letters. He thought this little note stiff and formal. He could not know how beaming a face had bent over it. He could not conceive that what he had done should render him eligible in General Vayne's eyes and demolish those formidable unacknowledged objections. He could not imagine that that long withheld consent had made her all at once shy of him — shyer than ever, when Mrs. Kirby sat by as she wrote and admonished her to remember that they were not engaged just now. Estwicke moodily compared the result with Mrs. Kirby's own affectionate effusion, its superlatives straggling half across the page. The contrast seemed significant. It was all over between them. He had told Marcia she must decide, and she had decided. And she wrote now only because they had been friends, and because she must, since his other friends wrote too — sooth to say more kindly. He regarded General Vayne's visit as the emptiest formality. Old Ridgeway, the merest acquaintance, had accompanied him, and there were many who came more than once. Estwicke's pride, too, was reasserting itself. He declared that he would humble himself to General Vayne and his daughter no more. He would go there never again, though his heart should break. He grew taciturn, and rebellious, and irritable, and the post-surgeon rubbed his hands and said that the patient was coming on finely and that a strong, fierce temper was the best indication of rapid convalescence.

Meantime, General Vayne, all unaware of the havoc his consistency had wrought in Marcia's life and the life of a brave man whom he admired, was reconciling himself with a good grace to that stern avenging dispensation which sends the " youth of flaunting feathers " close upon the heels of the father of a daughter. That opprobrious epithet "home-made Yankee" had been stricken from his vocabulary. He had substituted "loyal." Loyal! That was a word of noble significations. And he was a man peculiarly susceptible to the gracious charm of fine words.

Somehow the future seemed more ideally appropriate reconstructed on the basis of this word "loyal."

That notable issue of the "Daily Chronicle" was stale enough, when one day Tom Toole found his dinner wrapped in a fragment of it, as he sat eating from his tin pail in the brief interval of rest called "nooning." Between bites he read from it, slowly and laboriously. And as he read, the yard of the furniture factory, with its piles of lumber and its high palings; the city's hum; the strident voices of the street vendors; the heavy whir of the machinery that, even while it slackened and until it ceased, seemed to shake the massive building before him — all passed from his consciousness. Instead, he saw the long, sunlit stretches of the battle-field, beautiful and blooming beneath a summer sky. He heard the river sing, and remembered how the piers that stood in its midst roused its voice to a more passionate utterance, as if it too would tell the story of all that had happened here.

"An' hain't that thar old pier seen sights!" he exclaimed. "An' it's cur'ous fur it ter be this same man ter hev sech resky dealin's thar — this hyar Estwicke what looked so powerful like the t'other one — ef" — even in the sunlight and in the far away city he glanced dubiously over his shoulder — "ef thar ever war enny other one."

He munched for a time in meditative silence. Then he straightened the paper on the planks before him and began to spell out the closing sentence, sensible of a supplemental curiosity as to the man and boy whom Estwicke had sought to rescue.

The account of the officer's exploit had occupied a column and a half of fine print. But only a paragraph was needed to say that the man, Graffy Beale, a low fellow of the neighborhood, was fatally injured in the accident, although the boy had been pronounced out of danger.

Through the surprise throbbing in his quickening blood, through the agitation that mustered great drops upon his forehead, blistering the crumpled bit of paper as they fell, through the incredulity that sought to possess him because the familiar name looked so unfamiliar in print, Toole was mastered by a tyrannous recollection of that morning when Graffy had sat on the rock by the dusty milestone, and implored forgiveness, and a friendly word, and a hearty hand-clasp before they parted.

And for a friendly word he was bidden to look to the graves he had filled.

Was this the last word to be spoken between them? Had he indeed gone hence forever? The ignorant fellow was battling with that maddening sense of irrevocability which alone is potent to give to mortals a realization of how finite is opportunity, how infinite is eternity.

"But Graffy air the frien'liest pore critter 'in all this worl'!" he broke forth presently. "He ain't a-goin' ter hold no grudge agin nobody, nuther hyar nur hyarafter.

I hopes he knowed me that day, better'n I knowed myse'f. An' ef the Lord lets me I 'll tell him that, ef I kin git back thar in time."

Certainly conscience had little to do in Maurice Brennett's schemes. And when it became a factor, it was the conscience of another man.

CHAPTER XXI.

TEMPLE MEREDITH in New York — like "our army in Flanders" — swore terribly.

Miss St. Pierre's long-lost letter still lay, among the invitations to parties and weddings and other delicate and flimsy missives, in the darkness of his father's desk in Marston, to which the old gentleman's mistake had consigned it.

As Meredith received from time to time his mail, which was forwarded to him, he would eagerly scan the superscription of the envelopes, then, in deep disappointment, thrust the letters into his pocket, unread for hours. He had his own reasons for attaching a peculiar significance to her long-continued silence. The last letter he had written to her, which had apparently failed to elicit a reply, was one that could in no degree be considered in the same category with their previous correspondence as counsel and client. To be sure, it had some slight preliminary sentences, relative to matters of business, as a pretext, but then it meandered off into a strictly personal vein, and it filled four large and closely-written pages. Not a love-letter, by any manner of means; it merely breathed a respectful friendship, which, however, held a subtle but unmistakable suggestion of a latent faculty for vast expansion. Now this wily young lawyer had intended this as a tentative proceeding — in his own jargon, as a "fishing bill." He had felt, for the first time in his life, self-distrustful, and that he needed encouragement. Their intercourse had hitherto been on the basis of counsel and client, — peculiarly informal, professionally speaking, peculiarly formal in a social point of view. He had been altogether unable to decide in what esteem she held him, apart from his position as her adviser, apart from that vast legal lore on which she relied so implicitly. But if she should respond to his attempt to awaken a personal interest, he would take heart of grace.

So the fishing bill was carefully prepared and duly filed — and it caught nothing. He had hardly realized how fully he had expected an answer, how strong were his hopes, until days and weeks sped by and brought him only grievous disappointment. There was an extreme mortification in all this. And thus it was that Temple Meredith, smarting with wounded pride, blasphemed, and said in his wrath that he was the only damned fool (*sic*) in America who could contrive to get into the position of being rejected before he had offered himself. She refused even his friendship; no doubt she infinitely scorned those delicate intimations of a still deeper feeling which the young lawyer had carefully and craftily incorporated into the instrument. He remembered them all. He remembered them with a rush of blood to his face and a plunging heart. He remembered the foolish hopefulness with which he had drawn it up. He had thought it a masterly performance at the time. He had wished to avoid "rushing things" and speaking prematurely. And now she would not give him an opportunity of speaking at all. If he had not put his fate to the touch so soon — so fatally soon; if he could only have waited for a time! But no! and it was that evil thing, a lawyer's busy pen, which had brought all this woe upon him, and thrown him out of Cupid's court. And so he swore terribly.

The thermometer in New York was the wonder of the country during Temple Meredith's sojourn in that city.

He grew callous as to how long that sojourn should continue. At one time he contemplated writing to her to explain that he was prevented by business from keeping his promise to be in Chattalla on the 28th of June. But why should he write? what did she care how he came or went? That day was a long day in New York as well as in Tennessee.

When he returned home he received after a short interval a letter which had been forwarded to New York, arriving there after his departure, and following him to Marston. As he caught sight of the delicate chirography he seized it with eager hands, tore the envelope open, and while he read, dismay overspread his face. The fair writer curtly and coldly begged to call his attention once more to the matters contained in her previous communication.

"There is some terrible mistake here," he exclaimed. "A letter has gone wrong, and it has played the very deuce, I'm afraid. Did nothing come for me except the mail you forwarded?"

"No," replied his father decisively; "everything was sent on." After a moment's reflection he repeated, "Everything was sent on — except, I believe, some wedding-cards and such like."

"Where are they? By some chance the letter may be among them."

When at last the package was drawn from the pigeon-hole where it had been so methodically lost, Temple Meredith had no time for the somewhat unfilial criminations that had risen to his tongue. After anxious perusal of the inclosed letter from Fortescue's lawyers, he caught up the newspaper, glanced at the time-table of the Marston and Chattalla road, hastily made his preparations for the journey, and on the afternoon of the same day his card was brought to Antoinette. She had lapsed into despair. It had seemed impossible that she could ever hear from him again. The slow torture of the past few weeks had been sharpened with a keen sense of perpetuity. Now she felt stunned with surprised relief, and tried in vain to brace her nerves for what she must say to him and what he would say to her. Through the open door of the library he caught a glimpse, as she came across the empty drawing-rooms opposite, of her black-robed figure; a stray sunbeam gilded her blonde hair; her face was flushed, and he noted that expression of pathetic appeal which it had acquired in place of the sweet immobility it was wont to wear. Somehow that gave him a more adequate idea than anything else could have done of all she had suffered; it roused within him an unjust self-reproach. He could hardly endure to meet her as he rose hastily and advanced. She suddenly lost her self-control when she had entered the room. She leaned back against the door as if for support. She cast one glance upon him, and burst into tears.

Perhaps it was well for Temple Meredith that he was a lawyer, and expert by habit in marshalling together effective points and swiftly exploiting an argument. So well did he plead his cause that he had made the whole position of affairs, from the loss of the letter to the state of his feelings, perfectly plain to her in the few moments that they stood together by the door. And all the time he held her hand in his, and she did not attempt to withdraw it.

"What did you think of me?" he exclaimed at last, in retrospective dismay.

"I knew it was some strange accident," she faltered; "I couldn't believe you had forgotten me."

"Forgotten you!"

Then she turned away, and once more fell to sobbing. He looked at her in great anxiety. He began to understand that something was involved in all this of far deeper significance than those merely monetary interests. Something had happened during his absence to grieve her greatly.

He sat down beside her and once more took her hand.

"What is it?" he said, gently. "Tell me what it is that troubles you?"

She made no reply.

"I don't wonder that you hesitate to trust me, after all this," he continued. "I only wish I knew, so that I might say something to comfort you."

"Nothing can ever comfort me," she declared, in a burst of tears. "And yet I know it is false, whatever it may be. It's not that I believe it, but other people may. That's the reason I can't tell you. But I've intended to tell you. I've waited for you because I can't trust any one but you."

"Then tell me," he urged.

She was unobservant of the effect of her words as she sobbed through her pathetic little account of the scene with Brennett on the moonlit portico, and explained the interpretation she had placed upon his mysterious hints and his motive in hazarding them. She was hardly conscious that Meredith's hand, which still clasped hers, was trembling, and that there was a change in his voice intimating a tense repression of feeling. He did not interrupt her. He spoke only after she had finished her story.

"Where did you meet the man?"

"Here. That's the strangest of all. He seems to be a thorough gentleman as far as appearance and association go. They are all completely deceived as to his real character."

"Where is he now?"

"At Mrs. Percy's. He is making her son a long visit."

She looked up — an extreme surprise mingled with the tears in her eyes. Meredith in ominous silence had risen, and was glancing hastily about for his hat. His face was stern and hard. She divined his intention from its expression.

"I thought I might trust you," she exclaimed. "This is the reason I did n't tell General Vayne. He would have been rash. He would have taken my position into consideration only as his daughter's guest, who had been threatened and intimidated in his house. He would have felt that his own dignity was involved. But you! I thought *you* would care only for my interest. And now for the luxury of calling that man to account you will have a great sensation, and it will bring out the whole story, — the wicked fabrication that will seem the truth, — and it will drag my name into the newspapers. It will all seem worse than it is. You will have the satisfaction of horsewhipping or pistolling the man, because *you* are angry, and *I* shall have to take the consequences and the publicity."

Meredith paused. He could not overlook these considerations. He felt the weight of her argument. He stood, his hat in his hand and his intention vacillating.

"You must not see him at all," she persisted. "Promise me that you will not. You are angry on my account. You think you are fighting my battles. But you are taking the course of all others I most deprecate. Ah, it is hard, — hard that there is nobody who will think for me, and whom I can trust!"

He came back, and again sat down beside her. "Don't tell me that," he entreated. "It is the pride of my life that you have said to-day you could trust no one but me. I will do whatever you wish."

"And what I wish you to do," she exclaimed in increasing agitation, "is to see Fortescue's lawyers and make terms with them. Offer them whatever they will take. Get the compromise through. Get it through at once, and have it over."

He looked at her in surprise. "Don't you think you are very precipitate?" he said. "This affair is a most transparent device. The man is merely trying to frighten you into a compromise, so that he can collect his debt on Fortescue."

"I've thought of that. But can I risk it? Suppose we are mistaken. Fortescue knew my people before I was born. My father, my mother, they have been dead for twenty years. I never knew them. How could I disprove any lie he might tell? How do I know what innocent circumstance he may contort into such shape as to serve his wicked purposes. It's so vague; that makes it all the more terrible. That lie must touch them or it would be impossible to make it useful in coercing me into a compromise. The attempt proves that. Do you think I can keep the property at such a price, — the price of their good name? You see I have no choice."

"There is no secret, — not even a lie," said Meredith. "That rascal threw out the idea merely as a chance suggestion. If you would allow me to go to him I could wring from him a retraction of every word he spoke to you "—

"I will not, — I will not," she interrupted. "I have told you how disastrous that would be to me."

"I only want to convince you that the whole thing is only a most audacious attempt to extort money. I dare say Fortescue has never heard of this move. It is that incomparable villain's own device."

"But do you *know* it? Shall I risk everything on a

surmise? Will you take the responsibility of advising me to defy the man? It was such a bold thing. He could n't have known that I would n't ask questions. He was ready to tell the lie, and he was prepared to support it."

"But a compromise would give you no immunity. They would presently renew their demands and threats in the hope of extorting more money still."

He looked at her with earnest eyes. All the lawyer within him revolted at the idea of thus tamely submitting to blackmail. It seemed hardly less wicked than weak.

"Then they could take the whole property,—every cent."

"And still they might tell it."

"Then, you know, I could n't help it. It would be like a stroke of lightning. It would be my hard fate. But my duty would have been done. I should have stood between the dead and calumny as long as I could. I should not have chosen money rather than their good repute. I can't keep the property now. I can't haggle and barter over their graves. Oh, no; I can't do that."

Her soft lips were quivering; her eyes had filled again.

"Oh, don't distress yourself," he cried. "Don't talk about it any more."

"I can't think of anything else," she faltered.

"But don't cry. See here. I want you to tell me all that that man said about Fortescue's case. It may be useful. Tell me what he said."

It was not difficult for Antoinette to recall all the details of the conversation. She had gone over it often in the deep stillness of the perfumed summer midnight, as she lay awake and could not sleep because of her unquiet thoughts. She became more calm as she rehearsed it, and he grew graver still. A pretty strong showing he considered it, for he believed that Fortescue's visit to the United States during the suspension of the statute of limitations would not be held to operate as a removal of the disability. In his opinion the statute began to run against Fortescue only when he landed in New York early in the spring of '71. He resolved to observe special caution in his advice to Miss St. Pierre. If he should counsel her to refuse the compromise, it might chance that Fortescue would be able to sustain his claim to her whole estate, and the story of which he seemed disposed to make such unscrupulous use might prove, when spread abroad, as disastrous as if it were true. Thus she would lose heavily both in pecuniary considerations and in the more important matter of feeling. Meredith appreciated his weighty responsibility in view of this possibility.

"What is your opinion?" she asked at last.

He made an effort to shake off his anxiety for the present.

"That it will bear a good deal of tough cogitation," he said, with his imperturbable aspect. "Suppose we agree upon this: to postpone deciding upon the compromise for a week. That will give me an opportunity to look into the affair. I'll come again to Chattalla next Tuesday. Then we'll talk it all over again and determine on our best course."

She assented, and for a few moments sat gravely silent. Meredith noted her downcast eyes and troubled face. With an effort to conjure into it something of its wonted impassive brightness, he said, remembering her former ambition to explain things "like a man,"—

"How well you stated those points just now—positively like a lawyer."

She looked at him and smiled faintly.

"I couldn't have got them more distinctly from some 'big wig' arguing in court."

She laughed at this as at a jest. Still she was visibly flattered.

Her pride in her capacity for business suggested to him the recollection that it was a hollow assumption, for she was still unconscious that she owed him any money for his professional services. He thought of his father and the "golden rule of practice" in inward and unfilial merriment, and he offered himself a glorious bet that he was the only lawyer in America who had ever taken as a retainer his client's heart.

When he was gone at last it seemed to Antoinette, with her rigid sense of propriety, that it was incumbent upon her to confide to Mrs. Kirby, as her chaperon *pro tempore*, the circumstance of this very recent engagement to Temple Meredith.

"Now this is very nice — very nice indeed," said the old lady, beaming with gratification. "I don't know Mr. Meredith, but I have no doubt he is *all* a young man should be, for his grandmother was Leonora Archer — nice people, the Archers! And his mother was Louise Lapice — and they are a good family too — and I feel confident that you will be very happy."

It never occurred to Mrs. Kirby that a nice grandmother might, in the perverse course of events, have a grandson who was not at all nice. The grandmother she considered important in the premises, and thus she deftly argued. One pang of pity for Maurice Brennett's blighted affections — he was so talented! But then, she thought, brightening with reassurance, no doubt Temple Meredith was talented too, for was not his grandmother Leonora Archer!

And this was Mrs. Kirby's moan for Maurice Brennett.

She had no intention of betraying Antoinette's confidence. She fancied that a secret told to her was as safe as if it were locked in the bosom of the earth. She piqued herself on her trustworthiness. Thus she was prone to error through lack of precaution, for she set no guard upon her tongue, believing that member to be the most discreet organ of its kind.

It chanced that she spent the following day with Mrs. Ridgeway; the dust of her departing wheels was hardly laid upon the pike before her hostess was on the way to town in that swift and commodious fashion, known as "riding in the barouche." And in three hours all Chattalla was aware that the pretty Miss St. Pierre, who had made Miss Vayne such a long visit, was just engaged to a stranger — a friend of Horace Percy's — whom she had first met at Mrs. Percy's house.

And, singularly enough, this disclosure evoked a train of sequences fraught with disproportionate importance.

CHAPTER XXII.

MAURICE BRENNETT confided little to chance. He had found it a doubtful auxiliary. One lowering afternoon, however, it came to his aid in an unexpected emergency. It had moved him to decline an invitation from Horace Percy to drive to Chattalla, and an hour or so after his friend's departure it led him into the library.

The day was sultry; no wind stirred; the woods were still. A heavy cloud overshadowed the landscape like an impending curse; now and then it was cleft by a lurid flash of lightning, but as yet there was no thunder. The storm was in abeyance.

The grating of wheels on the gravelled drive struck sharply upon the silence. With an idle man's-languid interest in small details, he put aside the curtain and looked out. His heart stood still.

It might seem that there was nothing in the sight which met his eyes to elicit vivid emotion — only a well-dressed man, with a handsome face and a seigniorial manner, alighting from a carriage. But if a great painter had staked his life, his soul upon the grouping in his masterpiece, and the figures should become animated with a malicious free-agency, leaving their places on the canvas and involving all in ruin, his despair might be commensurate with what Brennett felt when John Fortescue, quitting his prescribed sphere, appeared suddenly on this new scene, dragging chaotic complications after him.

There was hardly a moment for reflection. There was hardly need for that moment. His best course — his only course flashed through Brennett's mind instantly. He caught up his hat, walked hastily out into the hall, and the two men met at the open front-door as Fortescue laid his hand on the bell-knob.

He drew back slightly. The gesture, almost imperceptible though it was, restored Brennett's self-confidence. There was no trace of discomposure now in his manner.

"You've come to see me, I suppose," he said coolly. "May I ask why?"

His agitation seemed to have subtly transferred itself to Fortescue, whose face changed.

"Hang it!" he said with husky uncertainty. "Shall I talk it out now and here?"

"If you like," Brennett replied, laughing a little, and eying him contemptuously.

Fortescue had known Brennett long and well. No one could know him well enough to divine how he quaked with the prosaic fear that some servant might see the carriage and come to usher in the guest — how cautiously he was pushing his advantage — how anxious he was lest he push it too far — how he deprecated what he invited, for a hasty word might ruin them both. Still it was imperative to cow Fortescue — to keep him down was the first consideration.

"Isn't there some place about here where we can talk without interruption, Brennett," said Fortescue, calling his name for the first time. "I don't want to meet people — I must see you alone. I must talk affairs over with you. I won't go on with the "—

He broke off suddenly. "I tell you now," he resumed, with a gathering frown, "I've come expressly to have it out with you."

"You can imagine what facilities there are here for the interview you propose," said Brennett, still harassing him. "There is the library, with the dining-room adjoining; there are the parlors, opening into a conservatory; there is my room, connected with Percy's by sliding doors."

"Oh, come out, come out!" said Fortescue impatiently. "We can find some quiet place about the grounds, or we can get into the carriage and drive away somewhere."

Brennett silently assented. As they walked down the steps he took out his cigar-case and offered it. Fortescue shook his head, hardly raising his absorbed eyes from the ground, and mechanically keeping by the side of his friend, who led the way through the shrubbery. Brennett was selecting a cigar for himself when they reached their objective point; they had emerged from among the evergreens into an open, grassy space, with only a great oak-tree in the centre; beneath its wide-spreading branches was an iron bench. Here a figure approaching in any direction could be observed at the distance of fifty yards, and their voices, even if raised in emphasis or anger, would be inaudible to any loiterer among the shrubbery beyond.

Brennett threw himself on the bench, and, with his cigar between his teeth, he glanced up at his visitor, who paused, leaning moodily against the bole of the tree.

"Now, see here," said Brennett, in a pleasant, deliberate voice.

Fortescue lifted his head with a hungry expectancy of look, almost pitiable in its intensity.

"Give me a match, can't you?" continued Brennett.

A cruel disappointment was sharply cut into Fortescue's face. There was something positively simple-hearted in his unsuspecting ignorance of the astute intention that had dealt this insidious thrust. It seemed to him that only his eagerness had led him into sanguine anticipation, and in his curt response, "Have n't one," there was no infusion of bitterness.

"Ah, I believe I have one myself." Brennett produced it and lighted his cigar; then, as he began to smoke, he carelessly eyed his despondent companion, still leaning against the tree, — more despondent, perhaps, for that sudden kindling of hope, as suddenly quenched, — more anxious, more nervous. Fortescue made an effort to rally.

"Now, Brennett, what have you to say to me?"

"To say to you?" echoed Brennett in surprised accents. "My dear fellow, not one word."

"Come, there's enough of that," retorted Fortescue fiercely.

"Did you journey all the way from the mountains merely to ask what I have to say?"

"I won't be badgered in this manner, Brennett. You had better draw off. I came here for money. You know that."

"You won't get it."

"Then I'll expose the whole affair."

"And incidentally give yourself up?"

Fortescue looked hard into his coadjutor's face. It was grave, but the brilliant eyes were lighted by some inward, sardonic laughter.

"And give myself up," he said slowly, "and, incidentally, you."

"You mistake your metal, my dear Fortescue. You have been a soldier, as we all know, but you are not the stuff of which martyrs are made."

"I don't see why I should be a martyr. I don't see why, in exposing you, I should necessarily give myself up." Fortescue paused, as if in doubt whether he should go further. Brennett's satiric face and gleaming eyes seemed to exert an unnerving effect upon him.

"I intend to cut the whole thing," he cried suddenly. "I have been shabbily treated from the first, because you fancy that I am completely at your mercy. I am not in your power. I have the ability to ruin you by a course which insures me immunity. I did *not* come all the way from the mountains merely to ask what you have to say, but to see Miss St. Pierre, — unless you find it prudent to come to terms."

Brennett pulled away comfortably at his cigar. The unconstrained calmness of his manner had not a suggestion of *bravade;* his attitude denoted a certain degree of easy attention; his bright eyes were fixed in listless quietude upon the line of shrubbery. But was his face paler than its wont, or did it catch the pallid reflection of a lurid gleam from the heavy clouds?

"See Miss St. Pierre," he exclaimed presently, looking up. "Of course you must. She is worth seeing, I assure you."

"Damn it!" cried the other furiously, "you know what I mean. I shall see Miss St. Pierre, and, by disclosing the whole scheme, secure her promise not to prosecute, — as far as I am concerned. I went into the affair reluctantly. I never half liked it, but I was so devilish hard up for the money you bribed me with. I never knew how serious it was. It seemed a sort of theatrical lark. I was exhilarated with the idea of personating that fellow and humbugging a town full of people. I knew I could do it. But I really did not appreciate what a swindle it was, for I was only half posted about the facts before I had committed myself. *You* were the originator of the plot; you alone will have to answer for it. I shall tell her the whole story, and throw myself on her clemency."

"Her clemency!" Brennett repeated the words mockingly. "The man who trusts to *her* clemency will find himself in the county jail, convicted of a conspiracy to fraudulently obtain property."

From this ignoble allusion Fortescue flinched. And certainly there was a barbed malice in its incongruity with all those fastidious intimations which hung about his presence — his attire, somewhat too elegant and elaborate, his impressive bearing, even his delicately white but strong and sinewy hand clenching itself upon the kid glove which he had drawn off. Hardly more incongruous, however, than the man was with himself, with those sordid appeals for money, with his coarse threats. He seemed so nobly endowed by nature. His superb physique in itself should have rendered mere existence pleasure. His strength, his stature, his animal spirits might have made life a long triumphal progress for some ambitious soul, niggardly equipped. All the sharply chiselled lines of his features, and those fine eyes that were so vicious and so handsome, bespoke a rare intelligence which could only be an added reproach to him and his failings. His special talents, and his voice, with its infinite susceptibility of inflection, would have given fortune and fame to another man, and a histrionic artist to the world. He was an example of perverted powers. He had all — yet lacked all in lacking that consecrating element, an abiding sense of honor.

Certain lines about his perfectly moulded lips might once have suggested an ingenuous sensitiveness — now they expressed an accomplished sensuality. There was a momentary lapse, however, into the old habit of their muscles as they trembled almost imperceptibly. Then they were resolutely stilled, and with the coarseness of these days he faced his coadjutor's suggestion and persisted.

"She will be under a certain degree of obligation to me for exposing the conspiracy and withdrawing from it before her interests are injured. She will have promised."

"This is the nineteenth century," said Brennett, "and yet here is a man willing to stake his liberty on a woman's promise. The world moves slowly."

There was a muttering of thunder on the still air. A vivid flash shot swiftly through the heavens from zenith to horizon and quivered in ghastly vibrations over all the landscape below. Fortescue lifted his eyes toward the black clouds as he spoke. "I left Bandusia with the resolve of seeing her at once. Even after I reached that little town yesterday I had no intention of ever appealing to you again. This afternoon I started out to that man's place — General Vayne's place — determined to have an interview with her and explain the whole affair."

He was still looking at the clouds. He did not note the effect of his words, or he might have seen that Maurice Brennett winced at the imminence of this danger of which he had had no premonition. His bright eyes were distended and brighter still. He lounged upon the iron bench in a relaxed attitude; one hand was on his hip; it might have occurred to a man more timid or more observant than his companion, that it was in significant proximity to his pistol pocket. He was an unscrupulous villain and he had been threatened with discovery and ruin. His quick, prophetic mind had sketched the outline of the possible scenes to come — a jet of red light projected into the somnolent atmosphere of this gray afternoon; a sharp report; a result that should be called a dreadful accident; frantic regret for the careless handling of a pistol supposed to be unloaded; always the most cordial relations existing between the parties. Thus the curtain should fall upon the "theatrical lark."

There was no change in his voice when he spoke. He asked a question as if the answer could in no degree concern him.

"And why did n't you go?"

Fortescue once more searchingly scanned the face before him. There was nothing in it to suggest how he had best modify the facts. He gave them unvarnished. "I discovered she was not there. Before I left the turnpike I met a carriage with two young ladies driving toward the town. I questioned the tollgate-keeper, who said that one was General Vayne's daughter and the other Miss St. Pierre. So I postponed the project, turned back, and concluded to try you once more before I throw up my hand."

"Throw it up, my friend. You can see her easily enough in the morning."

"I'll try it, at any rate," said Fortescue doggedly, his breath coming hard between his clenched teeth. "I'm likely to get nothing from you — perhaps she will pay for the information I can give."

"You don't know her!" exclaimed Brennett, laughing. "If you did I should admire your enterprise."

"I shall not ask her for money," cried Fortescue impetuously, veering instantly from his determination. "I shall only tell her the whole story and throw myself on her clemency. My testimony against you will give her all the revenge she wants."

"My dear Fortescue," said Brennett, still laughing, "you don't know your cousin."

"She is not my cousin. Stop that humbug. Don't call me 'Fortescue.'"

"Don't you call yourself 'Fortescue?' Tell me, what shall I call you?"

"What's the use of all that rot when we are alone?"

"Habit, my dear fellow — for the sake of habit. You would n't like it if I should accidentally blurt out among our acquaintances in New Orleans that you are my valued friend Edward Keevor — merely masquerading for mingled considerations of pleasure and profit as John Fortescue."

"And you need n't shout it now" — with an anxious glance toward the shrubbery.

"Why not? To-morrow you will fling yourself penitent before Miss St. Pierre, and meekly petition for immunity and mercy. The game is up."

The adventurer said nothing. He was thinking that if it were desirable to see Miss St. Pierre he should have done so without talking the matter over with Brennett. He was conscious of being unduly swayed by his coadjutor's influence when they were together, and yet he could not shake it off. His project, which he had believed so safe, so easy, began to present unexpected difficulties. Pitfalls were before him — he must tread warily. There was no prophesying how she would receive his disclosure. The story once told — he was absolutely at her mercy. As he reflected on his fast-fading resolve it seemed the maddest temerity to have contemplated risking himself upon the doubtful whim that might possess a woman whom he had never seen, and of whom he had heard nothing save what would augur the most disastrous results of his confidence.

He could not understand Brennett's indifference. It was simply inexplicable in a man fatally menaced, with every consideration at stake. It never occurred to him — who could feign so well — that another might play a part too. And he did not think Brennett in any special sense a courageous man — he did not credit him with the nerve to stolidly face an emergency like this. He believed himself possessed of far more force and pluck; he had relied on these endowments to shake his adversary's equilibrium, and now he himself was wavering. As far as he could judge he had made no impression. A new conviction was sending deep roots into his mind — his coadjutor had an alternative in contemplation. Perhaps there had been some change in the position of affairs of which he had not been notified. He quaked as he thought of his precipitancy, and the dangers into which he might have plunged. He felt enmeshed in hidden toils; his manner was changing from threatening sternness to despondent appeal. He stood for an instant longer beneath the tree, then he walked slowly to the iron bench and sat down beside his companion.

"Brennett," he said, "you have not treated me fairly in this matter. You have deceived me in more ways than one."

"If so, you have your redress. I don't say a word to dissuade you. Do whatever you think your interest requires."

"You kept me in ignorance of the extent of this swindle until I was fully committed. You knew I would n't take hold if I had understood. I never before did anything villanous — never half so bad, I mean. Ah, well — when a man once starts on the down grade of crime there 's not much chance of putting on the brakes. The gambling-house and the gates of hell — they are the *termini*, I suppose."

"This is edifying," said Brennett, with a curling lip.

"You are trying to exasperate me. You are trying to provoke me to an outbreak. You want me to become discouraged and to relinquish the whole matter, and go quietly back to France. You have succeeded in effecting a compromise, and now you are trying to evade paying me the five thousand dollars which you promised."

Brennett laughed. "What a fool!" he said contemptuously. "How could I effect a compromise without John Fortescue's signature?"

This was evidently a false scent.

"Then you have some alternative in view. What is the prospect for a compromise?"

"Better than ever."

"You have told me that before."

"It was true then — it is true now. The chances have steadily improved. Before long they will be merged in a certainty."

"I must have money, Brennett — in the meantime I must have some money."

"You won't get it from me."

"Then I'll split."

"Split then — and be damned to you!"

There was a pause.

"It is hard — hard! You promised at first that it should last for only two or three weeks, and I agreed to play the part for that length of time. It has lasted four months. It is a terrible strain."

"Nonsense. I don't believe you. I've seen you ape first one fellow and then another, and hardly make a gesture or speak a word in your own manner for days together. It's a natural gift with you. There's no art nor cultivation about it, and it can't be painful to exercise it. You are doing for money what I have seen you do a thousand times for pure tomfoolery. I have filled my contract with you to the letter. I told you that the time could not be positively limited. I paid you five thousand dollars — to undertake a little deception, as easy to you as lying — and I promised you five thousand more contingent upon effecting a compromise with Miss Antoinette St. Pierre. You want more money in the interval — which our agreement does not call for. I won't pay a cent."

"I run a frightful risk. Every day that this thing continues makes it more imminent. I am always oppressed with a sense of my danger."

"You run a frightful risk when you are drunk."

"But I haven't been drinking lately. I have sworn to be moderate. I thought at first that I could carry the affair off easily enough for a short time, but this long, long imposition has broken me down. And since that locket — you remember I wrote to you — since it has come from the grave to upbraid me I have been fearfully harassed; my nerves are disordered; I am beset with an idea that discovery is upon me. I am actually becoming superstitious," he continued, more wildly. "Brennett," — he paused impressively as he rose to his feet, while the thunder crashed from the clouds and the lightning rent the sky — "I am almost afraid to put it into words, but I have a curious sense of companionship. Often that man, John Fortescue, is with me."

Brennett glanced up with a satiric smile.

"You will not believe me," the other went on, in a broken voice and with a white, set face. "Why I should tell *you* I don't know — I saw him shot from his horse on that battle-field — I saw him hours afterward lying on the ground, dead — and — by the Lord in heaven — I met him on the streets of Marston yesterday."

He struck the iron bench in emphasis; the blow forced out the blood from his hand. He did not notice it in his excitement. He held it up, dripping and quivering, as he spoke.

"Like he was when I first knew him. Like he was twenty years ago. Brennett — Brennett, I thought I had lost my mind! I thought that it was only a diseased and morbid fancy. I purposely reeled up against it, like a drunken man, to try if the — the Thing was palpable — if it could speak!"

His face was illumined suddenly with the baleful glitter of the lightning; then it sank as suddenly into the moody shadow of the stormy clouds. And still he held up his hand, dripping with blood, and quivering with a pain of which he was unconscious. Brennett was looking at him with some speculation in his cool, critical eyes as to how he might turn these fantastic mental gyrations to his own use. "And it did speak?" he said.

"It did speak — and it spoke with his voice, but I could not catch the words. He threw me off with a gesture as characteristic as his tones. Then he walked on down the street with exactly the air and manner which I had been imitating as I had walked on up the street. It seemed to me so patent that I stared about to see if people had noticed it, but no one was looking at us."

After a moment the impostor once more broke forth wildly, —

"When I fell asleep I dreamed of him; I shall dream of him to-night. Some day I shall see him again. I know it. I feel it. I shall see him again."

Brennett laughed harshly. "You are a marvellously unreasoning creature. Does it never occur to you that the man was uppermost in your thoughts, and this fact invested some stranger with a fancied resemblance. I'll stake my immortal soul, too, that you had been drinking."

"I expected you to say that," his friend declared, with a heavy sigh. "I don't understand why I should tell these things to you, except perhaps because I can tell them to no one else. I don't look to you for sympathy. I am a fool, God knows, but I have never been given over to such abject idiocy as that."

Again he paused, white and haggard. He was in a strong tremor. He might have fallen but for the tree behind him.

"Brennett," he cried suddenly, "I am dead! I have lost my identity. I am a dead man! And this," he continued, striking his breast, "this is John Fortescue. *I* go about so lonely — so lonely among these crowds of living men. When my head aches, and my heart is bursting, and my conscience has fallen upon me with a fang, John Fortescue is hilarious and loud. He has a handful of winning cards — the bottled sunshine of champagne has kindled a riotous summer in his veins. His friends are fond of him for all his faults. They call him Jack, and swear he is the best fellow in the world! His father's old cronies come to him and beg him to reform. They take him home to dinner, and he meets saintly old ladies, who talk to him about his mother. And *I*, I don't know where *I* am! *I* look on at all of it from some outer darkness. My soul has given me the slip; God has forgotten it — it was so little, you know, it slid away, and was lost, just vaguely *lost* somewhere. For *this*, this is John Fortescue. They talk to him about his mother. And he listens. I don't, you know, for I never saw her. And I would rather face death than the recollection of my own mother. But he, he feels differently. It is very natural that he should."

Once more Brennett's sardonic laughter jarred the air.

"Don't think to work upon me, Ned, by your histrionic display. I have already the highest opinion of your ability in that line. I have given you substantial proof how I value your talents. You cannot extort further admiration, and, incidentally, another *honorarium* by this unexpected *coup de théâtre.*"

His words were like a douche of cold water to the adventurer. They chilled while they stung, and yet they brought up his blood with a rush, and steadied his nerves. He again walked to the bench and seated himself.

"Brennett," he said, laying his hand upon his friend's knee and speaking slowly as he looked into those bright eyes, "you are a man of acumen and excellent judgment — singularly quick in the vivisection of character, and adroit to a superhuman degree in exposing secret motives. And yet you think it possible that a man would try to profit by working upon your feelings; that I credit you with a heart — a heart! whose generous heat might mislead your cooler reason. I have long known that you have an ability to scheme which you call your mind; an all-consuming avarice, that you dignify by the name of ambition. You have a system of veins and valves and arteries through which flows a sluggish fluid that is not blood, for it was never warm — it can pulsate to no interest save your own. I could only reach your feelings by striking you. And I have a mind to strike you dead on the spot."

"There would be a prompt decadence of the drama if all mild, admiring spectators were subjected to dangers like this," sneered Brennett. He made no move toward his pistol-pocket now — the threat was empty of intention. He recognized the fact.

"I did not hope that I could by argument reach that hypothetical essence, your conscience, — by showing you how manifestly unfair it is that I should be forced to continue this personation through four months instead of the three weeks to which I agreed, and without any payment for the extra time and risk. I did not trouble you so long as I could live by the tables, but at that sequestered place in the mountains, where on account only of your insistence I remained, there is literally nothing going on, and I am sometimes at my wits' end for five dollars. But I did not intend to appeal to your conscience. If you have a conscience nobody would suspect it. If you have a soul — imagination cannot conceive the idea! If you ever had a spark of honor or honesty it was extinguished long before I first knew you — long before I first fell under your blighting influence. How it should attach men to virtue — the companions they meet in vice!"

"You're a rhetorician, Ned; doubtless able to write tragedies as well as play the high-minded though lugubrious penitent. Give over these handsomely rounded periods and tell me what you did expect to reach?"

"Your fears."

"I am mistaken, Ned; comedy is your forte. This is funny."

"And so I thought I would warn you that I intend to tell Miss St. Pierre."

"You won't do it," said Brennett coolly. "You have everything to risk; you have nothing to gain; and you will certainly lose the chance of five thousand dollars."

Still once more the adventurer scanned that impassive face. There was no mistaking its expression — it was an absolute indifference. He threw himself back with a hunted look; he hardly knew which way to turn. It was a great relief to give for a moment his attention to a trivial subject.

"How did I get that cut?" he said, looking in surprise at his hand, and sensible for the first time of the stinging bruise.

"In your excitement you struck your hand on that sharp edge," said Brennett. "I tell you now — for your own good, mind you — such agitation is dangerous. You ought to struggle against those fantastic illusions about Fortescue, or you'll pass the rest of your days in a strait-jacket."

The other did not reply. He was spent with the intensity of his emotions. His spirits were at their lowest ebb. He raised his heavily-lidded eyes and gazed despondently at the encompassing wall of shrubbery. Suddenly he became aware that a carriage was rapidly passing behind it, and he heard a hasty voice of recognition calling from the window.

He turned in languid inquiry to Brennett.

"That's Percy," said Brennett in answer to the look. "He has seen you. We shall have to go to the house, I suppose. If you intend to continue with the affair, you ought to try to rally and support the character."

"I intend to go on with it for the present," the impostor rejoined.

Certainly it was no mean order of ability which could conjure into that jaded, sordid face all those strong, yet subtle suggestions of vitality, and buoyancy, and a fine candor, and a generous ardor; that could put on, as a vestment, a demeanor in which high breeding and pride were blended with patent recklessness and a fantastic *bravade* of convention. One would have said that it was an inimitable manner as he walked with his friend toward the house. He was drawing his glove over his cut and bruised hand, and Brennett, watching him furtively, yet narrowly, felt a great weight lifted in the vanishing doubt as to how he would meet Percy.

He met Percy lightly enough, parrying with clever lies and excuses the young man's invitations which were insistent almost to the verge of rudeness. For the storm was breaking at last; the peals of thunder and flashes of lightning were instantaneous and nearly unintermittent; far away about the horizon the sombre masses of clouds were torn into fringes as the heavy rain began to fall. With feigned regrets the visitor sprang into the carriage, and it rolled away between the darkening earth and the flaring sky.

CHAPTER XXIII.

THE storm was over by the time he reached Chattalla. The wind and the breaking clouds were rioting through the deep blue sky. The moon had risen; wherever its rays fell they seemed to evoke a lily in the picturesque waste of a garden, that lay at one side of the little hotel; there were petunias hidden somewhere, and honeysuckle, their fragrance all freshened by the rain. His sore heart was instinct with tender recollections as he leaned out of the bar-room window, recognizing the fragrance of old-fashioned flowers, the pride of country gardens — he had not seen their like since his early childhood. It took him back for a moment, and in that moment he forgot the baffling wonder and dismay that had possessed him; for since parting with Brennett he had been groping blindly about in a maze of conjecture for those secret motives which he suspected. Now some long crushed germ of higher impulses was faintly stirring, perhaps with reviviscent possibilities, as he took his cigar from his lips and looked out into the dim leafy recesses, and sighed while he looked. He knocked the feathery ash from the weed, and in the motion changed his position.

It brought the interior of the bar-room before him, and with the glare of the lamps and the prosaic suggestions of the scene, returned his eager speculation as to the innocuous alternative which he believed Brennett held in reserve. This roused his exhausted faculties for another spurt.

The house was quiet, but from the purple gloom of th street came the insistent clamor of the village church bells, inconceivably discordant to ears accustomed to the more melodious sound of the bells of cities. This was not Sunday, but a "big revival" was in progress — the prevailing sensation amidst the monotony of life in Chattalla — and by reason of the dominant desire to know who had "got religion" it drew until even the saloons were almost deserted. Now and then, however, a languid drawl broke the stillness within the bar-room, and seemed the preconcerted signal for a group of loungers to noisily shift their chairs, which were already precariously tilted on the hindlegs, to spit profusely on the bare floor, and to raise slow meditative eyes to the speaker's face. Their conversation was of that retrospective character, peculiarly rural, in which facts perfectly well-known to each are severally rehearsed as if to satisfy some iterative mental craving. Often covert glances were cast at one of their number, expressive of curiosity, and an expectation of more pronounced symptoms of emotion than he exhibited. His grave, stolid face was half shaded by his slouched hat, his long, tawny beard hung down upon his breast, his legs were stretched out at length, his hands were thrust deep in the pockets of his brown jeans trousers. The talk was not cheerful, and seemed as incongruous as might be with the time and place. It consisted chiefly of details of the fearful "taking off" of an unfortunate called Graffy Beale. These chanced to involve the mention of General Vayne, whose name the adventurer caught as he lounged in the window.

"Firing the Gen'al's fields kep' Graffy in torment," said the bar-keeper, turning a huge quid of tobacco in his cheek. "An' yit 't war an accident."

"Never rested till they went an' fetched old Frank —

they tells me," said Tom Toole, shifting his heavy boots one above the other.

A third spat on the floor. "Jes' oughter hev seen Gen'al Vayne!"

"Ye war thar," said Toole affirmatively.

"I war," the eye-witness replied.

Long pause.

"Old Gen'al gits foolisher every day — talks like he war a millionaire yit," he presently resumed discursively. "All that thar good cotton burnt up fur nothin', an' he so scrimped fur money — Shucks! Mightily surprised he war ter find out that the fire started from whar Graffy hed hid in the old powder-magazine on his plantation — then sez he — sez the old Gen'al — 'I hope I may be forgiven ez freely ez I forgive you. My pore feller, I do not grudge one fibre of the cotton. I bear in mind your grievous straits. And, for God's sake, if you had shelter, or warmth, or security from me or mine, take it as the bounty of Providence, and be at rest!'"

The church-bells jangled out of tune. The breath of jasmine came in at the window. A mocking-bird was singing in the moonlight. Once more the roughly shod feet grated harshly on the floor, and the chairs were noisily moved.

"Shucks! Mighty big sinner now, old Frank is!" another submitted ironically. "What ails him ter git ter goin' round hyar jowin' 'bout furgiveness? What's he ever done ter be furgiven fur?"

"He fought a juel wunst," suggested a moralist, dubiously. "They say nowadays ez that is a sin."

"I reckon even the bes' men need grace," said the barkeeper piously.

"I beg your pardon," the adventurer struck unexpectedly into the conversation, "but you alluded just now to General Vayne's financial condition. I have some curiosity to know how he stands since the war."

This moment was the crisis in Maurice Brennett's affairs. If his coadjutor should leave on the next train for East Tennessee his scheme was perfect. On this chance he had reckoned when they parted. Only a few more days and there would come the full fruition of success — it was even more imminent than he thought, — for Miss St. Pierre had finally instructed her lawyer to compromise on any terms her adversary might dictate.

And all this intricate mechanism, of which free agents were the component parts, so delicately adjusted that the ruling characteristic of each acted and reacted on the others according to Brennett's volition, all was in an instant brought to naught because his accomplice's eyes chanced to rest upon Tom Toole, and the impulse of the moment led him to mingle in the rural gossip.

"How does he stand? how does General Vayne come on since the war?" he reiterated.

Tom Toole shook his head with slow impressiveness. The gesture operated as a melancholy annotation of his response. "Come on? He don't come on wuth a cent."

"It's a pretty good country you seem to have about here. I should think he might have pulled together in all this time. He ought to have more elasticity."

"He's flat *broke*," said the bar-keeper conclusively. "The value o' his property hes gone down ter nothink, scarcely, whilst his debts hev been growin' on thar interes'. When the hammer comes down it'll smash all in sight. Now, ez ter me, *I* never hed nothink ter lose. But it's a right stiff thing on the 'big rich,' sech ez Gen'al Vayne uster be."

"Oh, I dare say he will mend his fortunes. He is only middle-aged as yet. He is not on his last legs, you see.

There are chances before him. He may marry a rich widow. Let me tell you, never moan for a man who has a rich widow for a neighbor! He has a financial panacea, always ready to be applied with neatness and despatch."

There was a laugh of languid amusement among the rural loafers. Only Tom Toole sat silent and grave.

The speaker, too, laughed as he shifted his cigar between his teeth. "General Vayne has acumen in those matters, I should judge. He has hedged — neatly. I happen to know that he has a young lady staying in his house, visiting his daughter. Is it a coincidence that this young lady is very rich, in her own right?"

He had carried his point. He had wrenched the subject of conversation to Miss St. Pierre. He wanted to know what was said and thought of her in the village; a chance word might give him a clew — vaguely a clew — to something that would prove valuable. He had heard of her only through Brennett. It might be well to glean a point or two from some source more reliable and disinterested. It might lead to a knowledge of that suspected alternative which he believed rendered Brennett indifferent to the imposture, and the imposture futile. He did not know what use he could make of the vague "something" when he should hear it. He only felt blindfolded, and working in the dark, and his instinct was to lift the bandage.

"Ye 're a stranger hyar," said Toole, "an' I reckon ye don't know Gen'al Vayne. No man that ever knew him would believe *he* was dangling after rich wimmen fur the sake o' thar money."

"Oh no, I don't know him. He was only pointed out to me on the street."

"*I* know him — bet on that! I served in his brigade four year. I've known him on the battle-field an' in camp, in forced marches an' routs, in victories an' defeats.

What *I* don't know about that man ain't wuth findin' out. An' *I* say he 's a good soldier, an' a brave man an' a gentleman — *every inch!*"

"That 's a true word," said the bar-keeper, suddenly infected with Toole's enthusiasm.

"Fur a fack!" chorused the group, easily adapting their plastic mood to the gravity with which Toole contemplated the subject.

"I don't question it," the adventurer carelessly declared. "But gentlemen have married rich women. It may be a wicked thing to do. Still I am no judge."

And he laughed again.

"Gentlemen hev never married rich women fur the sake o' thar money — not ef *I* onderstan' the meanin' o' the word. A gentleman sech ez Gen'al Vayne don't invite a young lady ter visit his darter fur the sake o' draggin' in her fortin'. That 's what you hinted jes' now," Toole persisted seriously. He thought he owed much gratitude to General Vayne, who, despite his anxious financial straits, had furnished bail, had given with an open hand of his scanty store, had restored his humble friend to liberty, had trusted him when all the world was against him. But hitherto the indulgence of this sentiment had seemed a farce to Toole, so heavily did remorse weigh upon him for his share in that folly which had resulted in firing the battle-field and burning the cotton. He had never been able even to contemplate confessing how deeply he had injured his benefactor. Those words of comfort and forgiveness, which had sent Graffy in peace to the grave, were hardly less welcome to him. Now he no longer felt belied in any demonstration of respect and regard for the man who had done so much for him. He could not sit by and hear General Vayne disparaged. He was ready to make it his own quarrel. As a sudden recollection struck him he was imbued with a sense of triumph, and he re-commenced with the assurance of making this insidious detractor eat his own words.

"An' now I kem ter think of it, mister, I kin prove ter ye that ye air all cat-a-wampus on that p'int — 'kase this young lady — this Miss Sampeere, or Camphire, or whatever her name is — it's reported about town that she is engaged ter be married ter another man — a stranger hyar."

"A *stranger?* What stranger?"

Toole looked at him in surprise. He had drawn himself up to his full height; his teeth were clenched on his cigar; his breath was quick; upon his face was the pale anguish of suspense.

"Why," said Toole, with a reluctance which he hardly understood, "I don't know his name. I ain't sure he's hyar now, — he's a friend o' Horace Percy's, an' he stayed a good long spell down at Mrs. Percy's house."

"By the Lord!" exclaimed the adventurer wildly, bringing his hand down on the counter with a vehemence that sent a shiver through all the glasses, "what a dupe I have been! Engaged to him! There's the secret! That explains it!"

His pallor had deepened — his face was ghastly and rigid. A terrible passion was blazing in his eyes. It had set all his pulses a-quiver, and he shook visibly. He looked desperate, even dangerous. For an instant he stood in doubt, then started toward the door. One of the amazed, uncomprehending loafers threw himself in the way, striving to expostulate. "Hold on; give yerself a chance ter cool down, or ye may do something rash."

He silently flung off the countryman and plunged into the violet dusk of the street, which was still a-jangle with the discordant bells, and permeated with the fresh fragrance left by the summer rain, and veined with the glint of the moonbeams. His anger dominated over every faculty. He was barely conscious of throwing himself into a carriage and calling out an order to the driver. Then he was shut in with it, losing even the sense of motion as the vehicle rolled on and on through the darkness toward the vast, vague stretch of the battle-field. And so Brennett was going to marry the girl, and thus secure her fortune. All that was necessary had been to keep his coadjutor at a distance, counsel prudence, and excite fear. And this had cost him not one cent; on the contrary, he was cleverly beating his dupe out of five thousand dollars — the unsuspecting fool, whose futile and dangerous imposture had thus been left day after day without a word of warning at the mercy of accident. This was the favorable change for Brennett of which there had been no hint. This was the innocuous alternative. Perhaps the influence already secured over the girl was sufficient to make her doubt the plainest proofs which could be put into her hands of the conspiracy of her "lover"— he sneered at the very thought of the word — to rob her. But it might be that Brennett overrated this influence. It should be put to the test. He would risk his liberty — if need were, he would risk his life — to compass the ruin of the man who had deceived him. He ran over once more in his mind what he would say to her. It was a strong showing — stronger even than he had thought. No sane woman of reputable station would marry a man blasted like this. He could thwart Brennett's scheme, and wreck his hopes, and stigmatize him forever in the business world, even if, for the sake of what had been, she should refuse to prosecute.

But the price of this: It should cost as little as might

be. He would be cautious. He swore to himself that he would be cautious. He would, if possible, secure first her promise of immunity; if not —

He was looking out at the moon-flooded battle-field with abrupt realization of what he saw. Somehow, now that he was here again — here, where the battle was fought — the localities seemed to have dwelt strangely in his memory. On that elevation there had been a battery, and how the shells had rioted through the heavy timber to the west. He turned slightly — the heavy timber was gone. Where were the dead and dying men once strewn over this ground! — there seemed to him a flash as of bayonets from out a thicket as he passed. And suddenly — he lifted his head with an intent gesture and dilating eyes — a mellow, undulatory resonance drifted to him on the wind — clear, vibrating, infinitely stirring. His heart leaped to the familiar strain, and every nerve responded with a thrill. For was it not a distant bugle, sounding "boots and saddles." But, no, how could that be? The place — the associations it revived — these illusions were accounted for so readily. He heard, too, a shell shrieking down the night. He would have sworn it. But that also — that was his sensitive imagination. There stood Fort Despair — no doubt about it — mounted with heavy guns once, and fiercely repelling the fiercest assaults — but now assaulted only by the wind or the rain. And here was the long slope where John Fortescue and a score or two more fell, while the rest went on with that wild charging cheer — surely its echoes were in the air yet! It was some comfort to him now, singularly enough, that he had gone back afterward, under a hot cross-fire, to take his friend's dying hand. He felt its convulsive grip again. He put his own tremulous hand over his eyes for an instant. He was so wrong, so weak, so wretched.

And here, rising starkly into the night, was a great gaunt house, that he remembered too — as headquarters. A flare of lights came from the open window, and within was Antoinette St. Pierre holding strange possibilities in the lives of two men. And here was his resolution again in full force.

He did not hesitate. But he walked slowly up the pavement, giving himself time to quiet his tumultuous pulse and gather his faculties to sustain the personation. He would keep it up at first — it could do no harm and he might regret a different course. He noticed that a group of figures stood at the end of the long portico just without the lighted window. He hardly thought he was observed as he ascended the flight of steps. Then the clangor of the bell resounded through the house.

It seemed to General Vayne and Mr. Ridgeway, seated in the library, a moment of no special significance when Antoinette St. Pierre, delicately blonde and youthful in her mourning dress, was rising from her chair beside the table with a card in her hand. She glanced hastily at the name upon it and a hot flush mounted to her brow. The next instant ushered in a man of notably fine presence. His handsome eyes swept the other occupants of the room with a cursory glance. Then he bowed to her gravely.

"I have ventured to intrude," he began. But there was a stir upon the portico; a light shower was pattering down; the group without were entering at the long windows. As he spoke his eyes fell upon Captain Estwicke, who was holding back the curtain for the ladies to pass into the room while he stood motionless outside.

The impostor suddenly raised a tremulous hand.

"Coming again!" he cried wildly, pointing to the face, plainly defined upon the darkness and framed by the drapery of the window. "I knew you would! I have felt you with me when I could n't see you. But, Jack! Jack! why should you care? You know if you were alive you'd forgive it all and pass it by. You always loved me. You always said so — 'the best friend a man ever had.' You've *sworn* it! — *sworn* it a thousand times."

He held his right hand up as if in memory of an oath. He had pressed by Miss St. Pierre, and was advancing toward Estwicke, who still stood without the window, the curtain in his hand, motionless, and with a dismayed surprise aghast upon his face. The adventurer paused.

"We went through so much together. You have n't forgotten — surely, surely, you have n't forgotten. Don't look at me with those accusing eyes! you'll break my heart. You would never have looked at me like that in the old days. And I tried you often, and tried you hard. Ah, Jack! you're dead — that makes all the difference. A dead man forgets his friends. A dead man *has* no friends — that's what you think. You come back and find a fellow masquerading around the world as John Fortescue, when John Fortescue is dead, so cruelly dead, so long ago, on this black battle-field. But, Jack, if it could have hurt *you*, old man, I would have lain down in your place and let you take mine, rather than call myself John Fortescue."

Estwicke made a motion as if to step into the room.

"I'm not afraid of you!" cried the impostor, holding out both arms. "Give me your hand. I had its last clasp in life. Tell me you forgive me! Say the word! And let it all be as it was in the days when *you* were John Fortescue, and Edward Keevor was his best friend."

He laid his hand heavily on Estwicke's shoulder, and

General Vayne, impelled by a sense of danger, sprang to the window, and caught the stranger's arm.

"The man's a maniac!" he exclaimed. "What does all this mean?"

"Why that," faltered Estwicke, "that — John Fortescue — that is my name."

CHAPTER XXIV.

ESTWICKE stepped into the room in the midst of an expectant silence.

The touch of a strong, coercive hand upon the impostor's arm roused him to a realization of the situation.

"In the name of Heaven," he gasped faintly, "who are you?"

"I," said Estwicke tremulously, "I am — his son."

"His son!" The adventurer echoed the words in a passion of despair.

Only five minutes ago he had been assuring his fears of the caution of his intention. And yet he had wrested from Miss St. Pierre no promise of immunity. He had pulled down no temple of fancied security upon Maurice Brennett. He had betrayed himself, himself only, to a dozen witnesses, and among them this man, John Fortescue's son, of whose existence he had never before heard.

Instinctively, perhaps with no idea of flight, he turned toward the door. A moment earlier he might have seen more beyond it than the great, dimly-lighted, bare hall. He might have seen, lurking in the gloom, a hesitating shadow, with cruelly brilliant eyes, all their rapacious suggestions sharpening and intensifying as they looked upon the group within. But when those words, "his son," and their despairing echo, struck Maurice Brennett's intent ear, he slipped out softly into that night of changeful mood. And as he rode swiftly through the misty uncertainty of the moonlit battle-field he remembered the strong premonition that had beset him when first he saw John Estwicke's face, and again and again he cursed that fine and subtle sense which gave him so much and yet gave him no more.

There was no need for General Vayne to tighten his grasp upon the detected impostor's arm. The man was incapable of flight. He stretched out his hand to the table for support, or he might have fallen. He was white and shivering, his breath was failing. The faces bent upon him, each expressive of a righteous aloofness, seemed reeling fantastically about the room. And he looked at them, as they went in that giddy whirl, with a piteous deprecation of which he was unconscious. The group stood motionless, silent, watching him askance as if every human feeling and endowment were merged in that coldly accusing gaze.

Marcia never knew how it happened; her heart was suddenly all pierced with compassion; the sympathetic tears sprang into her eyes. The most potent instinct of her nature — to help, to comfort — was strongly constraining her. She made no question. She had no thought of the others, or of what they would think of her. She found herself putting a glass of wine into his trembling hand. "Drink it," she said, "you are faint. Oh, papa, papa, can't you even give him a chair in *your own house!*"

It broke the spell. There was a change of attitude in the circle, a breath of relief. He turned toward her with the glass untasted in his hand.

"I cannot thank you," he said brokenly. "I am not worthy to speak a word to you. You don't know me, or you couldn't pity me. I am too low for pity."

Her eyes were filling again, but she replied with prosaic little words, "You will be better after this."

"Yes," he said slowly, looking hard at her, "I will be better after this; I promise you that."

He placed the brimming glass upon the table. Once he had been a gentleman. Even now, far down as he had sunk, he could not drink wine in the house of a man who gazed at him with stern, condemning eyes.

"You understand it now," he said, addressing Estwicke. "It was a conspiracy to obtain money. The imposture was part of the scheme."

"How did you dare —?" Estwicke began angrily.

"It was no question of courage. Nothing was easier. I had known that man — John Fortescue — all my life. He had not been in New Orleans in thirty years before my little game. I had reason to believe that he was the last of his family. I had heard him say, a thousand times, he had no near relatives. He used to complain that there was not a soul upon earth to care if he were living or dead. The last ten years of his life we spent abroad together. We came back on account of the war. We took part in a few skirmishes, but in his first battle he was killed; the report said, 'missing.' I was captured, and remained in prison till the surrender, when I went at once to France. These circumstances came to serve my turn afterward. We were on the staff of General Crespeau, who was killed on the same day. There were not ten men who knew us well enough, during the short time we were together in the army, to have recognized either Fortescue or me a year afterward. Everything played into my hand, you see. I knew him thoroughly, through and through. I could imitate his voice, and gesture, and manner, without a chance of detection. I have a knack at that kind of thing. A casual resemblance in height and build and complexion helped to carry it off. I passed easily enough as John Fortescue among men who had not seen him for twenty odd years."

He recited this in a hard voice and an off-hand manner; he had mustered his effrontery to face it out. General Vayne's grasp was relaxing, for his attention had concentrated itself upon a phase of the story which touched him nearly.

"Captain Estwicke, — if that is your name," he said severely, "I think I am justified in demanding an explanation from you."

Estwicke turned, with sudden color flaring in his face, and his eyes flashing. His quick intuition had met General Vayne's covert suspicion, and he was tremulous with the shock of the collision.

"You shall have it!" he exclaimed. "My name — John Fortescue — was changed by law. When my mother died, within a year after her marriage, it became the scheme of my grandfather, Judge Estwicke, to effect a separation, permanent and complete, between my father and me, so that I might grow up to be 'correct,' like the Estwickes. A promise was obtained from my father never to interfere with me; never to see me; to keep his distance; because he was no fit custodian and exemplar for his own son. All the long heads of the family were put together, to make out a showing that might rid me even of his too notorious name; for his extravagant escapades, and gaming ventures, and wild courses had rendered the very words a stumbling-block and an offence to good men, like the Estwickes. My father's consent was forthcoming when Judge Estwicke pledged himself to make the change of name advance my pecuniary interests. And so it was done. The connection was cut like a thread. He left me forever, because I was little, and troublesome, and expensive — so the Estwickes afterwards gave me to understand."

It was all beginning to be plain enough to Edward Keevor. He listened with as intent an interest to the points touching upon his imposture, as if he could still serve a purpose by comparing the facts to the ingenious status which he had constructed and fitted to those circumstances that he had believed constituted an exhaustive knowledge of his friend's life. So the roystering John Fortescue had had a hidden heart-history, with some cruel suggestions in it, which he buried under years of revelry, and from which he separated himself by leagues of water and foreign lands. It was not strange that so proud a man should never have spoken to his boon companion of his dead wife, and her "correct" relatives, who held themselves better than he. But there was something curiously uncharacteristic in this voluntary alienation from his child, — he, so generous and hot-blooded, with his deep feelings and enthusiastic attachments. And the son, so like his father, was strangely unlike in this critical, censorious attitude.

The fire was dying out of Estwicke's eyes; he seemed dallying with some resolve. Twice he checked himself as he was about to speak, but his desire suddenly pulled away from his control and he broke forth impetuously, the tragedy of his feelings expressed, incongruously enough, in the hap-hazard phrasings of the day.

"I can't talk about this thing — it kills me! I thought I had no part in it. But it was settled at last by my own choice; and I never knew I had a choice to make. And he is dead. And I am here. He can never understand. It will always seem that I went back on him. I thought he had thrown me off; and it was all the other way, for they would never let me know. He had stipulated — he had stood firmly on that — he had stipulated that if ever my heart should turn to him, they must let me go. He looked for it, he said, for blood is thicker than water. And my heart did turn to him. He was my father; as I grew older, I wanted to know him — to be with him. *I* did n't care if he did live as all gamblers live — like a prince one day, and a beggar the next. *I* did n't care if he had left his reputation in every city on this continent! That's the account the Estwickes gave of him. And when I declared I would go to him, they made me think — for they would not tell me otherwise — that he cared nothing for me; that in all these years he had shown no interest in me, — never a line, or word, or sign. It was sharp; it cut me. And that idea that he had given me away because I was so little, and troublesome, and expensive — I could n't forgive him for that."

He paused for an instant and laughed sarcastically.

"Well, I cherished that idea, and after a time it possessed me. Only once it let go — only once, for a little while. It was just before this battle," — he made a gesture toward the black plain without. "I was aghast one day to realize that now and here I was nearer to him than ever before. I used to climb up on the parapet of Fort Despair at night, and watch the rebels' camp fires, and wonder which might be his, and whether he knew that I was here, and a terrible fear of meeting him as a stranger and an enemy laid hold upon me. A flag of truce went out one day and I wrote to him, and when the letter was finished I thought it all over again, and that idea that he had given me away lightly — *lightly* — as if I had been a choice puppy, beset me once more. It was too much like a choice puppy to go fawning around now without a word of encouragement. So I flung the letter into the fire. If I had stood up for him, if I had believed in him against all the world as I was bound — *bound* by every instinct of my blood to do, that letter would have reached him the day before he was killed. We should have understood each other then. He would have read it here where the battle was fought."

With an agitated gesture, as if he would clasp his missing right hand, General Vayne sought to interpose a word of deprecation. "Let me beg of you — say no more, my dear sir."

But Estwicke hastily interrupted.

"I saw him at last!" he cried, bitterly. "Oh, yes, I saw him at last. It was after an assault on Fort Despair, one of many attacks that day. They had charged again and again, with picked men. When it was all over I saw *him* lying on the ground — dead — *dead!* I knew him by my own likeness to him — by my repudiated sonship. It was as a prevision of my own end — it was like looking on my own dead face. It's a fine thing — oh, I tell you it's a fine thing for a man's conscience to acquit him of the crime of parricide on the plea of a lucky accident, — to have to thank a gracious God that a minie ball from the infantry was charged with his father's death rather than the shells which were bursting everywhere from his own battery."

He leaned against the window-frame, and turned his eyes out upon the night. The fire-flies flickered. A bird sang. Far, far to the vague horizon stretched the stern, savage old battle-field, indelibly marked with its own irrevocable history — the seal of woe set upon the country. And still, even in the haunted thickets, the very outgrowth of carnage, the bird sang, the fire-flies flickered.

After a moment he recommenced scornfully. "I suppose it was in the joint character of a victorious plunderer and an heir-at-law that I felt myself privileged to ransack John Fortescue's belongings in the captured train. And I found among them an old budget of letters from my grandfather and uncles, evidently carefully treasured, friendly, delightfully cordial letters, teeming with bits of news about *me*, — my health, my talents, my progress at school, as if these trifles were of deep interest to him. Now and then there was an allusion, in response to letters of his own, to those objectionable habits which used to grind the rigid and intolerant Judge Estwicke when John Fortescue was brought near to him as his daughter's husband, — invariably it was couched, not as one might speak to a coldly depraved man, but to a noble creature with fantastic generosities of character, and elastic impulses that carried him away, and sometimes astray. And these letters made a mystery — they began to poison my life. At last I wrote to my grandfather demanding the full correspondence that had gone on over my head while I knew nothing of it. And then I discovered that, from the first, my father's heart went out to me; that he kept himself posted, and was familiar with every detail of my life; that he consented to this 'cruel separation' only for my good, as he thought; that he relied implicitly on Judge Estwicke, and revered his 'great sagacity,' and humbly submitted his own judgment; that he was hard on his own faults, and was always trying to reform, on my account; that he patiently awaited and expected some sign from me, when the agreement would be broken and he could take me back; that the years brought him only disappointment, and he bore it meekly, and said he deserved nothing, and that I was doubtless far better off, growing up 'steady,' with studious habits, and among such good influences. And I thought he never wrote. And he thought his own son never cared. And the end was that we met here, where the battle was fought, when he had lain down with his tragic, empty heart, and did not rise again."

He paused. His voice was faltering.

"I cannot sufficiently regret," said General Vayne, with grave constraint, "that I forced this explanation upon you."

Estwicke turned sharply.

"I don't know what I have told you!" he exclaimed. "I am misleading you! I am misrepresenting the good man who did everything for me — who had no motives but his self-sacrificing interest in my welfare, and his fear that my father's influence and example would ruin me. I was a burden — a dead weight from first to last. My grandfather in his old age worked early and late, and took from his dutiful sons to give to me, for my mother's share of his little property had been advanced during her married life, and had slipped through John Fortescue's hands at the card-table. And here, in the presence of these people who never knew Judge Estwicke, I am maligning him and holding him up as cruel, and treacherous, and hard, when the only sin of his long life — if it were a sin — was to save me. Don't you see what a traitor I am? Don't you see I can't justify myself without aspersing him. I went back on my father, or if I try to persuade myself that I did not, I go back on the man who deprived his own children to give to me. Do you wonder that I don't talk of these things — that I can hardly bring myself even to think of the chaotic sarcasm of John Fortescue's fate. The most honorable man that ever lived systematically deceived him. 'The best friend a man ever had,'"— he quoted the words with a sneer, — "has robbed him of his identity, and is masquerading around the world with his name. And here is his own son, masquerading around the world — without it!"

He laughed harshly as he turned away. He was resolving to say no more. He wondered now that he had spoken at all, except to give the curt explanation required. Why should he have bared his heart with all its long-rankling wounds, for these strangers to gaze upon.

He scarcely listened as Keevor addressed him. The man, panoplied in vice though he was, had yet one vulnerable point. He had been honestly fond of his friend. Even after so many years the feeling hampered his imposture, it stirred unaccustomed chords of remorse and repentance, it hung round him with strange superstitions, at last it betrayed him.

There was genuine emotion in his voice and an eager appeal in his manner. "I can't attempt any extenuation," he said. "There is none to make. But at first it did not seem the gross sacrilege that it does now. It was rather a relapse into an old habit. I had often imitated him to his face. He used to laugh. He thought it was clever. The realization of what I have been doing only came upon me by degrees. And I was kept in ignorance of what a swindling job it is until I had been plunged deep into it."

Estwicke made no answer and not a sign of attention until Keevor was about to recommence, when he raised his hand with a gesture of contemptuous expostulation, stepped out of the window, and walked off down the portico.

As Keevor turned away, crushed and cowed, his eye fell upon Miss St. Pierre. She was still standing beside the table, and still turning his card nervously in her hands. The sight of her suggested the reflection that now she would hold her property secure — after his father's death the law allowed Estwicke only three years from January, 1867, in which to bring suit, but he had evidently been in ignorance of his rights, and by the lapse of the prescribed term the remedy was barred forever. So thoroughly had the impostor identified himself with the part that he had played, that with a strange doubleness he experienced a vicarious disappointment because at last the Fortescue heir would receive nothing.

And it was Maurice Brennett who would profit by this! He would marry her; he would gain the fortune he coveted, and around which he had woven the fine web of his schemes. With sudden anger in his face and voice, Keevor spoke to her, resolved to frustrate Brennett yet, if it were possible.

"I was not the originator of the plot to rob you," he said. "It was a device of Maurice Brennett's; I acted under his instructions throughout. I came here to tell you that, to warn you how you place confidence in him. I can give you proofs of what I say; I can put papers into your hands. It was a conspiracy to obtain money."

She was pale and agitated, and a little frightened. "I suspected that all the time," she said simply.

She could not analyze the look he bent upon her. A pang shot through his heart. He had for his fancied wrongs causelessly ruined Brennett; he had defeated the scheme in which they had both lavished a world of ingenuity; and he had indeed given himself away. "A friend of Horace Percy's," the countryman had said, and he must infer no friend save one. He stood silent, feeling thwarted and beaten and bruised.

She had seemed on the point of speaking again. But at first she was only conscious of a painful bewilderment, of mentally fumbling for something she greatly desired to say. Then she realized that she was no longer at the mercy of that dastardly lie with which Brennett had threatened her.

"If you will prove his complicity," she cried impetuously, "if you will give testimony that will convict that man, you shall go free! I will fix it upon him! I will pursue him to the ends of the earth!"

She became suddenly aware that the others were gazing at her with astonished eyes — she hastily averted her own. As she turned slightly she caught sight of a great, swift light that had sprung up on the horizon. It incomprehensibly paused for a moment, but she gave it no heed. Then it glided on as before. It was the head-light of the up-train for Marston. Her caution had held her anger and revenge in leash too long. At that instant Maurice Brennett had signalled the train, and now it was bearing him far away into the darkness. The thorough search made for him afterward was futile.

Keevor received with stolid composure the promise of immunity for which he had hardly dared to hope. "I shall wait in Chattalla until I hear from you. If I am permitted," he turned to General Vayne, "I shall go."

He bowed at the door with courtesy as elaborate as if he were an honored guest taking leave. He went out from the dim hall into the moonlight. The wind was high, and the haunted thickets tossed in wild commotion. A great wave of martial music rolled over the plain. It broke into weird shouts and cries, and the earth shook with a strong tremor. The outline of Fort Despair defined itself aggressively against the western horizon. The gusts passed, the sounds fainted, his foot-fall was dying in the distance. And then, Estwicke, still standing on the portico, could hear only the tumultuous beating of his own passionate heart, which had wrought with its exacting sensitiveness such cruel havoc in its lot. He did not see that the light curtains were suddenly a-flutter, and a girl's slender white-robed figure glided out. But under the touch of her hand upon his arm his whole nature softened like the rock that the prophet smote. He looked down at her through gathering tears that came few and painfully and stood burning in his eyes and did not fall.

"You see what you have escaped, Marcia," he said gently. "I am a man whom no woman might safely trust"— she lifted her face, eloquent with an indignant protest —"a recreant to natural affection. There are not many such. I am a man whose life must be made up of remorse and self-reproach, his best alternation a callous forgetfulness."

"I ask no greater happiness than to share his life," she declared suddenly.

He turned and caught her in his arms.

"Oh, if I could only take the great joy and comfort that you are to me, without grudging it for his sake, remembering what his life was, and what I helped to make it. If he could only know how it all happened, and how I feel, and "—

"He must — he does!" she cried solemnly, like one inspired.

Estwicke looked hard at her. Light opaline clouds were sweeping across the sky; pallid mists shifted about the battle-field and caught the glimmer of the moon, and through its mystery and through its glamour her face shone as the face of an angel.

"Why do you say that?" he asked, his credulity half-constrained by the force of her conviction.

"Oh, God is so good!" she exclaimed.

He slipped her hand through his arm, and together they turned toward the east and the future.

C. J. PETERS & SON, STEREOTYPERS, BOSTON.

www.ingramcontent.com/pod-product-compliance
Lightning Source LLC
Chambersburg PA
CBHW030543300426
44111CB00009B/836